Making Sense of
Men's Magazines

MAKING SENSE OF MEN'S MAGAZINES

Peter Jackson
Nick Stevenson
Kate Brooks

Polity

First published in 2001 by Polity Press
in association with Blackwell Publishers Ltd

Editorial office:
Polity Press
65 Bridge Street
Cambridge CB2 1UR, UK

Marketing and production:
Blackwell Publishers Ltd
108 Cowley Road
Oxford OX4 1JF, UK

Published in the USA by
Blackwell Publishers Inc.
350 Main Street
Malden, MA 02148, USA

ISBN 0-7456-2175-9
ISBN 0-7456-2176-7 (pbk)

A catalogue record for this book is also available from the British Library and has been applied for from the Library of Congress.

Typeset in 10.5 on 12 pt Sabon
by SetSystems Ltd, Saffron Walden, Essex
Printed in Great Britain by MPG Books Ltd, Bodmin, Cornwall

This book is printed on acid-free paper.

Contents

Contents

Acknowledgements

We would like to acknowledge the ESRC's financial support for this project (award number R000221838) and the co-operation of editors and focus group participants, without whom this study would not have been possible. While most of the material is published here for the first time, parts of chapter 4 have appeared in the *European Journal of Cultural Studies* (Stevenson et al., 2000a) while different parts of chapter 5 have appeared in *Environment and Planning D: Society and Space* (Jackson et al., 1999) and in an edited collection on *Commercial Cultures* (Stevenson et al., 2000b). We are grateful to the editors and publishers for permission to reproduce this material here in revised form.

We would all like to thank Rebecca Harkin at Polity who waited patiently for the manuscript and Louise Knight who saw it through to publication. Thanks also to the anonymous readers for their constructively critical comments on earlier drafts of the manuscript. Finally, we'd each like to take this opportunity to express some personal thanks.

Peter Jackson would like to thank Peter Wood for providing a home-away-from-home in London during the interview phase of the project, and colleagues in Sheffield and elsewhere for their comments on earlier drafts, some of which were presented at seminars and conferences in Belfast, Dallas-Fort Worth, Hull, Liverpool, Kentucky, Minneapolis-St Paul, Oxford, Roskilde, Sheffield, Southampton and Sussex – thanks to those who extended the invitation, provided hospitality and engaged in discussion about the project. Peter would also like to thank Deborah Lee and Samuel Lee Jackson for providing the kind of loving support and distraction from academic work that gives life real meaning.

Nick Stevenson would like to thank his father for continually explaining to him what being a man is all about. He would like to thank his friends David Moore, Anthony Elliott, Paul Ransome, Jagdish Patel, Alex MacDonald, Rob Unwin and Mike Kenny for offering a diversity of 'alternative models'. He would also like to thank Lucy James for being Lucy James.

Kate Brooks would like to thank Matthew Taylor, whose good friendship has, over the years, taught her more about the complexities of the male psyche than perhaps she needed to know; Linda Evans, for her generosity, humour and support during this project and many other times; and Leigh Fiorentino, 'as it can't have always been easy sharing an office with me and more than 100 "lad mags"'. Also those who helped set up focus groups, in particular Jo and Glen Brooks-Herbert, Lydia 'Knit one, purl one' Read, and Roger Sabin, whose help on yet another project is very gratefully appreciated. Finally, and most importantly, heartfelt thanks to Mark Neath, for pretty much everything and in particular for 'never, ever, referring to me as "the missus"'.

1

Introduction

During the 1990s a new generation of men's 'lifestyle' magazines was launched which redefined the UK magazine market. The sales of early titles such as *Arena* and *Esquire* were rapidly outstripped by such titles as *Loaded* and *FHM*, as images of the 'new man' were replaced by an emphasis on more 'laddish' forms of masculinity, associated with drinking, sport and sex.[1] Within a few years, these titles had established a mass market and were, in some cases, outselling the most popular women's magazines. The pace of change is indicated by successive newspaper headlines, which heralded the arrival and increasing popularity of laddish forms of masculinity ('We're all lads now', *Guardian*, 13 July 1998), only to pronounce the Great British Lad on the brink of extinction a few years later ('They think it's all over', *Guardian*, 29 June 2000).

This book sets out to explain the phenomenal success of this new breed of men's magazines not only in commercial terms but also in terms of what their success tells us about the changing nature of contemporary masculinities. Unlike most media commentators, we have sought to avoid taking a moralistic stance towards the magazines, not wishing simply to condemn them as sexist and irresponsible. But neither do we want simply to celebrate the new forms of masculinity associated with the magazines, as signalled by media references to the 'Loaded' generation. Instead, we have set out to explore the ambivalent spaces that the magazines occupy, associated with a shift from 'new man' to 'new lad'. We argue that the magazines have provided their readers with what the sociologist Ulrich Beck (1992) refers to as a form of 'constructed certitude' in the face of men's increasing anxieties about their lives in the late 1990s and early years of the twenty-first century. We show how the magazines offer men advice about their health and well-being, about their social lives and sexual relationships, and about the changes they are encountering at home and at work. That men are ambivalent about this advice is signalled by the ironic tone in which the magazines present such information to their readers. We argue that the predominant tone of the magazines is one of 'harmless fun' and that readers adopt a similar attitude, never wanting to appear to be taking the magazines too seriously. While the media have represented the content and style of the magazines in a uniformly negative way ('Dumb and dumber', *Guardian*, 2 June 2000), we highlight the discursive spaces that the magazines have opened up, providing a public forum for thinking about masculinities in new and potentially more democratic ways. The unprecedented commercial success of the magazines in the 1990s suggests that something has changed in the way that men can be addressed as men, promoting new ways of seeing and new ways of being a man. This book explores such changes through an analysis of the production, content and readership of the new generation of men's 'lifestyle' magazines.

We interpret the changes in the UK magazine market as a reflection of (and as an active force in shaping) men's changing gender relations and identities, popularly represented as a shift from the new man to more shamelessly laddish forms of masculinity. Rather than seeing the magazines as a simple response to some generalized crisis of masculinity, however, we trace the specific ways that different individuals and groups of men have attempted to 'make sense' of the magazines and associated changes in commercial culture. We interpret the magazines' success as a response to a series of wider social changes in men's working lives and social relations. These changes have become a central figure of recent developments in popular culture, including the success of novels such as Nick Hornby's *Fever Pitch* (1992) and British television programmes such as the situation comedies *Men Behaving Badly* and *Game On*, the sports quiz *They Think It's All Over* and chat shows like *Fantasy Football*.

Little more than a decade ago it could be confidently asserted that 'men don't buy magazines', apart from pornography or special interest magazines on sports, photography or motoring (*Campaign*, 29 August 1986).[2] Within five years of this assertion *Loaded* had become a runaway success, winning multiple awards from the publishing industry. A few years later, *FHM* had overtaken *Loaded* in sales terms and was outselling the most popular women's magazines, *Cosmopolitan* and *Marie Claire*. Men's 'general interest' or 'lifestyle' magazines had become the fastest-growing sector of a very buoyant magazine market.[3] Top-shelf magazines like *Penthouse* were repositioning themselves as lifestyle titles, and magazines for younger women, such as *Minx*, *Sugar* and *Bliss*, were trying to emulate the success of men's magazines such as *FHM*, *Loaded* and *Maxim*, with girl power heralded as the female equivalent of laddishness.

The research project on which this book is based was designed to encompass several phases in Richard Johnson's (1986) 'circuit of culture', linking production issues and editorial decisions with the actual content of the magazines, following this through to issues of readership and interpretation. While we include a discussion of the publishing business as part of our analysis, our principal focus is on how different individuals and groups of men use the magazines to help them make sense of changing gender roles and relations.[4] By 'making sense', we do not mean to privilege our own analytical abilities as academics, but seek to describe the active capacity of ordinary people (inside and outside the academy) to make their lives culturally intelligible. We wish to stress the everyday nature of this creative cultural work, where meaning does not reside within the text waiting to be 'read off' from the magazines. Instead, our focus group evidence confirms that people are able to engage actively with the text in the process of meaning creation. Besides their simple pleasures in the text, our focus group evidence confirms that the participants also possessed (to varying degrees) an analytical ability to interact critically with the magazines. The process of 'making sense' involves an ability to draw meaningfully on a range of cultural resources, including the range of discursive repertoires that we describe in detail in chapter 5. These repertoires are often highly mediated forms of public knowledge (as we demonstrate in chapter 2) but their articulation in specific circumstances is always subject to negotiation, involving contestation as well as compliance.

In practice, our understanding of the process of 'making sense' involves an analytical distinction between the *discourses* on which men and women draw in talking about the magazines and the *dispositions* they have towards these discourses (a distinction that we elaborate upon further in chapter 5 and in the Appendix). This allows us to adopt a rather more nuanced approach than has been common in recent media coverage, which has tended to portray the magazines in a rather one-dimensional way – as evidence of the general dumbing down of public culture and of the resolutely laddish nature of contemporary masculinities. While there is much to criticize in the magazines, particularly in terms of their representation of women (discussed in more detail in chapter 4), our approach has tried to avoid a tone of moral outrage or blanket condemnation, aiming to explore the ambiguous and contradictory spaces that are opened up by the magazines. This is particularly noticeable in terms of their coverage of men's health and lifestyle issues including their fashion pages, where men's bodies are increasingly represented as objects for other men's gazes and as a suitable subject for the successful marketing of haircare, skincare and other beauty products. We interpret these spaces as open and contested, evidence of potentially significant changes in contemporary masculinities, even though these changes are taking place in (and are arguably restricted to) the highly mediated world of commercial culture. It is this, we claim, that gives the magazines their wider social and cultural significance and which justifies our interest in them.

Given our emphasis on various stages in the 'circuit of magazine culture', the book includes detailed empirical material on most aspects of the men's magazine market. We should emphasize, however, that this is not a reader-centred study of men's magazines, in the sense that it does not provide systematic evidence on the readership of each of the magazines (contrasting *Loaded* readers with readers of *Men's Health*, for example). Instead, we selected focus group participants to provide a wide range of opinions about the magazines, trying to build up a picture of how different individuals and groups of men (and a smaller number of women) 'make sense' of the magazines and associated changes in commercial culture.

In their discussion of the magazines, several of our focus group participants drew directly on discourses that circulate within other media – including newspapers, television and club culture – illustrating the connections that exist within different circuits of contemporary culture (Johnson, 1986; Mackay, 1997). There is, then, an element of artificiality in structuring the book according to the 'circuit of magazine culture' from production through content to consumption, and we have tried to break from this linear logic where appropriate by emphasizing the connections and contradictions between different phases in the circuit and the 'leakages' that disrupt any simple model of 'encoding/decoding'. As our analysis of the focus group material (in chapter 5) confirms, meanings are rarely imposed on readers in a singular or uncontested way. While it may be possible to infer 'dominant' or 'intended' readings of the magazines, there are many ambivalences in how the magazines are read and talked about, even if this rarely takes the form of active or organized 'resistance'. Likewise, our analysis of the editorial interviews (in chapter 3) suggests that the publishing industry is a highly fractured and fragmented world which defies any simple analysis in terms of 'hegemony' and 'resistance'.

Reading magazines

While there are several impressive studies of women's magazines (e.g., Ballaster et al., 1991; Beetham, 1996; Hermes, 1995; McRobbie, 1991; Winship, 1987), there is as yet very little academic work on the men's magazine market. In this section, therefore, we aim to give a summary of previous work on women's magazines and to provide a wider context for the relatively few existing studies of men's magazines.

Given the preponderance, until recently, of women's titles within the magazine industry (accounting for around a third of all magazines published), it is perhaps no surprise that academic research has focused on women's magazines, from Cynthia White's (1970) historical research to Hermes' (1995) more recent study. Reflecting on the suggestion that magazines were, at least until recently, a 'feminine form', Beetham (1996) argues that they not only defined their readers as women, but that they helped bring into being the very women they addressed, whether as the 'fair sex', the 'lady' or the 'new woman'.[5] In an essay originally published in the late 1970s, however, Angela McRobbie argued that there were 'no male equivalents' to the wide range of women's magazines currently available:

> Male magazines tend to be based on particular leisure pursuits or hobbies, motorcycling, fishing, cars or even pornography. There is no consistent attempt to link interests with age, nor is there a sense of natural or inevitable progression from one [magazine] to another complementary to the life-cycle. Instead there are a variety of leisure options available [to men], many of which involve participation outside the home. (1991a: 83)

Our research suggests that this was no longer the case by the mid-1990s, with the proliferation of men's magazines and a clear sense of progression from sports and music titles among teenage boys to more general lifestyle titles as they get older.

Much of the early research on women's magazines, informed by (and in some cases antagonistic towards) the work of the Centre for Contemporary Cultural Studies in Birmingham, was cast within an encoding/decoding perspective (Hall, 1980), with an emphasis on 'decoding' the text through various theoretical manoeuvres rather than through more direct encounters with readers. McRobbie's 1978 study of the 'romantic individualism' encoded within *Jackie* is a classic example of this genre. The essay is described by McRobbie as offering 'a systematic critique of *Jackie* as a system of messages, a signifying system and a bearer of a certain ideology . . . which deals with the construction of teenage femininity' (1991a: 81–2). According to McRobbie, magazines like *Jackie* served to introduce girls to adolescence. Their ideological work represented 'a concerted effort . . . to win and shape the consent of the readers to a particular set of values' (82). While McRobbie stopped short of describing the magazines as 'a mouthpiece for ruling-class ideology' (85), she emphasized their role as 'a powerful ideological force' (88). McRobbie was therefore openly hostile to the magazines for their portrayal of a 'cloyingly claustrophobic environment' (84) characterized by 'monotonous regularity', 'narrowness' and 'repetition' (117–18). With only one paragraph on how young women actually read *Jackie*, her method was semiological, privileging her own reading of the magazines over more formal content analysis and without giving any direct 'voice' to the readers themselves. Four sub-codes were identified and relentlessly pursued: romance, personal/domestic life, fashion and beauty, and pop music. Only in the concluding paragraph does McRobbie admit that 'this does not mean that its readers swallow its axioms without question' and that we need to know more about how girls read *Jackie* and how they encounter its ideological force (131).[6]

McRobbie addresses the one-sidedness of her earlier analysis in a subsequent essay which, like our own research, aims 'not to denounce . . . but to understand' the popular appeal of the magazines (1991b: 184). This later essay traces the changes in magazine content and in academic practice between the 1970s and 1980s, including 'the spaces these magazines offer for contestation and challenge' (ibid.: 186). McRobbie documents the decline in romance and the ascendancy of the commercial culture associated with pop music and fashion epitomized in the shift from *Jackie* to *Just Seventeen* as the best-selling magazine for teenage girls. Acknowledging that feminists such as Janice Radway (1987) and Janice Winship (1987) had shifted their attention 'away from texts and meanings, to the readers and their different and complex readings' (1991b: 137), McRobbie opens up her analysis a little more to the pleasures of the text.

Winship's study was among the first to reject the dismissal of women's magazines as a simple instance of patriarchal oppression, aiming 'to delve beneath this simple and dismissive description in order to both explain the appeal of the magazine formula and to critically consider its limitations and potential for change' (1987: 8). She approached the magazines historically, arguing that a combination of advice and entertainment had been characteristic of the genre at least since the nineteenth century (citing *The Lady's Magazine* of 1799, which announced its dual role to provide 'use' and 'amusement'). Her book focused on the place of magazines in women's lives and the social processes and cultural codes which shaped their meaning. While celebrating the (double-edged) pleasures of the text, she was critical of the magazines' ideological commitment to individual success and competitiveness among women, exploring the possibility of breaking the nexus between constructions of femininity, desire and consumption. The book delved deeper into the business of magazine ownership and production than previous studies, focusing particularly on *Woman's Own*, *Cosmopolitan* and *Spare Rib*, and examining specific features such as the 'triumph over tragedy' story, horoscopes and agony aunts as well as cover images, 'sell lines' and advertising. Despite its emphasis on the pleasures and contradictions of magazine reading, there was still very little direct engagement with other (non-academic) readers.

Drawing particularly on Winship's work, McRobbie (1991) contrasts a negative view of the internal logic of the problem page (characterized by unsisterly individualism) with a more positive assessment of its external logic (how the magazines are read and giggled over collectively). While McRobbie acknowledges this move away from 'the text in all its ideological glory' (1991: 38), actual readers also fail to make an appearance in her analysis. She is even critical of those, such as Janice Radway (1987), who have attempted to access readers' views for being over-reliant on the statements made to the researcher by her informants. More recently, McRobbie (1999) has explored the development of 'in yer face' teen magazines like *More* and *19*, which offer frank information about sex and represent girls as both lustful and enjoying sex. Like men's magazines, many of the features are ironic and borrow the confessional shock-horror style of the tabloid newspapers. McRobbie launches a critical defence of the pleasures and diverse subjectivities articulated by these magazines against their detractors on the Left and the Right. Rather than seeing the magazines as either ideologically or morally corrupting, McRobbie prefers to view them as an exercise in reflexivity. She argues:

> This new form of ironic femininity allows readers to participate in all the conventional and gender stereotypical rituals of femininity without finding themselves trapped into traditional gender-subordinate positions. Irony gives them some room to move. (1999: 53)

In this respect, McRobbie's arguments come close to our own on men's magazines. As we argue in chapter 4, the ironic content of the magazines allows men to experience many of the powerful fantasies that are traditionally associated with masculinity. However, as we also argue, the irony in men's magazines does not involve a reversal of gender positions (although it reveals a great deal of anxiety) and its excessive nature often borders on cynicism.

As described above, Janice Radway's work signals an important break with text-centred approaches, emphasizing the agency of 'ordinary readers' as well as the internal contradictions of the text. Radway's work grapples with the tension that her readers feel between the pleasures of the text and the uneasy sense that reading romantic fiction reinforces patriarchal ideology with its fantasies of male chivalry, female subordination and the all-encompassing world of romantic love.[7] Radway argues that reading romantic fiction is 'a collectively elaborated female ritual through which women explore the consequences of their common social condition' (1987: 212), emphasizing how women construe their reading as a declaration of independence from their socially-determined domestic responsibilities. For Radway and her informants, reading romantic fiction 'connotes a free space where they feel liberated from the need to perform [domestic] duties that they otherwise willingly accept as their own' (ibid.: 92). Rather than insisting that romantic fiction is fundamentally conservative or incipiently oppositional, Radway explores the ambiguities of the genre. She also demonstrates that women's readings are embedded in their social lives and that their media use is 'multiply determined and internally contradictory' (7–8). As we also attempt in chapter 5, Radway endeavours to isolate a variety of patterns or regularities among the diversity of readings she uncovers (including notions of fantasy, guilt, luxury, self-indulgence, 'reading for instruction' and compensation). Among this diversity of readings, Radway suggests, 'similarly located readers learn a similar set of reading strategies and interpretive codes which they bring to bear upon the texts they encounter' (81).

A related approach is adopted by Elizabeth Frazer (1992: 195), who uses a concept of 'discursive register' ('an institutionally, situationally specific, culturally familiar, public way of talking') to argue that teenage readers of *Jackie* engage in frequent and dramatic shifts in register without those registers being necessarily contradictory. Based on a series of group discussions with 13–17-year-old girls, she demonstrates that readers are rarely 'victims' of the text. Notions of ambiguity and contradiction are therefore increasingly prevalent in recent approaches to magazine reading. In a similar vein, Hermes

(1995: 3) writes of the mixture of pleasure and guilt involved in reading women's magazines, while Ballaster et al. (1991) reject the stark choice between 'bearer of pleasure' and 'purveyor of oppressive ideologies'. Prefiguring our own approach to men's magazines, they assert that:

> the identification of 'contradiction' . . . fails to embarrass either editors, writers or readers . . . The success of the women's magazine is no doubt connected with its ability to encompass glaring contradiction *coherently* in its pages. (1991: 7)

In an important essay (originally published in *Cultural Studies*, 1987), Mica Nava further develops this argument about the contradictions of contemporary consumerism. Rather than seeing new forms of consumption as politially diversionary, evidence of a capitulation to the forces of conservatism, Nava prefers to see recent political history as an intense struggle 'played out on the terrain of cultural forms and signs' (1992: 163). She suggests that the fashions and styles of masculinity and femininity depicted in magazines and other popular forms have no inherent meaning but are immensely plastic codes whose meanings are constantly being reworked. Thus, she argues, 'Feminists in the 1980s have argued . . . that women can read glossy magazines critically and selectively [without disavowing] more traditional feminine identities and pleasures' (ibid.: 165–6). She goes on to identify the progressive possibilities of new forms of subjectivity, new areas of authority and expertise for women that have been enhanced by consumer society and a heightened awareness of entitlements outside the sphere of consumption. The sense of contradiction is fundamental to these developments, whereby 'the buying of commodities and images can be understood both as a source of power and pleasure for women . . . and simultaneously as an instrument which secures their subordination' (166). Focusing specifically on the style magazine *Arena*, she concludes that we need a less guilt-ridden, more popular politics of resistance which seeks out the vulnerable points of contemporary commercial culture, avoiding the kind of accommodative response that simply rationalizes our desires.

Recent work on magazine reading addresses these dilemmas and contradictions, though an earlier emphasis on the text to the exclusion of actual readers is now in danger of being replaced by the opposite tendency: an emphasis on readers to the neglect of content and editorial design. For example, Joke Hermes's (1995) work focuses on readers as the producers of meaning with almost no attempt to distinguish between the various magazines they read.[8] Criticizing the over-emphasis on the text in earlier studies, Hermes identifies what she calls 'the fallacy of meaningfulness' (1995: 16): the assumption that all forms of popular media carry significant meanings. In contrast, Hermes insists on the everyday and mundane character of magazine reading for the majority of her readers (accessed via eighty in-depth interviews). Magazines are leafed through during gaps in their readers' everyday routines; they are easily put down rather than invested with any deeper significance. In this account, magazine reading emerges as 'a low-priority means of spending leisure time or unoccupied minutes' (ibid.: 20) rather than having any greater cultural or political significance. Rather than offering a single 'academic' reading of the text, her approach involves identifying the interpretive repertoires through which different women make sense of the magazines – an approach that we adopt (and adapt) in our own identification of different 'readings' in chapter 5.

Compared to the richness of feminist work on women's magazines, previous work on men's magazines has been much more limited. Mort (1988, 1996) situates his analysis of the emergence of such lifestyle magazines as *Arena, i-D* and *The Face* firmly in the context of the 1980s consumer boom. Against the tendency for over-abstraction which he detects in recent cultural studies, Mort details the professional networks and alliances that sustained these emerging popular and commercial forms. He describes specific 'topographies of taste' (whether in relation to the retail spaces of Soho, the commercial epistemologies of contemporary advertising agencies such as Bartle Bogle Hegarty, or the visual philosophies of stylists like Ray Petri and Neville Brody) and their historical trajectories (from Montague Burton – the 'Tailor of Taste' – to Next for Men, or from the nineteenth-century gentleman to his late-twentieth century counterpart: the yuppie or gay urban *flâneur*. Besides the growing visibility of a specifically homosexual marketplace, Mort also charts the emergence of a homosocial gaze, particularly in the fashion spreads of men's lifestyle magazines. According to Mort, the fashion pages of magazines such as *Arena* and *The Face* were designed as narratives to be 'cruised' rather than as conventional clothes advertisements, opening up a space, with its own visual codings, that attracted increasing numbers of straight men as well as those who identified as gay or bisexual. The figure of the 'new man' features prominently in Mort's cultural history, providing a partial exception to the rule of men's general reluctance to be addressed collectively as men. The figure of 'the lad' – 'the archetypal product of democracy and affluence' (1996: 41) – gets much less attention, however, and could be seen as a repudiation of the 'fashionable sexual ambiguity' (ibid.: 71) that was depicted in this earlier generation of men's magazines.

Mort's emphasis on the 'dialogue of the eyes', which signals a bond of intimacy between men – a homosocial rather than an exclusively homosexual gaze – is taken up in Sean Nixon's (1996) study of masculinities, spectatorship and contemporary consumption. Here and elsewhere, Nixon (1992, 1993, 1997) explores the 'new visual codings' of masculinity in menswear retailing, advertising, market research and magazine culture. The analysis of visual culture is extremely acute, focusing in particular on the role of fashion photography in *The Face* ('the world's best dressed magazine'), *Arena* ('a new magazine for men') and *GQ* ('the men's magazine with an IQ'). Like Mort, Nixon insists on the particularity of what he describes in terms of institutional practices within specifically metropolitan spaces. He draws on a psychoanalytical account of spectatorship, building on Laura Mulvey's (1989) reworking of Freud and Lacan, together with a Foucauldian emphasis on technologies of looking and practices of the self. Nixon describes his account as a cultural history of a very specific moment in the mid- to late-1980s, focusing on the figure of the new man, with very little discussion of the subsequent emergence of more laddish forms of masculinity in the 1990s.

Finally, Tim Edwards (1997) includes a case study of men's lifestyle magazines in his account of men's fashion, masculinity and consumer society. Edwards seeks to locate his study in terms of specific social, economic and political changes, noting, like Mort and Nixon, that it has become more acceptable for men to be consumers of various lifestyle products, to look at themselves and other men as objects of desire. Again (like Mort and Nixon), Edwards suggests that it is the *perception* of male sexuality that has shifted rather than sexual *practice* itself. While the study broadens out into a consideration of the increasing commodification and aestheticization of everyday life, it is rooted in the expansion of men's fashion that took place in the 1980s, together with associated developments in the commercial and institutional practices of marketing and advertising. Edwards concludes that the magazines 'have very little to do with sexual politics and a lot more to do with new markets for the constant reconstruction of masculinity through consumption' (1997: 82). His interpretation of the magazines as an 'overt legitimation of consumption', characterized by an uncritical endorsement of 'aspirationalism' and 'near pornographic' content (ibid.: 75–6) adopts the kind of judgemental tone that we are keen to avoid. Rather, in what follows (and particularly in chapter 5), we aim to represent in men's own words how they 'make sense' of the magazines and associated changes in commercial culture, emphasizing the ambivalences and contradictions of these accounts rather than adopting a tone of moral outrage or condemnation.

Following the launch of GQ in the late 1980s, media commentary adopted a similarly judgemental tone about the emergence of new forms of masculinity (Chapman, 1988; Moore, 1989). Some of these accounts were overtly hostile to the figure of the new man, seeing it as a pretence or as a purely commercial development:

> [C]onsumption is being redefined as an activity that is suitable for men – rather than simply a passive and feminised activity – so that new markets can be penetrated. More products are being aimed at young men and shopping is no longer a means to an end but has acquired a meaning in itself. (Moore, 1989: 179)

Contemporary academic accounts were more sympathetic, with Frank Mort writing enthusiastically of:

> the spaces and places of the urban landscape which are throwing up new cultural personas – on the high street, in the clubs, bars, brasseries, even on the terraces. It seems as if young men are now living out fractured identities, representing themselves differently, feeling different in different spatial situations. We may not like all of the net result. But there amid the broken glasses and the buddy talk are some distinctly new profiles. (1988: 218–19)

While all of these accounts have helped to contextualize our own research, none of these authors has much to say about the emergence in the 1990s of more laddish forms of masculinity and their associated commercial cultures.[9] As with previous feminist research on women's magazines, there is also a characteristic emphasis on visual and textual representations of masculinity rather than an empirical engagement with different readings of these changing representations.

Theorizing masculinities

We approach masculinity in this study as a discursive construction that assumes different forms in different places and at different times (cf. Jackson, 1991; Mangan and Walvin, 1987). While some constructions are socially dominant, hegemonic masculinities are articulated in relation to a wider set of power relations and are always contested. For this reason, we prefer to speak of *masculinities* in the plural, and to put the relationship between gender and power at the centre of the analysis (cf. Brittan, 1989; Connell, 1987). While some have defined masculinity as 'the gender of oppression' (Hearn, 1987), others have sought to show the way that constructions of gender are *mutually constitutive* with other social constructions, associated with concepts of race, class or sexuality, for example (Chapman and Rutherford, 1988; Hall, 1992; McClintock, 1995).

Approaching masculinity as a construction, we share Judith Butler's (1990, 1993) emphasis on gender as socially regulated performance.[10] While Butler's emphasis is on the embodied nature of such performances (and on the discursive limits of 'sex'), the performance of gendered identities includes the kind of *discursive practices* that are the focus of our study. As Butler insists, the performance of gender is recursively monitored and subject to regulation through patriarchal institutions and ideologies. While these structures may be negotiated or actively resisted, it is through their regulation that gender is rendered culturally intelligible.

While our approach in this study focuses on the discursive construction of gender (accessed through focus group and interview evidence) we do not dismiss the value of more ethnographic approaches to masculinity (as illustrated in the work of Bell et al. (1993), Cornwall and Lindisfarne (1994) and Mac an Ghaill (1996) among others). Our approach may lack an ethnographic understanding of reading practices, but it goes beyond most recent research on masculinity and the media (e.g. Blount and Cunningham, 1996; Craig, 1992) where the analysis remains at the level of textual or visual representation rather than attempting to grapple empirically with how those representations are negotiated and contested by particular individuals and groups of men. As such, we share Edley and Wetherell's (1997) interest in analysing the 'identity talk' through which specific masculinities are constructed and contested. Like them, we approach masculinities as a social accomplishment, treating the inconsistencies and contradictions of contemporary masculinities as something to engage with rather than to be prematurely resolved (hence our emphasis on ambiguity and ambivalence in chapter 5). While Edley and Wetherell analyse their material in terms of discursive regimes, interpretive repertoires, cultural narratives and subject positions, our own interpretation revolves around an analytical distinction between *discursive repertoires* and *discursive dispo-*

sitions. Put simply, we aim to understand the range of discourses on which different individuals and groups of men draw in making sense of the magazines (their discursive repertoires) and the different kinds of investment that they have in these discourses, embracing them or rejecting them for example (their discursive dispositions). While we are sympathetic to Edley and Wetherell's social psychological approach – drawing on the kind of psychoanalytic perspective advanced by Rutherford (1992) and others (particularly in our analysis of magazine content in chapter 4) – we wish to maintain a sociological perspective on the expression of masculinity within the institutions of late-modernity, as explored by Beck et al. (1994) in general, and by Carrigan et al. (1985) with specific reference to contemporary masculinities.

The analysis we advance in the remaining chapters draws heavily on Beck's (1992) concept of 'constructed certitude', arguing that the magazines provide men with a kind of conceptual map for navigating safely through their contemporary gender anxieties, whether in relation to their health, their careers, their sexual relationships or their place in 'consumer culture' more generally. We also draw on Bourdieu's (1984) notion of 'cultural capital' as a way of distinguishing between different ways of 'making sense' of the magazines, arguing that different class fractions (defined in terms of their access to economic and cultural capital) have different orientations towards the magazines, reinforcing our view that it is unhelpful to approach the magazines in terms of a singular moral stance. It is these ambiguities and contradictions that are at the heart of our attempt to 'make sense' of the magazines.

Finally, we wish to situate our study historically in the late 1990s, when the empirical research for this project was conducted. We have argued that previous research on changing masculinities and their associated commercial cultures, such as those in the collection by Chapman and Rutherford (1988) and in the work of Mort (1989, 1996) and Nixon (1992, 1993, 1996), deal with a slightly earlier period than that considered here. By the late 1990s, the new man was no longer a prominent media image, having been replaced by a (relatively narrow) range of more laddish representations. Britain, too, was a different place from the late-Thatcherite period of rampant consumerism evoked in these studies, with its celebration of enterprise and the free market. The election of the New Labour government in May 1997 heralded a period of change in British commercial culture. Under the banner of 'Cool Britannia' (Smith, 1998), the club and music scene experienced an economic boom associated with the international success of bands like Oasis and Blur (commonly associated with the label 'Brit Pop'). A darker, nostalgic sense of national yearning was revealed, associated with the death of Diana, Princess of Wales (Merck, 1998). However, these events could also be linked to more visible public displays of emotion, a new ethical agenda encompassing difference, and the capacity of the popular realm to attract mass attention and identification.

We are therefore keen to situate the discursive construction of gendered identities in terms of changes in the wider social structure, where masculinity is often represented somewhat simplistically as 'in crisis'. As Connell (1995) insists, there is little evidence of a general crisis of masculinity, in the sense of a systematic crumbling of patriarchal structures of power. Indeed, the sociological evidence marshalled by Segal (1990) and others suggests that the pace of change in gender relations is actually very slow. It may, however, be possible to detect a series of more minor crises for particular groups of men in specific contexts: in terms of educational under-achievement (compared to young women), for example. It may also be possible to trace the consequences of longer-term social trends, such as the decline of manual employment and the security of a job-for-life, on formations of masculinity among young working-class men (cf. McDowell, 1991). While we do not provide a systematic analysis of these changes here, they are undercurrents in our analysis of different readings of the magazines in chapter 5 and also underpin the uncertainties that characterize the work cultures of the magazines' editorial staff, analysed in chapter 3.

Consumption, the media and audience studies

Our study also connects with recent changes in the study of consumption (reviewed by Miller, 1995), where there has been a renewed emphasis on the agency of 'ordinary consumers', including an increasing focus on the active role of readers in the creation of meaning. Commenting on the recent interpretative turn within media sociology, James Carey (1989) argues that there has been a corresponding move away from functional approaches. By functional analysis, Carey means research that concentrates upon whether or not the mass media reinforce or disrupt the status quo. A more symbolic approach to cultural forms, he suggests, would seek to examine the interaction of symbolic meanings within communication.

In terms of media sociology, the most important domain of

analysis has addressed questions of meaning, ideology and resistance. For example, Hall (1980) famously argued that there is a basic distinction between the social processes that encode and decode media texts. Cultural forms can be said to be encoded through a specific historical mix of institutional relations, professional norms and technical equipment. On the other hand, the decoding strategies employed by the audience are similarly dependent upon social structural relations, political and cultural dispositions and access to the relevant technology. While Hall's essay states the dual nature of textual production, it is most often remembered for the emphasis it places on three forms of reading strategy: preferred, negotiated and oppositional. More recently, David Morley (1992) has suggested certain problems with the original 'encoding/decoding' model derived from Hall's writing.[11] The difficulties experienced with this approach can be defined as follows: (i) the notion of a preferred reading invokes the idea that the message content is governed by the conscious intentionality of the message sender; (ii) the 'encoding/decoding' metaphor invokes a 'conveyor belt' of meaning, rather than the possibility of radical discontinuity between these levels; (iii) decoding suggests that the audience attends to the text and produces meaning, whereas if the text has little resonance for the reader it could in fact be ignored; and (iv) preferred meanings are easier to detect within texts that have a single closed narrative. Other more open texts, such as soap operas, which rely upon a plurality of narratives and relatively unfixed subject positions, may resist a dominant hegemonic reading by the theorist. Many of these features have been important to our understanding of the magazines. First, the idea of a 'preferred reading' has been difficult to detect given the fragmented and discontinuous nature of magazine texts. While we were able to detect, within certain magazines, a shared concern around the 'new lad', the magazines were themselves difficult to stitch together ideologically. Second, the idea of the 'meaningfulness' of the magazines was also difficult to gauge. It was not always clear to us whether our focus group participants were commenting on the surrounding media debate or on the magazines themselves. Furthermore, we also heard plenty of evidence that the magazines were not read in any concentrated manner but in terms of a variety of less 'committed' reading strategies. Finally, in our conversations with editors, and in our content analysis of the magazines and our focus groups, it was indeed difficult to detect the direct passing on of meanings and ideologies. Hence, as we argued above, we prefer instead to talk of complex circuits of culture rather than one-way flows of information.

Elsewhere, John Fiske has also built upon the writings of Hall and others. His central argument is that the 'power bloc' produces uniform mass-produced products which are then transformed into practices of resistance by the 'people'. As Fiske argues 'popular culture is made by the people, not produced by the culture industry' (Fiske 1989: 24). To be considered popular, therefore, commodities have to be able to be mass-produced for economic return, and be potentially open to the subversive readings of the people. The music of Madonna or men's magazines are not simply a standardized product that can be purchased through the institutions of global capitalism, but a cultural resource of everyday life. The act of consumption always entails the production of meaning. The circulation of meaning requires us to study three levels of textuality while teasing out the specific relations between them. First, there are the cultural forms that are produced to create the idea of a media event. For men's magazines these include internet sites, books, posters, road shows, radio interviews and newspaper articles. At the next level, there is a variety of media talk in popular magazines and newspapers, television programmes and radio shows all offering a variety of critical commentary upon the magazines. The final level of textuality, the one that Fiske claims to be most attentive to, involves the ways in which cultural forms become part of our everyday lives.

While Fiske draws from a range of cultural theory, most notably semiotics and post-structuralism, the work of Michel de Certeau (1984) has a particular resonance for his approach. For de Certeau, popular culture is best defined as the operations performed upon texts, rather than the actual domains of the texts themselves. Everyday life has to operate within the instrumental spaces that have been carved out by the powerful. To read a fashion magazine, listen to a punk album, put on a soccer supporter's scarf or pin up a picture of Derby County is to discover a way of using common culture that is not strictly prescribed by its makers. The act of consumption is part of the 'tactics' of the weak that, while occupying the spaces of the strong, convert disciplinary and instrumental time into that which is free and creative. The specific tactics that evade instrumental modes of domination, or what de Certeau sometimes calls cultural 'poaching', in practice never become reified, as they are constantly shifting and thereby able to evade detection.

While these dimensions remain important, they neglect more structural aspects of cultural production, distribution and ideology, rendering magazine use overly meaningful, and proscribing consumption as resistance. Instead, our focus comes closer to that of writers like Janice Radway (1987) in seeking to make links across the different dimensions of media analysis, while being open to the different uses and meanings of popular culture. Radway notes, along with others such as Gray (1992), that women's enjoyment of romantic fiction can only be accomplished once they have successfully negotiated the cultural derision of their husbands, as well as their own sense of guilt. The 'guilty pleasures' involved in romance reading are emotionally sustaining in a male-dominated social order that seeks to discipline women into subordinating their own needs to those of significant others. Their reading operates in a compensatory way, offering them, via the text, the emotional support they are denied in their personal relations with men. The romantic escape, however, is also dependent upon a form of utopian receptiveness where the reader has the feeling of her own needs being met in a caring and receptive way. Paradoxically, the romance helps sustain the women ideologically in patriarchal relations, while holding out the possibility of more nurturing human relationships. It is, then, in the tradition of more ambivalent studies like Radway's that we seek to position ourselves. We would be just as critical of populist writers like Fiske, who view the audience as always involved in resistant readings, as of earlier studies which ignored the perceptions of the audience altogether. But we are also aware of the pitfalls of approaches that are only concerned with cultural meaning, thereby neglecting more mundane aspects of practice in respect of magazine cultures (Hermes, 1995). However, we would not go as far as some in suggesting that it is time for a completely different paradigm of media research (Abercrombie and Longhurst, 1998). Rather, this study seeks to build on the existing literatures within research on the media, consumption and magazine reading.

Outline of the book

Our analysis begins with a discussion of recent media debates about the growth of the British men's magazine market. These debates are situated within an account of the magazine publishing industry, including a brief discussion of earlier generations of men's and women's magazines. We document the proliferation of new men's magazines in the 1990s and the dramatic growth in their sales. These changes were the subject of constant media speculation during the 1990s, accessed here through our collection of more than two hundred articles and press-cuttings. We argue that the media generated a range of discourses about the alleged 'crisis of masculinity', including contested representations of the new man and the new lad, on which members of our focus groups were then able to draw in discussing the magazines and associated changes in masculinity. Media commentary, like the magazines themselves, has thus both shaped and reflected wider social changes. Chapter 2 also allows us to break away from a strictly 'linear' approach to production–content–readership to show a variety of connections within the circuit of magazine culture. For example, we illustrate the connections between different branches of the media; how editorial content is shaped by readers' reactions to previous issues; and how readers themselves work actively to reshape the meanings they attach to the magazines according to different social contexts. While the media helped to consolidate the 'naturalness' of laddish forms of masculinity, in contrast to which other forms (such as the 'new man') came to be seen as artificial constructions, we conclude that the media's focus on laddish masculinities (and on *Loaded*, in particular) oversimplifies the range of masculinities that our focus group participants were able to articulate in and through their reading of the magazines. In place of a model of hegemony and resistance, signalled in terms of the 'encoding' and 'decoding' of media messages, we prefer to identify a circulation of discourses between the magazines and their readers, which are reflected in and shaped by the wider media discourses identified in this chapter.

Chapter 3 is based on an analysis of our interviews with Andy Clerkson (editor of *Stuff for Men*), Mark Higham (editor of *Escape*), Mike Cones (editor of *GQ*'s Body and Soul section), Adam Porter (editor of UpLoaded, *Loaded*'s website), Gill Hudson (editor-in-chief at *Maxim*), James Collard (editor of *Attitude*), plus published interviews with several other editors, included Mike Soutar (founding editor of *FHM*) and James Brown (founding editor of *Loaded* and subsequently editor of *GQ*). The chapter highlights the tensions and contradictions that are central to the editorial process. These include an attempt to commodify the aspirational aspects of men's lifestyle as a way of appealing to advertisers, while simultaneously trying to speak directly to readers as the 'authentic' voice of the magazine. We demonstrate that the magazines faced a dilemma as they attempted to move from the niche markets of the 'style' press (established by *i-D*, *Arena* and *The Face*) to address a mass audience whose profile was very poorly understood. We conclude that the success of the magazines depended on the way these various tensions were addressed, commodifying men's gender anxieties through editorial material that provides useful advice in a witty and accessible manner, often using an ironic mode of address to avoid the charge of being 'sad' or taking things too seriously.

Chapter 4 provides a discussion of the magazines' editorial content, concentrating on their stylistic and narrative content. Combining sociological and psychoanalytical frames of analysis, we focus on the magazines' coverage of personal relationships as a key to their sexual politics and on their coverage of men's health issues. Our analysis demonstrates that softer, more caring versions of masculinity (associated with media images of the new man) have been displaced by other harder images of masculinity, characterized by laddish behaviour such as drinking to excess, adopting a predatory attitude towards women and a fear of commitment. Through a close reading of a selection of stories in *FHM*, *XL* and *Maxim*, we suggest that the adoption of an ironic mode of cultural commentary serves to subvert political critique, with those who object to the predominant (sexually objectified) ways of representing women easily dismissed as missing the point, much as feminists have previously been described as 'humourless'.

Throughout the book, in fact, we take a sceptical approach to the alleged irony of magazines such as *Loaded*, arguing that their tone of 'knowing' sexism may serve as a way of deflecting potential criticism. Irony is, of course, always double-edged, capable of exerting political critique but always in danger of undermining the very seriousness of that critique. The tone of magazines such as *Loaded* can therefore be thought of more critically as a means of handling the contradictions of contemporary gender relations where older-style patriarchal relations are crumbling but where men may still strive to maintain conventional power relations between the sexes. The chapter also shows how, occasionally, the magazines depart from their characteristic emphasis on phallic certitude to admit varying degrees of sexual anxiety. More commonly, however, the magazines offer a mix of irony, practical hints, calculative reason and playful misogyny in their approach to personal relationships.

Rather than simply condemning the magazines' treatment of personal relationships as shallow and misogynistic, however, we view them (within certain limits) as offering a source of pleasure and amusement but also as deeply ambiguous. In adopting an ironic or cynical tone, they provide a means of temporary escape from the contradictions of contemporary gender relations, evading the need to engage with the more uncertain scripts that those relations increasingly demand.

We also analyse *Men's Health* magazine, which is representative of a more niche-marketed aspect of magazine production. Aimed at a slightly older audience, *Men's Health* was of interest to us, as it has resisted the more obvious excesses of lad culture, expressing advice in an instrumental rather than an ironic tone. However, as we argue, while it articulates a more responsible version of the masculine subject, it also instrumentalizes masculinity by employing a hierarchical discourse of scientific expertise. In particular, we draw attention to the ways in which the magazine focuses on the idea of an uncertain future through metaphors of the body as machine, notions of speed and performance, and the displacement of concerns about human ageing and bodily decline. We end the chapter by considering the magazines' ambivalent political significance.

Chapter 5 examines the way the magazines are read and talked about by different individuals and groups of men, based on our analysis of the focus group transcripts. We identify a series of *discursive repertoires* that men use to 'make sense' of the magazines. These include notions of 'surface and depth', 'honesty', 'naturalness', 'openness', 'harmless fun', 'change' (or 'backlash'), 'seriousness' and 'women as Other'. We then draw on Ulrich Beck's (1992) notion of 'constructed certitude' to demonstrate how the magazines can be seen as a kind of magical resolution of men's anxieties and apprehensions (whether arising from job insecurity, the demands of feminism or other sources of uncertainty).

We then turn our attention to the different *dispositions* which different individuals and groups of men take towards the previously identified discourses, including 'celebration', 'compliance' and 'hostility', an 'apologetic', 'deferential' or 'defensive' approach, a 'vulnerable', 'distanced' or 'rejecting' disposition, and an 'analytical', 'dismissive' or 'ironic' stance. Identifying this range of dispositions helps us to highlight the ambivalences and instabilities in the ways the magazines are read, rather than assuming that all men have an equal investment in the magazines or are equally complicit in the magazines' dominant representation of laddish masculinities. (Our analysis therefore departs significantly from recent media representations which emphasize a depressingly homogenized dumbing down of masculinity to its most uniformly laddish form.) We then draw on Pierre Bourdieu's (1984) notion of cultural capital to show how the different discourses and dispositions are distributed among different groups of men, reflecting their differential power, including the power to hold and express an opinion. The chapter concludes by arguing that the magazines occupy an ambivalent space in both a metaphorical and a material sense. Metaphorically, the magazines provide their readers with a conceptual map for traversing some of the complexities of contemporary masculinity and commercial culture. Materially, the magazines provide a kind of public forum where

issues of men's health, personal relationships and bodily appearance
have not previously been so widely discussed. In this sense, then, we
argue that the magazines have played an important role in shifting
the discursive geography of contemporary masculinities, helping men
to develop their practical and discursive competencies in a more
reflexive and publicly mediated way.

In the Conclusion (chapter 6) we draw the empirical evidence
together, returning to some of our key ideas about constructed
certitude, cultural capital, irony and ambivalence. We reassert the
historical specificity of our argument regarding changes in the magazine industry and popular culture during the 1990s, and we return to
our understanding of the operation of cultural power, not in terms
of media hegemony and reader resistance or compliance, but in terms
of the resonances between discourses that circulate among the magazines, their readers and wider media debate. We show how the
magazines have encouraged men to 'open up' previously repressed
aspects of their masculinity (including attitudes to health, fashion
and relationships) but how this increasing openness has its attendant
risks and anxieties. We contrast our own findings with those of two
studies of men's magazines, by Sean Nixon (1996), who sees the
magazines as a reflection of changes in masculinity, and Tim Edwards
(1997), who argues that the changes have little to do with changing
gender identities and much more to do with changing commercial
cultures. Our own interpretation treads a middle path, arguing that
the magazines represent a commodification of men's current gender
troubles, opening up the potential for radical change but using
humour, irony and other devices to distance men from any significant
commitment to personal or collective change.

Rather than condemning the magazines as a space in which older,
reactionary forms of masculinity are being celebrated and reinscribed
(albeit in an ironic tone), we wish to interpret the magazines' cultural
significance in more ambivalent terms. Like other forms of commercial culture (Jackson et al., 2000), the magazines are poised uncer-
tainly, with the creative and radical potential for reworking
traditional forms of masculinity constantly undermined by commercial imperatives. The commercial success of the magazines, in terms
of the pressure for increased circulation and advertising revenue,
suggests that this equation is likely to be resolved in favour of more
reactionary ('laddish') versions of masculinity. While this is particularly the case in terms of magazine content and editorial control, our
focus groups provide evidence of a variety of 'readings', including
those which display greater ambiguity and reflexivity towards the
masculinities currently represented in the magazines. It is in this

sense, we would argue, that the magazines signify the *potential* for new forms of masculinity to emerge even as the magazines are simultaneously reinscribing older and more repressive forms of masculinity.

2

The Media and the Market

Sometimes I'm not happy being a bloke in the late twentieth century. Sometimes I'd rather be my Dad, he never had to worry about delivering the goods, because he never knew there were any goods to deliver.

(Nick Hornby, *High Fidelity* 1995: 102)

This chapter introduces the history of magazines as a specific cultural form which, despite some early exceptions, soon came to be regarded as a predominantly feminine genre. It charts the history of magazines for men from the eighteenth and nineteenth centuries, focusing particularly on the development since the late 1980s of a new generation of men's 'lifestyle' magazines. Documenting the commercial success of these magazines in the 1990s, as the number of titles proliferated and as sales soared, the chapter explores the way they were discussed in the newspapers and other media. The chapter argues that these media debates, together with the magazines themselves, provided a key context for thinking about contemporary masculinities, including a range of discourses that resonated strongly with the variety of readings we uncovered in our focus group research (discussed in chapter 5).

The magazine market

Magazines have had a central place in popular print culture at least since the beginning of the nineteenth century when the magazine emerged as a distinctive cultural form: literally a 'storehouse' or 'repository' of material by various hands, as distinct from the single-authored serial or periodical.[1] The earliest magazines developed alongside newspapers in the late seventeenth century, including such titles as *The Gentleman's Journal*, which dates from 1692 and which described itself as 'a Letter to a gentleman in the country, consisting of News, History, Philosophy, Poetry, Musick, Translations, etc.' (Davis, 1988). While some of the earliest titles were aimed explicitly at male readers, the magazine soon came to be regarded as a specifically feminine genre.[2]

The historical development of women's magazines is described in detail by Margaret Beetham (1996) who traces the establishment of such characteristic features as the agony aunt and the fashion plate, together with a simultaneous concern – often held in uneasy tension – for dutiful domesticity and romantic desire. In the magazines that Beetham reviews, useful tips on good housekeeping (of varying degrees of practicality) appeared alongside romantic fiction (of varying degrees of sentimentality). Much of the feminist literature on magazine reading (discussed in chapter 1) has addressed this same tension, highlighting the way that women's magazines forged a 'space for women' while simultaneously reinscribing conventional gender roles and relations through patriarchal notions of compulsory heterosexuality, romantic love and the apparent inescapability of the nuclear family.[3]

Despite some early precursors, such as *The Gentleman's Magazine* (founded in 1731), which circulated in the upper-class world of the gentleman's club throughout the nineteenth century, and *Blackwood's Magazine* (founded in 1817 and known affectionately as 'The Magga'), magazines for men are of comparatively recent origin. Apart from publications such as *Playboy*, which celebrated the liberal sexual mores of 1950s America and helped legitimate what Barbara Ehrenreich describes as 'a consumerist personality for men' (1983: 171), magazines for men generally catered for a special interest market in photography and film, and sports and motor cars, where the appeal to readers' masculinity was largely unstated and taken for granted. Newspapers, too, might be defined as an implicitly masculinist form of print culture, though their readership has been in steady decline for several decades.[4]

A significant predecessor of the current generation of men's magazines, *Esquire*, was launched in the United States in the 1930s for a predominantly male readership, containing short stories by authors such as Ernest Hemingway and F. Scott Fitzgerald. According to Kenon Breazeale (1994: 4), the magazine's founders, David Smart and William Weintraub, both had a background in menswear and saw the magazine as a vehicle for advertising men's apparel. Editorial content was a virtual afterthought. Though its editor Arnold Gingrich claimed the *New Yorker* and *Vanity Fair* as inspiration, *Esquire*'s immediate precursor was the trade press and business magazines like *Fortune*. Despite its literary pretensions, *Esquire* has been criticized for its misogyny, having been keen to distance itself from women and from what Gingrich described as 'the whiff of lavender' (homosexuality) in its desire to court men as consumers: 'the challenge was to contrive a balance, or better put, a tension, between a sub rosa assertion that the magazine was enjoyably salacious and a more overt claim that it was absolutely respectable' (Breazeale, 1994: 11).[5] Through an arch tone and a characteristic use of ironic humour, *Esquire* worked to veil these contradictions, balancing titillation and reassurance, fine arts and cheesecake. When *Playboy* was launched twenty years later (in 1953), Breazeale argues that men could be addressed directly as consumers without having to denigrate women, as *Esquire* had previously done in order to establish its distance from the feminine world of consumption: 'We like our apartment. We enjoy mixing up cocktails and an hors d'oeuvre or two, putting a little mood music on the phonograph and inviting in a female for a quiet discussion of Picasso, Nietzsche, jazz and sex' (*Playboy*, 5 January 1953: 3). Meanwhile, with stories such as 'What men don't like about women' (July 1939), 'Ladies are lousy drivers' (January 1941) and 'Clamorous Janes' (October 1945), *Esquire* stands accused of having been responsible for 'some of our era's most aggressively one-dimensional representations of women' (Breazeale, 1994: 1).

Some of the same tensions recurred in Britain when the idea of launching a 'general interest' magazine for men was first mooted. Despite the success of the gentleman's tailoring magazine *Man About Town*, which ran under various titles from 1953 to 1968, and several gay magazines like *Spartacus* in the late 1960s, the British publishing industry was distinctly cautious about men's magazines.[6] Though *Arena*'s founding editor, Nick Logan, argued that 'since the 1960s men have been interested in fashion and style' (*The Times*, 6 September 1989), others were less sure. According to Mark Boxer, editorial director at Condé Nast:

I think there's a problem with men's magazines. Men are already well served for sport, the City and politics by newspapers. . . . They're now getting freebies sent to Diners Club and American Express card holders. There is too much to read already. The one area there might be a gap is for a style magazine – but in that area Englishmen are uneasy, they don't admit to taking fashion seriously. (*Observer*, 26 April 1987; quoted in Nixon, 1996: 138)

The major publishing houses had been scared off by the failure of *The Hit*, IPC's first men's title, which was launched in 1985 but collapsed after six issues.[7] NMC had published *Cosmo Man* as a supplement to *Cosmopolitan* in 1984 and Condé Nast already had a successful men's title (*GQ*), published in the US since the mid-1980s. This nervousness about the British men's magazine market resurfaced in 1988 when Condé Nast launched a British edition of *GQ*. Though titles like *L'Huomo Vogue* and *L'Homme Vogue* had been used in Italy and France, Condé Nast preferred to distance the British edition from its sister magazine. According to Sean Nixon: 'The name *GQ* was favoured over *Vogue for Men* because of the feminine connotations of the latter' (1996: 141). There were similar fears about the magazine's appeal to straight readers, with press reports (*Independent*, 10 January 1990) that the editor had been given the task of 'hetting up' the magazine's editorial content for its British readership.

One important exception to most of the above trends was the launch in 1978 of *Achilles Heel*, a radical journal run by a collective of socialist men who were interested in men's consciousness-raising and other forms of anti-sexist politics (see Seidler (1991) for a selection of articles). With its close links to feminism and interest in men's liberation, the magazine was never commercially very significant. But it provided an important forum for debates about changing masculinities, including a discussion about the significance of the 'new man' and 'the new men's glossies' ('Fact or Fad?' *Achilles Heel*, Winter 1992–3).

As this brief history suggests, the new generation of men's general interest or lifestyle magazines was launched into a relative vacuum in the early 1980s. Their immediate predecessors were style magazines such as *i-D* (published by Time Out), *Blitz* (Jigsaw) and *The Face* (Wagadon), all of which flourished in the 1980s, together with teenage music magazines such as the *New Musical Express* and *Smash Hits*. As others have noted (Mort, 1996; Nixon, 1996), several of the first men's magazine editors had a background in the style and music press, notably Nick Logan at *Arena*, who had previously worked on *Smash Hits*, *NME* and *The Face*, and Mike Soutar at *FHM* who had also worked at *Smash Hits*.

While the major publishers prevaricated, a small independent publisher, Wagadon, entered the market in 1986 with *Arena*, edited by Nick Logan. Once its success was established, the main publishers

Table 2.1   The British men's magazine market in the mid-1990s

Title	Date launched	Publisher	Publisher's related titles
Arena	1986	Wagadon	The Face
GQ (Gentlemen's Quarterly)	1988 (GQ Active, April 1997)	Condé Nast	Vogue, Vanity Fair, House & Garden, etc.
Esquire	1991	National Magazine Company	Cosmopolitan, Harpers & Queen, etc.
Attitude	1994	Northern & Shell	Penthouse
FHM (For Him Magazine)	1994	EMAP	Q, Mojo, Select, etc
Loaded	1994	IPC	Marie Claire, Home & Gardens, Women, etc.
Men's Health	1995	Rodale Press	
XL for Men	1995	EMAP (formerly Stonehart)	Q, Mojo, Select, etc
Maxim	1995	Dennis Lifestyle	Stuff for Men
Stuff for Men	1996	Dennis Lifestyle (acquired by Haymarket 1999)	Maxim

followed suit, aiming to get a share of the burgeoning men's market and to create a range of men's titles to match their established women's magazines (see table 2.1). Until the late 1980s, however, the received wisdom in the publishing industry was that 'men don't buy magazines', or at least that :

> men don't define themselves as men in what they read [but] as people who are into cars, who play golf, or fish. . . . Successfully launching a general interest men's magazine would be like finding the holy grail. (Campaign, 29 August 1986; our emphasis)[8]

Within ten years, however, men's magazines had become 'The fastest growing of all consumer magazine markets [with] currently the highest profile' (Key Note 1996).

Table 2.2   Retail sales of men's magazines by type of outlet, 1994–6

	1994		1996 (est.)	
	(£m)	(%)	(£m)	(%)
Confectioners, newsagents and tobacconists	5.12	46	14.02	44
Newsagent chains	3.59	32	9.56	30
News-stands	1.24	11	3.19	10
Subscriptions	0.45	4	2.23	7
Garage forecourts, supermarkets, etc.	0.83	7	2.86	9
Total	11.23	100	31.86	100

Source: Mintel (1997)

Since the early 1990s, the market has developed in a truly spectacular way. A 1997 Mintel report on men's lifestyle magazines describes a 400 per cent growth from 1991 to 1996 in a sector that it estimated to be worth £30.9 million in cover sales revenue, predicted to grow to £68 million by 2000. Mintel's analysis of retail sales also suggests that men's magazines have a higher proportion of subscriptions than women's titles (though we found very few subscribers among our focus group participants) and higher sales via garage forecourts than most women's magazines (see table 2.2).

While there are some similarities in content and style among the magazines included within our study, there are also some significant differences. Some titles (including *GQ* and *Esquire*) are more 'upmarket' in terms of content and readership; others are resolutely 'downmarket' (including the market leaders, *FHM*, *Loaded* and *Maxim*).[9] Some have a specific focus: on extreme sports (*Xtreme*), health (*Men's Health*) or computing (*Escape*). Others have spun off from the success of their parent magazines to address a more specific niche (such as *Stuff for Men* from *Maxim*, or *GQ Active* from *GQ*). All are addressed, at least implicitly, to a heterosexual readership, with the exception of *Attitude*, which specifically targets gay men. Some of the magazines, notably *Loaded* and *FHM*, have achieved a genuinely mass circulation (with monthly sales of several hundred thousand); others have a much lower circulation.[10] The titles included here are all monthly (or in some cases, bi-monthly) magazines, costing between £2 and £3. They vary from around 120 to 300 pages

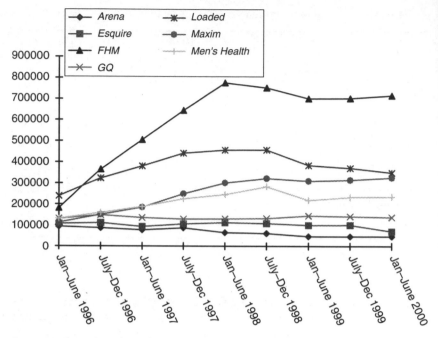

Source: Audit Bureau of Circulations

Figure 2.1   Magazine circulation

in length, with advertising accounting for between 20 and 40 per cent of their pages.[11]

Circulation figures confirm the growth of the sector, first dominated by *Loaded* and later by *FHM* (see figure 2.1). They also show significant expansion among some of the more upmarket titles, such as *Men's Health*, as well as the relatively static or declining sales of some of the longer-established titles (such as *Arena* and *Esquire*). As competition has increased, the market has clearly begun to segment into a small number of mass-circulation titles and numerous specialist or niche markets. The most recent figures (for July–December 1999 and January–June 2000) might even suggest that the expansion of the men's magazine market has peaked, with sales of most of the leading titles showing a decline.[12] At their peak, however, men's magazines generated a vast amount of media commentary, which we now go on to discuss.

Contemporary media debates

The unprecedented commercial success of men's magazines in the 1990s gave rise to a series of media debates which sought to relate their astonishing popularity to the alleged crisis of masculinity that was constantly being discussed in the media during the course of our research. These debates were, in turn, reflected in the discourses that were articulated by our focus group participants (discussed in chapter 5). As has been discussed elsewhere (Barker and Brooks, 1998), research into people's pleasures in popular cultural forms can mean negotiating with the 'disciplinary discourses' of the media by which talk of such pleasures is constrained. Popular action films, Mills and Boon romances, comics, TV sitcoms, for example – and now men's lifestyle magazines – all carry with them possible value judgements of their worthlessness, or indeed harm, to those who enjoy and consume them.

When we began to analyse the transcripts of our focus groups, we were aware that the participants often acknowledged, either explicitly or implicitly, humorously or otherwise, the possibility that we as academic researchers were judging their responses to these new magazines. A common response or defence of one's reading pleasures was the disclaimer, 'I'm not sad, but . . .', and a common criticism of our assumed position as academics was to claim that we were being overly analytical and therefore not getting the (ironic) joke.[13] However, we also found a considerable number of people who were willing to celebrate or at least to speak openly about what they saw as the more positive elements of the magazines. This could have been because we were in some way positioned as representing the magazine industry, or indeed as a way of subverting the hierarchies of power and knowledge involved in the research process. That is, despite the low regard that many have for popular magazines within our culture, many of the focus group participants felt confident enough to speak up for the magazines and defend their pleasures.

In chapter 5 we make a distinction between two different forms of public talk about the magazines, identifying the discursive repertoires through which individuals and social groups make the magazines meaningful, and the dispositions which describe their degree of commitment to those discourses. A certain repertoire may, for example, be acknowledged, rejected, satirized and so on. The distinction allows us to draw attention to the role of researcher effects (which are discussed at greater length in the Appendix) and to acknowledge the wider social processes through which these forms of public talk are constituted. In this case, we suggest that media discourses about the magazines constitute one of the key sites for the formation of this public talk. The focus group discussions to which we turn in chapter 5 can then be seen as a reflection of the participants' reactions to us as academics (and our assumed agenda) and as a series of (sometimes critical) reflections on the discourses that were currently circulating more widely in the media.

Sean Nixon (1996: 4) argues that television and press advertising, menswear retailing and men's magazines were 'key sites of cultural circulation' for imagery of the new man. This chapter moves on from Nixon's discussion of visual representations to focus on the discursive representations of 'new' masculinities, looking at some of the key sites of cultural commentary. For the duration of the project, more than 200 articles and press cuttings on the magazines and the crisis of masculinity were collected from as many sources as possible, including newspapers, other magazines and the internet. It is in these sites, we argue, that struggles over rival systems of classification can be located with competing versions of masculinity emerging in these texts, to be labelled, debated, discussed, championed and rejected.

Because we are concerned here with media representations of the magazines and the part those representations played in debates on masculinity in crisis, this chapter will not address any similar debates which took place in the magazines themselves – these are dealt with in chapter 4 – nor the considerable media attention on the editors themselves, particularly *Loaded*'s editor, James Brown – which is discussed in chapter 3. Whilst the changing themes of the debate did not occur in a strictly linear fashion – some publications were heralding the end of the new lad before others had even acknowledged his existence – the intention here is to group such themes loosely in a way that makes best sense of them.

Masculinity in crisis?

Much of the media debate centred on the notion that, as definitions of masculinity were now in question, masculinity itself must be in crisis (cf. Horrocks, 1994). The explosion of new representations of masculinities has been well documented in academic studies on men's magazines, including Edwards (1997), Mort (1996) and Nixon (1996), in historical perspectives on gender, such as Bourke (1996), Faludi (1992, 1999) and Kimmel (1987), and in other places as diverse as *Take a Break*, *US Business Week*, *Achilles Heel* and

Kilroy. Indeed, the notion that masculinity is in crisis is so widely assumed, Kimmel (1987) argues, as to have become a cultural commonplace both here in the UK and in the United States.

Certainly, such debates on masculinity and contemporary men's magazines can and did function as disciplinary discourses to some of those attempting to describe or defend their pleasures in what others clearly regarded as trash. However, we attempt to go beyond seeing these debates in terms of media effects or consumer resistance, in order to begin to conceptualize how people *use* the media: how, in this instance, they draw upon and engage with such media debates in their articulations of their discursive repertoires. In this way, we can conceptualize the relationship between magazines and their readers (and, indeed, non-readers) in terms of ambivalence rather than via more simplistic and cumbersome notions of resistance or effects.[14]

According to *Achilles Heel*, the new man was 'born in the 1970s . . . professional, usually white, heterosexual and between 25 and indeterminate middle age. He is . . . having somewhat of an identity crisis as his girlfriend(s) discover feminism' (Winter 1992–3). The 1980s and early 1990s saw an unprecedented amount of media attention on the meanings of masculinity and the possibilities of the new man. *The Times*, for example, saw masculinity as 'the issue of the nineties' as feminism had left men 'struggling for an identity' (31 May 1991). Craik argues that, in general, the new man was a 'contradictory composite' (1994: 197), particularly where the marketing of men's fashions was concerned. The new man was 'not only aware of fashion but an active consumer in the pursuit of his sense of self' (ibid.: 198). The epitome of this complex representation was, according to Craik, the early 1980s advertisements for British Pure New Wool, in which a man in a woollen jumper prowled the urban streets as a 'wolf in sheep's clothing'. Soft yet strong, sensitive yet sexy, cool yet caring, the success of the new man and his pullover, and the subsequent growth of the men's fashion market heralded the emergence in the late 1980s of these new men's lifestyle magazines.

Mort, among others, was optimistic that magazines such as *GQ* and *Arena* might offer new ways of looking both at and for men:

[Y]oung men are being sold images which rupture traditional icons of masculinity. They are stimulated to look at themselves – and other men – as objects of consumer desire. They are getting pleasures previously branded taboo or feminine. A new bricolage of masculinity is the noise coming up from the fashion house, the marketplace and the street. (1988: 94)

However, the wolf in sheep's clothing was not welcomed by everybody. The *Guardian* queried, 'does the New Man exist outside the realms of TV advertisements?' and concluded, 'those guest appearances of Family Man in . . . advertisements are evidence of how men like to see themselves these days, not of a serious commitment to equality' (20 June 1990). In June 1988, writing in *New Socialist*, Rowena Chapman similarly argued that 'in reality the new man served consumer capitalism very well . . . [he] represents not so much a rebellion but a reform in masculinity'. The *Guardian* saw these reforms towards the traditionally feminine spheres of domesticity and consumerism as a sign that 'having secured the heartland of the public, men are now moving onto the private', whilst Chapman ominously concluded that 'men change in order to hold onto power, not to relinquish it'.[15]

Critics of the new man focused on a set number of themes. First, the sensitive but stylish new man was middle class. This meant that, on the one hand, he was dismissed as part of another 1980s image, the expensively dressed, shallow-minded yuppie. In his account of the 'inside story of *Loaded*', one-time editor Tim Southwell recalls that *Arena*, *GQ* and *Esquire* had been 'around for a while and they were laughably out of touch . . . none of us read them. They just seemed obsessed with fashion' (1998: 17). On the other hand, the middle-class new man of the *Achilles Heel* variety was, by definition, a wimp: his attempts at Political Correctness and sympathies with feminism rendered him 'apologetic . . . feeble' (*Mail on Sunday*, 12 February 1995), with 'pathetic, po-faced views' (*Independent*, 7 February 1995). Feminism and designer fashion were both thus simultaneously dismissed as middle-class, yuppie trends, which the early fashion lifestyle magazines can be seen to represent. Second, the new man's self-consciousness, whether in the men's group or the fashion houses, rendered him undesirable to women, as if, it seemed, once men become aware of 'being-looked-at', of their position as a passive object of potential female desire, they become sexless, pretty boys, wimps. A man can only be an object of desire if he appears not to realize he is so, and women can thus only actively desire by taking sneaky, voyeuristic peeks – from Nick Kamen in the 1980s, casually undressing in the laundrette, oblivious to the stares, to the semi-naked window cleaner of the 1990s who appears not to notice the women crowding in the office window as he blithely passes by on his daily 11.30 Diet Coke break.

Self-consciousness here equals lack of spontaneity, and lack of any possibility of active male sexuality. Rosie Boycott, once editor of *Spare Rib*, then editor of men's magazine, *Esquire*, on the impossibilities of 'equal' sex, declared in the *Mail on Sunday* that 'women can't *bear* the idea of a bloke who goes to the supermarket and buys the nappies . . . You want to be equal in the office, but who wants equal sex?' (1 January 1995). The point was underlined by *More!* magazine's quiz to find out the best type of potential boyfriend, which described the new man as 'more likely to enjoy going to the theatre with a female friend' than watching an 'Arnie movie with his girlie' and warned that, eventually, 'his unwillingness to be spontaneous will drive you potty' (15–28 January 1997).

Finally, the new man was a hypocrite, an 'unreal' man, dishonest about his desires. 'Young men', according to the *Mail on Sunday*, were 'coming out of the politically correct closet and admitting all that nappy changing stuff was baloney' (1 January 1995). Identifying the new man as hypocritical or dishonest provided a space for the emergence of more unapologetically laddish forms of masculinity. In an article in *The Face* (February 1986), for example, Julie Burchill described the characteristics of this form of masculinity, 'the lad', as 'on the make' in both a social and a sexual sense. Similarly, Sean O'Hagan's article on the 'New Lad' in *Arena* (May 1991) was based on a debunking of 'this supposed "new man" with his phoney nappy changing . . . ways', according to its current editor, Kathryn Flett (*Observer* 13 November 1994).

O'Hagan's article began by describing the new man as a 'stillborn species', a 'myth', an 'advertising concept' catering to 'female wishful thinking'. Now, O'Hagan writes, the new man is a joke, a figure of fun. However, just because the new man does not exist doesn't mean that things haven't changed between men and women: O'Hagan heralds the birth of a 'slippery sub-species which has emerged as a muted response to the embarrassing vacuum left by the New Man's ignominious non-appearance'. What we are dealing with here, is 'a would be New Man who can't quite shake off his out-moded, but snug fitting, laddishness'. The generic term to describe him is 'New Lad': 'basically, the New Lad aspires to New Man status when he's with women, but reverts to Old Lad type when he's out with the boys. Clever eh?'. The New Lad is, O'Hagan warns, 'pretty flaky' but he is nevertheless 'a damn sight more fun than the New Man and a damn sight more progressive than the Old Lad, who, incidentally, is still going strong – loud, proud and utterly unreconstitutable'.

Thus the apparent failure of new man icons of masculinity could be said to be due to their inability to overcome the common-sense notion that male self-reflexivity, whether in terms of personal style or personal politics, was somehow 'unreal' and 'phoney'. To analyse at all was to over-analyse, to take it all too seriously, as if 'real men'

– to borrow the Nike slogan – 'just do it'. (These themes are a staple of our focus group discussions, reported in chapter 5.)

O'Hagan's article concludes with a warning that 'ultimately, there is something sad about the New Lad ... basically we didn't have the will, nor the nerve, to seriously consider such a radical shift in our consciousness. Basically, to steal a recent advertising slogan, the New Lad is "the best a man can get"' (O'Hagan, 1996). This so-called lost moment is largely ignored or forgotten in the popular press's subsequent enthusiasm for more laddish versions of masculinity.

Whilst it was the tabloids in particular which championed the new lad and the supposed 'blokelash' against feminism and the navel-gazing new man, they were not by any means the only ones pleased to herald this new version of masculinity. Writing in *The Sunday Times*, for example, A. A. Gill declared: 'there's no need to bark on about inequality' – indeed, he saw sexism in this post-feminist age as 'no more than a fantasy bred by a few embittered maiden aunts' (*Sunday Times*, 10 October 1994). In a similarly enthusiastic celebration of what could indeed be termed a 'back to basics' approach to masculinity, the *Mail on Sunday* (1 January 1995) printed a list of 'Lad Facts': what they eat (pub snacks), what they don't ('formal meals'), who were 'top lads' (George Best, Primal Scream) and who were not (John Major, Cliff Richard), what they liked (Tarantino, 'a laugh') and what they didn't (marriage, snobs) – and the magazine that came to epitomize these trends was, of course, *Loaded*.

Learning from Loaded?

According to its one-time editor Tim Southwell (1998), *Loaded* was formed as an antidote to new man imagery. *Loaded*'s success was phenomenal, and changed the face, and certainly the covers, of the men's magazine market. *Arena*'s original strapline was 'success with style', and, indeed, early covers of men's lifestyle magazines included, somewhat unbelievably now, public figures such as Michael Heseltine, whilst the cover of *Loaded*, with its strapline 'for men who should know better', featured semi-naked female celebrities, such as fashion models, pop and soap stars. By 1997 *Arena*, *GQ* and *Esquire* had began to emulate *Loaded*, as *GQ*, for example, regularly featured Caprice, the latest Wonderbra model and 'It' girl.

It is no surprise that the tabloids were keen on the lad culture of *Loaded* and its imitators. Both employed a sense of 'permissive populism' and a particular discursive notion of 'fun' (Hunt, 1998). Just as the tabloids focus on sex, sensation, scandal and sport (Sanderson, 1994), so too the defining interests of lad culture were depressingly similar, no matter where they were listed: 'The traditional staples of male life: fast cars, loud music, competitive sports . . . great looking babes and lots of booze' (*Mail on Sunday*, 1 January 1995); 'beer, birds and bad language' (*Guardian*, 10 October 1994); 'football, lager, birds' (*More!*, 15–28 November 1997); 'football, beer, sexy women, sports' (*Herald Tribune*, 28 November 1996); 'women, fast cars, sport' (*The Australian*, 18 June 1997); 'scantily clad babes, sex, sports' (*Observer*, 11 August 1996); 'sex, lager and football' (*Independent*, 19 April 1997); 'football, clubbing, women, drink' (*The Bookseller*, 18 April 1997); 'football, beer, sex and rock' (*Daily Telegraph*, 15 May 1997); 'boozing and getting laid' (*City Limits*, quoted in *Achilles Heel*, Autumn 1991); 'sex, fashion, music, cars, shopping' (*Marketing*, 10 February 1994); and 'birds, beer and football' (*The Big Issue*, 23–9 March 1998).

Both the tabloids and the new lads' magazines share a fascination for conventionally attractive female celebrities from popular TV shows and advertisements, and an idealistic, nostalgic notion of the good old days of white, working-class (male) Britishness. This sense of nostalgia was frequently referenced in *Loaded* via 1970s sit-com characters and the Golden Age of football and footballers (mainly George Best), and indeed by world war imagery, as in the *Sun*'s infamous reporting on the England–Germany game in the 1997 European championships.[16] Both share what Sanderson (1994) terms the 'merry violence' of blokey, jokey colloquialisms ('Nice work fellah!') and a sense of humour that tends towards sexism, racism and homophobia.

Resisting the political?

For the tabloids, then, there was no sense of masculinity in crisis, as the new lad was a straightforward return to more honest representations of masculinity, a long-awaited backlash to political correctness and humourless, sexless feminism, a (reactionary) return to happy heterosexual hedonism. Indeed, the *Mail on Sunday*, echoing A. A. Gill's observations, dismissed the very notion that masculinity was in crisis at all, describing it as 'dreamt up by crew cut North London feminists . . . [and] academics with ideological hang ups' (1 January 1995). These responses are, however, more complex than they might initially seem. The attempt to naturalize one particular version of

masculine identity during a period of social change has obvious
political connotations (as we discuss in chapters 4, 5 and 6 in terms
of the notion of 'constructed certitude').

This sense that Other People – particularly academics – are unable
to appreciate the harmless fun of the magazines is an important
point, and one to which we will return in our discussion of magazine
content in chapter 4. The tendency for academics, particularly in
cultural studies, to over-analyse the obvious is a common cause for
tabloid mirth. Studies on films, comics and magazines are usually
derided as foolish, ivory tower nonsense: these things are fun, to be
enjoyed just for a laugh, and any response other than that is sadly
missing the point. Likewise, Tim Southwell articulates this rejection
of any notion of crisis, in his inside story of *Loaded*. Here, once
again, it is academics and sensitive feminists who 'saw *Loaded* as
Beelzebub's shopping list in print' (1998: 42). It is they who are in
crisis, so caught up with political correctness and over-analysis that
they can no longer appreciate the harmless fun of Caprice, George
Best and similar laddish icons.

This resistance to the political can possibly be explained through
the way the magazines are positioned within a culture of consumption. The informal symbolic creativity that is required to 'make sense'
of the magazines in this interpretation depends upon a sense of play
rather than work. Thus, to offer a political reading of the magazines
could be perceived as a form of symbolic violence, seeking to silence
some of the more informal pleasures of the text. In this interpretation,
to have a politics of consumption is to deny the fun and creativity
involved in reading the magazines (cf. Willis, 1990). As we discuss in
chapter 5, this has obvious implications for our focus groups: regardless of our intention to be as exploratory as possible, we might have
been perceived as tied to a humourless and technocratic agenda that
sought to deny pleasure and semiotic plurality. That is, it was not so
much political conservatism that we were discovering as a resistance
to different forms of moralism.

A related reason could be the differential availability of political
registers of thinking. Following Elizabeth Frazer (1992), we might
argue that the way we interpret the magazines depends upon the
different styles of talk and knowledges to which we have access, and
which of those are deemed appropriate for using in conjunction with
magazines. In our society, commercial and leisure cultures are often
viewed as being a form of harmless fun, as a defence against those
who would like to stop people from enjoying themselves. As above,
then, politics is read as a form of humourlessness. Such critiques not
only point to a limited understanding of politics, but also highlight

the need to develop a popular politics that takes pleasure seriously, as many feminist writers have suggested.[17] In this reading, politics simply stops us having fun. And, as we have argued, it was these kinds of populist sentiment that tabloid newspapers built upon throughout the 1980s and 1990s in the construction of a popular common sense.

The formation of a counter-culture?

Although a number of Loaded's original writers came from Arena, such as Mick ('Dr Mick') Bunnage and Sean O'Hagan, the magazine's reference points were drawn not from the style press and women's glossies, but from various other (often counter-cultural) forms, particularly those which its young male readership were likely to share. These include – as documented by Nixon (1996) and Mort (1996) – music (Primal Scream's 'Loaded' gave the magazine its title, and editor James Brown came from the NME), 'alternative' writings such as the 'Gonzo journalism' of Hunter S. Thompson, and fanzines (again, a number of the magazine's writers had started out writing fanzines – amateur, anarchic, non-commercial fan magazines – including Southwell).

In his work on fanzines for what he calls 'paracinematic' or 'trash' cinema,[18] Jeffrey Sconce uses Bourdieu's term 'autodidact' to describe 'a person who invests in unsanctioned culture . . . because he or she can "afford" to' (Sconce, 1995: 379). In other words, one who is usually 'middle class and university educated', and subsequently has 'double access to high and low culture' (Gripsrud, 1989: 199), who is thus able to celebrate 'trash' whilst simultaneously displaying cultural capital in the skilled ways in which this trash is, usually ironically, appreciated (by 'men who should know better'). As Hunt (1998) remarks in his discussion of the 'low culture' of the 1970s, 'only a select few will "get" the counter-aesthetic virtues of Curse of the Swamp Creature' – and, likewise, as Southwell discovered, only those sharing the reference points of the magazine's writers will 'get' Loaded.

In his disarming account of Loaded's attempt at a roadshow, Southwell vividly describes the problems of potential misreadings of the magazine writers' message by its enthusiastic punters:

Basically what we had in mind was for us to . . . regale the audience with tremendous tales of publishing and derring-do . . . our attempts to do any regaling however were cut short by a rowdy three front rows who – plastered on all the free alcohol we'd supplied (duh!) – hurled a variety of abuse in our direction . . . these geezers just didn't get it at all. (Southwell 1998: 233–4)

He quotes another writer also on stage:

They were just pissed up and obnoxious . . . I thought we'd attract people who were into the writing, who were into the humour, who got the point of it . . . But . . . we did play into their hands [by introducing 'Page 3' girls on stage] . . . we gave them a reason to be Neanderthals. (ibid.: 234–5)[19]

Loaded has various roots: the explosion of the DIY rave music scene in the 1980s and its emphasis on anti-authoritarian hedonism, the supposed backlash to middle-class ideologies of political correctness, perhaps also the nostalgic 1990s retro fashion for all things '70s,[20] and possibly most significantly, given many of *Loaded* writers' backgrounds, the counter-culture of (maga)zines. Zine writers are, as Duncombe argues, in the main 'young . . . culturally if not financially middle class. White and raised in a relatively privileged position within the dominant culture' (1997: 8). The type of zines celebrating 'derided cultural forms' exist, according to Duncombe, both out of enjoyment of so-called trash cultural forms, and as a critique of middle-class taste criteria. Essential to a zine's success is its position on the edge of mainstream culture and within a knowing middle-class counter-culture.

Southwell had believed that it was obvious that *Loaded* had a 'cultural agenda' of 'witty and irreverent journalistic style' which would have surely put off the 'truly Neanderthal end of the British male evolutionary scale'. However, the subcultural sensibility of irreverent, satirical journalism, and *Loaded*'s particular idiom of an ironic reworking of tabloid discourses, do not travel well into mainstream success. The various roots of the magazine inevitably render it ambiguous – on the one hand, supposedly ironic counter-culture with *Viz*-like, comic humour; on the other, tabloid-like sexist soft porn belonging on the top shelves. The magazine's very position on the newsagents' shelves illustrates this ambiguity – sometimes on the top shelf, sometimes next to *FHM*, sometimes alongside 'adult comic' *Viz*.

A male malaise?

If *Loaded* had come to represent a more honest, post-new-man version of masculinity, it now came to represent a particular form of male malaise. Many of those who had originally celebrated *Loaded* as offering an alternative to political correctness and aspirational yuppiedom, became disillusioned. Journalist Jack O'Sullivan, for example, described how 'the press will publish any story that is a variant on the theme of *Men Behaving Badly*, any writer whose underlying assumption is that men are useless'. He continues that this is in no small part attributable to men's magazines such as *Loaded*, which:

> takes pride in portraying us . . . as witless, porn obsessed, drunken serial shaggers. . . . [T]his championing of male sexual desire is a breath of fresh air after that stillborn, asexual being the New Man. . . . But New Laddery, in slavishly adopting its own negative feminist stereotype of men, exposes its own bankruptcy. It has no positive vision for men (*Independent*, 28 April 1997)

Living Marxism editor, Mick Hume, similarly argued that 'it is harder and harder to find depictions of male heroes these days', as virtually every representation of men in the media branded them 'inadequate, weak or evil' (*Living Marxism*, May 1996). Even girls' magazine, *More!*'s six-page Lads Special wondered, 'mad for lads . . . but do you want a lout for a lover?' (*More!*, 15–28 January 1997).

Conversely, as *Loaded* gathered its critiques, new magazines for women appeared on the shelves, influenced by *Loaded*'s success. *More!*, *Minx*, *Frank*, *So*, *Bliss* and *Fresh!*[21] all promised more irreverent wit, irony and 'attitude' than traditional fashion- and beauty-based magazines. *That's Life*, for example, labelled itself as a female version of *Loaded*, promising a regular 'near to the knuckle chuckle' at the expense of men, and an 'affectionate pop' at the male sex.

The high media profile of these magazines, as indicative of a new generation of sexually confident and independent women (epitomized by the Spice Girls and 'Girl Power'), combined with the growing critique of *Loaded* as a prime example of the negative media representations of masculinity, served to further the notion that single men were (in) trouble. In June 1997, for example, both *Bella* magazine and the *Independent on Sunday* ran features on the increasing number of male anorexics, asking if 'the new wave of glossy magazines for men' had anything to do with it (*Independent on*

Sunday 8 June 1997; *Bella*, June 1997), and a report on Blur's Damon Albarn's apparent depression also made links to *Loaded*. Magazines like *Loaded*:

> have provided a popular solution to the identity crisis for today's man: become a new lad. But . . . there is something sad about it . . . [with] the media celebrating male youthful behaviour there is no encouragement for men to leave their laddish phase, which sets up the potential for future crisis (*Independent*, 3 February 1997).

In May 1997, the *British Medical Journal* featured the results of a study on depression. As the female rate had fallen, the number of men suffering had risen. Men were now, the *Guardian* concluded, behaving not badly but 'sadly' (18 May 1998).

Before long, *Loaded* came to stand for all that was wrong with masculinity. Living as a lad 'is ultimately a sad life . . . it stunts your growth, narrows your horizons and numbs your intelligence' (*Independent on Sunday*, 23 March 1997). Whilst *Loaded* had dominated the market and media debates (it was the most successful in terms of sales figures until eclipsed by *FHM* in 1996), the magazine 'for men who should know better' came to represent the whole genre of magazines and readers: Home Secretary Jack Straw for example, referred to 'delinquent' youths as part of a '*Loaded* Generation' (*Independent*, 30 April 1998).[22]

Although the men's magazine circulation figures continued to climb, the focus on semi-naked 'babes' caused some advertisers to rethink their relationship with the publications. In the same month that *FHM* hit record circulation figures, Chanel announced it was to pull out of advertising in the magazine because of the magazine's 'image', and Calvin Klein was also reported as 'concerned at the soft pornographic element' (*Guardian*, 28 August 1997). The *Daily Mail* reported this withdrawal as part of the 'backlash against publications which tap into the so-called New Lad market of sex, alcohol and football' (28 August 1997). Earlier that year, Paul Raymond Publications, who own *Mayfair* and *Men Only*, had criticized men's lifestyle magazines as taking over their market without being seen as 'top shelf magazines'. 'At least our magazines are honest', a Chief Executive is reported as saying (*Independent*, 25 May 1997). *Loaded*'s version of true and refreshingly honest masculinity was now seen as dishonest because its position was ambiguous – not quite ironic comic or retro fanzine, not quite men's fashion glossy, not straight tabloid sexism, and not quite soft porn. Thus, *Loaded*'s ambiguity meant that the new lad could no longer be taken for granted as the obvious, true version of 1990s masculinity.

New versions of masculinity began to take the place of *Loaded* Lad. In April 1999, for example, *Later* appeared on the shelves, also published by IPC, and edited by Phil Hilton, formerly of *Men's Health*. This new version of 'what men are really like' attempts to combine both the self-reflexivity and health concerns of *Men's Health* with the hedonism of *Loaded* – '*Later* Man is *Loaded* Lad grown up: someone who still wants a laugh but has responsibilities too' (*Guardian*, 27 April 1999). *Later* Man sounds somewhat similar to Millennium Man, dreamt up at a 1996 marketing conference: a man who can also, finally, laugh with and not at his responsibilities. 'He is as happy to have a laugh with his mates down the boozer as he is to cook a fine meal for his girlfriend' (*Independent*, 20 October 1996). This had been tried before with another (short-lived) men's magazine, *Deluxe* ('you want to party hard . . . but be able to look yourself in the eye in the morning') and also by the editor of *The Face*, Richard Benson, who came up with Soft Lad – who finds 'the individualist aspiration of old eighties man too shallow, and the you 'n' me sensitivities of seventies New Man too deep'. Soft Lad was, according to Benson, 'Seeking Ordinary, Fundamental Truths' in the changing world of the late 1990s (*Guardian*, 15 December 1997). It remains to be seen if any of these become as successfully 'naturalized' as the 1990s 'new lad'.

Conclusion: the instability of hegemonic masculinities

This chapter has examined recent media coverage of the new generation of men's lifestyle magazines and their dramatic impact on the dynamics of the magazine market more generally. The rapidly expanding market and the media frenzy that surrounded the magazines provides a crucial context for our study. We have shown, in particular, how *Loaded* came to stand for the whole genre of men's magazines within contemporary media discourses, even as its sales were overtaken by *FHM*. The media's reduction of the magazine market to a lowest common denominator (in the guise of *Loaded*) runs counter to the differentiation that the magazine editors insisted on (as discussed in chapter 3). The media's emphasis is justified to some extent, however, as *Loaded* did have a powerful effect on the other magazines. As the first of the new generation of men's magazines to reach a mass market, it pulled more fashion-conscious and arts-orientated magazines such as *Arena, Esquire* and *GQ* 'down-market' as, for a time, the figure of the new lad achieved a kind of cultural hegemony. As always, however, that hegemony was intrinsically unstable.

In particular, we have seen how the media detected a 'crisis' of masculinity in relation to which the magazines can be seen as a successful commercial response. Here, we wish to draw our own conclusions about the 'crisis' of masculinity and the significance of the alternative images of masculinity that appeared during the 1990s. We do not wish to argue that the crisis was a media construction with no link to the world beyond the text. But nor do we accept that the crisis of masculinity can be mapped unproblematically onto wider changes in British society, with recent social and economic changes providing a neat explanation for the (re)emergence of more laddish masculinities. We argue for a more complex understanding of the nature of crisis as a hegemonic struggle which focuses on the way that media representations, in the magazines themselves and in wider media commentary on the magazines, were internalized and made sense of by magazine readers. It is in this sense that we are prepared to speak of a general crisis of masculinity – rooted in the media and its consumption – rather than in terms of a 'crisis' with deeper roots in the economic restructuring of British society.

This, in turn, raises wider questions about the relationship between culture and economy. We reject answers to these questions that rely upon notions of base and superstructure, or notions that inadequately link the text to society. Analyses which stress the determining power of 'the economic' or the specificity of 'the cultural' do not enable us adequately to make sense of men's lifestyle magazines. This does not mean that the magazines are immune to questions of profitability (see chapter 3) or that the content of the magazines is unimportant (see chapter 4). Rather, our analysis strives to make sense of the relations between the economic and the cultural as mutually constitutive. That is, the practices of markets and economics are profoundly cultural and cultures in commercial settings are predominantly manufactured (cf. du Gay, 1996; Kenny and Stevenson, 1998). In this particular study, however, we are less concerned with traditional forms of political economy which would seek to unravel the interconnections between corporate ownership, control and capital accumulation. While this remains a legitimate area of research, we are more concerned with the ways in which the economy is being 'culturalized'. By this, we mean that our study seeks to understand the ways in which the aestheticization of goods and lifestyle cultures feed into the production, content and consumption of men's lifestyle magazines. That is, the circuits of information that comprise our study include both continuous and discontinuous discourses connected with economics (the emergence of flexible specialization), cultural industries (niche marketing and the spread of popular representations in respect of sexuality), society (shifting gender and sexual relations including the role of feminism), the impact of media commentary (analysed above) and the discourses involved in consumption. These are the informational co-ordinates of our study that cannot be adequately captured by older-style political economy or more purely constructivist concerns. Hence our emphasis upon the informational circuits of contemporary culture is intended to open out a more complex field of study than might otherwise have been the case.

Having clarified our theoretical approach, let us briefly re-examine media constructions of the alleged crisis of hegemonic masculinity. In this particular era of social, economic and cultural change, what we understand by work, family and sexuality can no longer be assumed, but are open to question. Thus, issues of relationships and gender identities become part of the cultural commentary of the press. As we have argued, each new version of masculinity struggles to become the true version: the one that becomes most widely accepted as common sense, according to the dominant values of the press. Thus, when we discuss new versions of masculinity, we are talking about a struggle for coherence as new versions emerge and are classified, and the process by which certain systems of classification become not only clearly distinguishable but gain more ideological resonance over other rival systems. Connell (1995) describes this process as 'hegemonic masculinity': not a static phenomenon, but an historically changeable social practice of patriarchal dominance. So, whilst this particular crisis is understood and talked about in the media as specific to the 1990s in Western society, with, for example, the emphasis on men 'being free to be honest again' after the apparently oppressive gains of feminist political correctness, the notion of a crisis itself can be seen in wider terms as a hegemonic function of patriarchal power, which comes to the fore in times of social and economic upheaval, such as post-industrial, post-Thatcher '90s Britain.

For Suzanne Moore and others, all this recent media commentary is evidence that the crisis of masculinity is largely confined to the media. As Moore observes: 'in the real world men are still in charge of big companies, still in charge of newspapers, still in charge of institutions' (*Independent*, 16 May 1998). Similarly, Suzanne Franks (1999) points out that whilst the 'cultural commentary' on work in the 1990s may well be that of women getting jobs and power in the workplace whilst men, unemployable and undermined, are in 'crisis', the economic reality is that women are doing more jobs because of the expansion of low-paid, temporary, part-time, service-sector jobs.

Our own analysis has not pursued the evidence of social and economic change leading to a generalized crisis of masculinity. Instead, we have demonstrated the pervasiveness of the notion of crisis in media commentary on changing masculinities and the way that these discourses are reproduced in people's talk about the magazines (a theme that is further amplified in chapter 5). We do not resort to the language of 'hegemony' and 'resistance', as in an earlier tradition of cultural studies, but to an examination of the circulation of discourses in different kinds of media, to the naturalization of those discourses in popular understandings and to an analysis of the ambivalences and contradictions that characterize those understandings.

We emphasize, for example, that the magazines are distinctive in terms of their mass appeal and the way that they are linked intertextually with other cultural forms such as soap operas, films and football. Second, the magazines have a definite 'after feminism' feel to them. By this, we mean that the magazines' ironic knowingness and sexual jokiness anticipates (and attempts to disarm) their critics. This could be seen as an attempt to reinvent 'natural' male heterosexuality after its deconstruction. However, the more visible nature of diverse sexualities in modern societies is reproduced within the magazines. For example, *Maxim* (June 1995) carried a feature on 'What can a lesbian teach you about sex?' using irony and jokes to tell men that they need not worry too much, before urging them to become less obsessed with 'The Big Production'. This underlines our argument that men's lifestyle magazines and masculinities are part of a changing and contested social field, part of a culture within which different forms of sexuality have become increasingly visible, if not generally acceptable.

We have not set out to establish whether the crisis of masculinity is 'real' or not, nor to establish where it is taking place, in the media or more widely. Nor are we setting forward any kind of generalization about the media's power (neither the power of magazines, nor the power of other forms of media to define those magazines). As we argue in chapter 5, few of our focus group participants would define themselves as committed readers of the magazines, but almost all were willing to engage in debates about their general significance. In this chapter, we have tried to move forward from traditional, and overly simplistic, encoding and decoding models, conceptualizing readers and non-readers in the now somewhat laboured terms of 'effects', 'harm' and 'resistance'. Instead, both here and in successive chapters, we have sought to explore the ways in which participants took up key themes from these mediated forms of 'public talk' and incorporated them within their own discursive repertoires. As such, the cultural commentaries reported in this chapter can be conceptualized as part of a wider circuit of magazine culture together with the magazines' content and readers' responses to them. The degree to which those themes are taken up, and the often ambivalent ways in which they are used, acknowledged, defended and/or rejected is central to our analysis of how readers and non-readers alike 'make sense' of the magazines.

3

Editorial Work

This chapter addresses the production phase in the circuit of magazine culture, focusing on the editorial work involved in producing men's lifestyle magazines. Drawing on a series of interviews with the editors and on a range of secondary material, the chapter reflects on the discourses and practices of magazine publishing, highlighting the tensions and contradictions that are central to the editorial process. From an editorial perspective, the magazines can be seen as part of the commodification of lifestyle, which engages (sometimes quite warily) with the notion of laddishness, walking a fine line between the niche market that was established by the style press and the mass appeal of more downmarket titles such as *Loaded* and *FHM*.[1] In the following account, magazine publishing emerges as a risky and unstable business where editors are striving to follow trends in popular culture (established elsewhere) while seeking to create their own independent readership. While the magazines may all look similar, superficially at least, and while readers may be relatively indifferent as to which title they read in any particular month, the editors we interviewed were keen to differentiate themselves from their competitors, to establish an independent identity for their magazine and to emphasize their close knowledge of their readers and their personal identification with the magazine.

When most of the magazines were launched in the early to mid-1990s, the editors had little sense of how big the market for men's lifestyle magazines might be. As one editor told us: 'I don't think anyone knew how it was going to go. . . . We thought, yeah, sounds like a great idea, but it could bomb and sell 20,000 or it could go crazy and sell 200,000' (Andy Clerkson, *Stuff for Men*). Not only did the magazines represent a balancing act between mass and niche markets, they were also positioned in a relatively unknown space, between standardized and more unstable cultural locations. There was much uncertainty about whether the magazines were merely following the *zeitgeist* of changes in commercial culture (associated with the rise of club culture, for example, or changes in men's fashion retailing) or whether they were setting a new agenda for contemporary masculinities. Our analysis suggests that the magazines and their editors are caught within this tension, attempting to commodify changes in gender identities and relations that are themselves extremely unstable (cf. Jackson, 1995). The analysis in this chapter is therefore consistent with our subsequent analysis of different readings of the magazines and of associated changes in masculinities (in chapter 5) where we emphasize a range of discourses and dispositions that we characterize as fundamentally ambivalent. As with our analysis of the focus groups, our analysis of the editorial interviews concentrates on the discursive analysis of *what was said* and *the way it was said*, rather than examining editorial practices per se. As such, the chapter engages with our own expectations and how the editors related to us as researchers rather than treating the interview material as a means of unmediated access to the editors' working lives. We also wish to situate our analysis in relation to previous research on the social relations of power within the cultural industries and in media research more generally.

Magazines and cultural power

The mass culture thesis within media studies was based upon the idea that culture had been converted into an industry. In Adorno and Horkheimer's (1973) original formulation, the sphere of culture was argued to be becoming increasingly like that of production with instrumental reason coming to administer and control a superficial media and consumer culture. The culture industry, it was argued, had a negative effect on the audience: repressing difference, manufacturing sameness and reproducing conformity. More recently, through the work of Fiske (1987), Morley (1988) and others, media and cultural studies has taken a less pessimistic view of modern audiences and their semiotic complexity. While such moves are welcome, the extent of the modern media's ideological power remains an open question, a critical idea of cultural power (and ideology) being dependent upon the notion that certain linguistic signs symbolically reinforce or leave unquestioned material relations of domination.

Our argument here is not intended to lead back into an unproblematic reading of the power of the culture industry, since it is evident that the media continue to have the power to define 'what everyone is talking about', even in these so-called postmodern times. But, we would argue, the images, discourses and frameworks of understanding that we borrow from the media in order to make sense of our everyday lives are embedded in wider cultures of production and media circulation. In this respect, we have found the metaphor of 'circuits of culture' to be helpful (Johnson, 1986). By this, we mean that ideologies and cultures disseminated by the media draw upon a multitude of sources and simultaneously influence and are influenced by civil society. For example, the idea of the new lad could be located in a number of media texts, including advertising, television programmes (such as *Men Behaving Badly* and *Fantasy Football*), rock stars (such as Damon Albarn and Liam Gallagher) and such like, with men's lifestyle magazines being perhaps the most prominent cultural form. This is not to argue that the media do not have an ideological effect, but to stress that circuits of culture are complex, leaky and difficult to trace in a fast moving global culture (Stevenson, 1999a; Jackson et al., 2000).

In terms of our understanding of the processes of production, we point beyond more traditional accounts of political economy (Kenny and Stevenson, 1998; Stevenson, 1999b). We do this by seeking to tie an appreciation of wider processes of commodification (the concentration of ownership patterns, product differentiation and so on) into a research process that reveals both the risks and the creative engagements of the editorial and production processes more generally. Rather than viewing the editors and production staff as either grinding out an ideology in conjunction with the structures of late capitalism, or as sustaining a mythology of editorial control and freedom, our study seeks to position the editorial process in terms of the structuration of the practices and discourses of magazine production (Giddens, 1984). It is not a question of 'separately' understanding magazine production in terms of the editors' ideological role, their linkage into broader frameworks of informational capitalism or their shaping of consumption and readership. In this respect, Lash and Urry (1994) argue, modern capitalism has been reorientated around increasingly flexible modes of production (where power is relocated through the dominance of certain distributors), while becoming more heavily reliant upon product design. This creates a situation of uncertainty in terms of the development of new markets for new products and the status of the editors themselves.

The move from a manufacturing to a service economy has been

accompanied by growing individualism, a weakened state and more multiple markets. Economic success or failure is now determined more by product innovation, retailing and design rather than earlier concerns with processes of production. Flexible specialization means that cultural institutions are better able to pick up on the shifting patterns of consumer spending and lifestyle. As Sean Nixon (1997) points out, the role of information in the design process helps shape the cultural meanings and values that become associated with a product and leads to the segmentation of mass culture into niche markets. The introduction of flexible specialization in certain sectors of the cultural economy creates a more symbiotic relation between producers and consumers than existed in previous periods of capitalist development. As we shall see, design-intensive, flexible capitalism, for the editors at least, is a source of opportunity (for cashing in on the considerable success of the magazines) and of uncertainty (in terms of job insecurity and mobility). The editors, then, are placed in the paradoxical situation of simultaneously creating and following trends in modern consumer culture. Bearing in mind these more theoretical projections, this chapter seeks to understand the interconnections between the development of the market in men's magazines, the work and discursive cultures of the editors and the links with broader processes of consumption.

The circulation of magazine and other visual cultures can also be linked to other dimensions of contemporary society. As Beck (1992), Castells (1997) and Melucci (1996) have all argued, the 'cultural' dimension can no longer be conceived as an add-on after the 'real' dimensions of politics and economics have been satisfactorily explained. Whether we are talking about the risk society, network capitalism or the politics of social movements, ideas of symbolic challenge and exclusion remain central. The power to name, construct meaning and exert control over the flow of information within contemporary societies is one of the central structural divisions today. Power is not solely based upon material dimensions but also involves the capacity to throw into question established codes and rework frameworks of common understanding. That is, we should seek to form an appreciation of the ways in which 'ordinary' understandings are constructed, of issues of interpretative conflict and semiotic plurality more generally. However, this cannot be achieved without also appreciating how dominant systems and institutions seek to establish the power of master codes, meaninglessness and dominant viewpoints. Thus we need to understand the cultural power of the magazines in terms of particular circuits of information which are genuinely mediated by a diversity of media forms and

Table 3.1   Editorial interviews, 1997

Editor	Magazine	Interviewer	Date of interview
Andy Clerkson	*Stuff for Men*	NS/PJ	19 March
James Collard	*Attitude*	PJ/KB	22 July
Mike Cones	*GQ Body and Soul*	NS	13 May
Mark Higham	*Escape*	NS/PJ	14 May
Gill Hudson	*Maxim*	NS/PJ	13 May
Adam Porter	*UpLoaded*	KB (phone interview)	22 April
Jerome Smail	*Xtreme*	KB (email interview)	9 June

popular experience. Whether we are describing the reactions of
ordinary readers, the editorial team or the content of magazines, we
are seeking to understand the way that mediated forms of understanding have transformed everyday life. As Castells argues, modern
media cultures operate in:

> a system in which reality itself (that is, people's material/symbolic
> existence) is entirely captured, fully immersed in a virtual image setting,
> in a world of make believe, in which appearances are not just on the
> screen through which experience is communicated, but they become
> the experience. (1997: 373)

Hence, in a global, fast-moving world, power is increasingly likely to
be exerted through the material dimensions of semiotic cultures. In
network systems power comes through the inducement and persua-
sion of information and images generating new opportunities, risks
and desires (Urry, 2000).

Interviewing the editors

The remainder of this chapter is based on a series of interviews with
editorial staff at a number of the leading men's magazines (see table
3.1). While some of the more prominent editors declined to be
interviewed, their views are represented through published interviews
in the national press. Our analysis reflects the situation at the time
of the interviews in the spring and summer of 1997 when media

discussion of men's lifestyle magazines was at its height (see chapter 2). Symptomatic of the rapid pace of change in the magazine industry, several of those we interviewed are now no longer in post. Some magazines have folded, others have been launched and new editorial staff appointed. Some of these editorial moves were extremely high-profile events, such as James Brown's much-publicized move from *Loaded* to *GQ* in April 1997. This was followed after only eighteen months by an equally public departure from *GQ* as a result of what the *Guardian* described as a series of 'errors of judgement and taste' ('Browned off', 22 February 1999) including his notorious reference to the Nazis (and Field Marshal Rommel in particular) as 'icons of style'. Given the volatility of the magazine market and the frequency of editorial changes, attempting to track the turnover of editorial personnel was no easy matter (see table 3.2 for a selection of recent changes).

Our analysis of the editorial interviews reflects this high level of editorial turnover and job insecurity (both within and between the main publishing companies). We focus on the multiple balancing acts that editorial work involves, including the possible conflict between editorial freedom and creativity versus the need to attract and retain advertising revenue; and the desire to provide useful advice and information versus the need to be entertaining. All of these issues are addressed in different ways by different magazines. Rather than being answered in a once and for all fashion, our interviews reveal how these issues are a source of constant tension for editors and for those in the magazines' advertising and marketing departments.

As a consequence of these tensions and instabilities, we do not interpret the history of men's lifestyle magazines as a kind of unilinear evolution, whether in terms of the new visual codings of masculinity (Nixon, 1997) or an ever-increasing emphasis on laddishness, for example. This is in contrast to recent media commentary which has focused on 'The rise and rise of the laddery from "Loaded"' (*Independent*, 19 April 1997), the tendency for men's magazines to become 'ever more crass and undemanding' (*Independent on Sunday*, 25 May 1997) and the increasing homogeneity of the men's magazine market following the 'dumbing down' of magazines such as *Arena*, *GQ* and *Esquire* ('We're all lads now', *Guardian*, 13 July 1998). Recent publishing history cannot be represented in such simple, linear terms. Rather, we suggest, it should be seen in terms of a series of unstable shifts back and forth, as magazines attempt to find an appropriate voice in which to address their readers without antagonizing advertisers, searching for a distinctive position

Table 3.2   Editorial turnover

Editor	Position	Career change	Replaced by
Rosie Boycott	Editor *Esquire* 1992–6	Previously editor of *Spare Rib*; moved to edit *Independent on Sunday*	Peter Howarth
James Brown	Founding editor *Loaded*	Moved to *GQ* (replacing Angus MacKinnon)	Derek Harbison and subsequently by Tim Southwell at *Loaded* and at *GQ* by Bill Prince
James Collard	Founding editor *Attitude*	Left to edit *Out* (best-selling US gay title)	Adam Mattera
Phil Hilton	Editor *Men's Health*	Left in 1999 to become founding editor of *Later*	Simon Geller
Peter Howarth	Editor *Esquire* since 1996	Previously style editor at *Esquire* and editor of *Arena* 1994–7	Ekow Eshun (at *Arena*)
Alexandra Schulman	Editor *GQ* until 1991	Moved to *Vogue*	Michael VerMeulen
Mike Soutar	Editor of *FHM* 1994–7	Left to become managing director of KISS FM in 1997 and in 1999 to oversee *Maxim* in the US	Ed Needham
Michael VerMeulen	Editor *GQ*, 1991–5	Died of drug overdose 1995	Angus MacKinnon

within the marketplace while simultaneously trying to maximize sales. These tensions are, we argue, a reflection of the contradictions and ambivalences of contemporary masculinities as well as a reflection of the dynamics of commercial culture. We suggest that the magazines that have best recognized these tensions and ambivalences have been most successful commercially, whether through *Loaded*'s strategy of seeing life as a perpetual holiday ('getting away with it', in Tim Southwell's (1998) memorable phrase), through *FHM*'s formula of being 'funny, useful and sexy' – paraphrased in the *Guardian* (17 February 1997) as 'funny, useful and selling' – or through

Maxim's irreverent lists of 'How to . . .' achieve anything and everything without having to try too hard.

Rather than treating the editorial interviews as a source of unmediated information, unaffected by our presence as researchers, we view the editors' comments as another reflection of the balancing act they are called on daily to perform. Their own lives, as reflected in the interviews, epitomize the kind of work cultures which are portrayed in the magazines as a mixture of anxiety and exhilaration, whether this is treated as a source of humour (as in *Loaded*), as an invitation to escape (as in *Escape* and other extreme sports magazines), as an incentive to maintain bodily fitness (as in *Men's Health*), or as a reason for pursuing a more aspirational lifestyle (as addressed, in different ways, in magazines like *Esquire* or *Stuff for Men*).

Editorial insecurities

Contrary to our initial expectations, most of the editors we interviewed had relatively little commitment to men's issues and limited experience of the men's magazine market prior to taking their current job. Throughout the interviews they were dismissive of our invitation to analyse the sociological significance of the magazines. Their self-image emphasized gut instinct over painstaking research, valuing spontaneity and editorial flair over what they perceived as the excesses of academic reflection and analysis. Rather than being advocates of any particular cause, most of the editors were journalists with a range of professional skills and experience, having worked for a variety of different magazines prior to their current involvement with men's lifestyle issues.[2] For example, prior to editing *Escape*, Mark Higham had worked in the magazine industry for eight years, editing six different magazines (including responsibility for launching three new titles). His previous titles were mostly computer magazines like *Computer Arts* and *PC Guide* rather than lifestyle titles. Mike Cones had been a playwright and TV writer with a part-time job in a health club, having also worked as a freelance journalist before joining *GQ*. Andy Clerkson had worked on a variety of other magazines including *New Socialist* and *City Limits*, prior to joining *Stuff for Men*. He had also been sub-editor of a computer magazine (*Computer Buyer*) and editor of *Home Entertainment*. Jerome Smail had previously edited *Cycling Today* and worked on *XL* and *What Mountain Bike* before joining *Xtreme*. Adam Porter had been at *Loaded* for about a year, having written freelance for the magazine since the third issue. Such is the turnover of editorial staff in the magazine industry that Gill Hudson, who had edited *New Woman* before joining *Maxim*, was well aware of her status as 'the longest standing editor of all the men's magazines – after two years' (and the only remaining female editor after Rosie Boycott's departure from *Arena* to edit the *Independent on Sunday*).

Most of the magazines have a very limited core staff, employing a large number of freelancers to handle design issues as well as to write specific features. For example, *Stuff* had only 12 core staff, with 27 freelancers contributing to its first issue. While the larger companies can do more of the editorial, marketing and production work in house, smaller magazines such as *Escape* function with a small team of half a dozen core staff, plus 'loads of freelancers and various artists that come in as well as production people' (Mark Higham). As Ekinsmyth (1999) demonstrates from her interviews with magazine workers (writers, editors and graphic designers), freelance work is particularly prone to instability and risk, though some of her interviewees emphasized the independence and flexibility of freelance work over the (sometimes exaggerated) benefits of a permanent job with a single employer.

The level of turnover and staff mobility between magazines contrasts with the picture that emerges elsewhere in the literature, where the editors of the early men's magazines are portrayed (and tended to portray themselves) as heroic figures, dedicated to the creation of a particular magazine. This is particularly true of Nick Logan's role in launching *The Face* before moving on to create the first successful men's lifestyle title, *Arena*. This entrepreneurial rags to riches story is described by Frank Mort in terms of 'publishing mythology':

> [*The Face*] was launched almost single-handedly by its editor, Nick Logan, with as little as £5,000, withdrawn from his local Halifax Building Society in east London. For much of the early 1980s it was run by only two permanent journalists, while Logan's wife, Julie, handled the accounts and subscriptions from home. The magazine's first offices were the depths of a 'cubby hole in Soho'. (1996: 23)

The launch of *Arena* in November 1986 is often described in similar terms, with Logan, rebuffed by the major publishing houses, eventually persuading the smaller independent firm, Wagadon (who already published *The Face*) to take the risk.[3] This sense of an heroic quest needs to be set alongside a more prosaic account of Logan's accumulated professional expertise. While he may have been 'profoundly charismatic' (Mort, 1996: 35), Logan had acquired years of publishing experience, working on the *West Essex Gazette*, *New Musical Express*, *Smash Hits* and *The Face* before launching *Arena*. Our interviews also suggest that other editors are better characterized as hard-nosed professionals who happen to be working on men's life-style magazines rather than as having an evangelical commitment to men's issues.

The insecurities of the publishing industry are exacerbated by the lack of clearly demarcated roles and transparent institutional structures: 'I'm not sure how many people there are in this company [Dennis Lifestyle Publishing]. It's very different from the old days when people wanted to be journalists and then you rose up through [the ranks], and people decided to put you in management' (Andy Clerkson, *Stuff for Men*). Some staff welcomed the air of informality that characterizes working practices in the publishing industry. For example, Mike Cones (at *GQ*) claims to have been recruited 'purely by chance', following 'a very drunken lunch' with former editor Michael VerMeulen whom he had happened to meet while working in a local health club, while *Loaded* is the archetype for this kind of informality. An advertisement for a new features editor at *Loaded* begins: 'In search of some serious freakdown?' and ends 'You must have a sense of humour and we'd prefer it if you didn't put vinegar on your chips.'

The magazine was reputedly 'invented' by James Brown and Tim Southwell during drunken celebrations after a football match in Barcelona. Southwell provides many similar examples where working for *Loaded* 'felt like we were being paid to lounge about' (1998: 25), including his account of 'what could loosely be termed a "features meeting", where we sit about and say stuff, hoping that a magazine will emerge. . . . Usually our meetings occurred by complete accident' (ibid: 3–4).[4] The other editors to whom we spoke were also keen to present an image of themselves as spontaneous and instinctively 'knowing' rather than relying on formal knowledge or market research.

Several of our interviewees resented the fact that they felt remote from important decisions, which were taken, according to Mike Cones, by the 'people upstairs on the fourth floor'. Cones had little say in his appointment as editor of *GQ*'s Body and Soul section (originally published as a biannual supplement to the main magazine): 'I was just told, "we want a health and fitness magazine . . . and you're going to edit them".' Cones referred disparagingly to the 'number crunchers' who take financial decisions without appreciating the organic way in which magazines grow: 'There will be somebody in America who will look at the facts and figures, they'll look at the circulation, they'll look at the revenue and costs and that's how you're judged initially.' While some editors appreciated the creative opportunities for networking with other people in the media – 'London's great . . . where the media happens . . . everyone's really close together down here, so there's a lot of input' (Mark Higham, *Escape*) – others were conscious of their lack of power, security and support: 'No one seems to give a shit one way or another' (Mike Cones, *GQ*). Cones particularly resented the way Angus Mac-Kinnon's dismissal as editor of *GQ* had been handled:

> I know it wasn't actually a surprise to us here that Angus left but it was the shabby way it was done . . . a lot of people having meetings and going round behind everyone else's back to make sure that James Brown [his replacement as editor] was in the bag before Angus was fired.

While Tim Southwell does his best to maintain an image of working for *Loaded* as 'the best party you'd ever been to, the best holiday . . . the greatest goal you'd ever scored' (1998: back cover), the magazine's success can also be explained in plainer commercial terms. Alan Lewis, *Loaded*'s editor-in-chief, is unusually frank about this: 'If I'm totally honest . . . the whole idea of us [at IPC] starting a men's magazine was ad-driven. *GQ*, *Arena* and *Esquire* had been around for a while [and] contained loads of ads that we weren't getting – clothes, fragrance, booze, cars, etc.' (quoted in Southwell, 1998: 16).

A similar tension between editorial independence and the commercial imperative to maximize sales and advertising revenue ran throughout our interviews. Yet, given that men's lifestyle magazines can be linked to powerful commercial concerns, how might we understand these discourses of fun and play? One argument might be that the emphasis upon 'craziness' is mobilized to hide the inevitably more rational features of the workplace. The incorporation of masculine fun (which, after all, is a staple feature of the magazines) gives the impression that staff are not really working at all. Narratives of charismatic individuals, drunken lunches and laddish celebrations not only reinvent the more stoic masculinities associated with Fleet Street, but temporarily hide the fact that the editors are all involved in rational bureaucratic modes of organization. The editors, then, are able to preserve the authenticity of the magazines and the creativity of their own roles by hiding these features from view.

However, another argument would be that such representations of the workplace also point to changes within contemporary capitalism. That is, while there are undoubtedly features of displacement, the editors' remarks are also indicative of deeper shifts within work-based cultures. The work cultures of men's magazines typify a world of work where, to quote Richard Sennett (1998: 87), 'to stay put is to be left out'. In the age of network capitalism, renewed emphasis is placed upon occupational mobility, flexibility and the importance of information within product design. This is a culture where established knowledges age quickly. Such a world requires energetic workers who thrive on uncertainty and risk-taking. To be successful in such an environment, editorial staff need the ability to be able to wrap themselves in the latest information codes, while not being so committed to them that they cannot respond to changes in the workplace or wider public cultures. Hence the public front of playfulness does more than hide more instrumental realities. It indicates the willingness of magazine journalists with careers in the cultural industries temporarily to reinvent themselves to fit into the culture that has come to be associated with men's lifestyle magazines. This has to be done at short notice before the necessity of reassembling themselves for new occupational challenges (Bauman, 2000). In the meantime, however, the ability to be able to speak the language of laddish frivolity indicates a certain commitment (which can of course be rapidly withdrawn) to the magazines. This positions the editorial staff somewhere between depth notions of belief and cynical forms of manipulation. To work in the magazine industry means never knowing where you are going to end up, and what lifestyle you will be asked to endorse, however temporarily.

Commercial imperatives versus editorial freedom

Editorial freedom was often perceived to be in conflict with the need to maximize advertising revenue. Gill Hudson (*Maxim*) argued that the early lifestyle magazines were advertiser-led:

> No one knew whether there was an audience out there. So, if you don't know if you have a readership, what you have to do is make sure of your advertising, so these things were just produced for the advertisers: thousand pound cuff-links, ninety million pound cars. Just absolutely 'out-there' which, of course, advertisers love.

Other editors insisted that they were driven by 'gut instinct . . . you just feel that something needs to happen' (Mark Higham, *Escape*), rather than by market research or commercial pressure to generate advertising revenue. Editors know that they are replaceable, and one way of asserting their indispensability is to claim that they uniquely understand their readers and speak in the voice of the magazine. There are, in fact, clear parallels between the editors' talk in terms of unreflexive practice ('just doing it') and readers' talk about buying and reading the magazines ('you just go in and grab one off the shelves').

Editors' talk also has an element of machismo, emphasizing spontaneity and sociality (the drunken lunch), with creativity arising from an appropriate 'devil-may-care' attitude rather than from cautious reliance on market research, driven by the need to maximize sales and advertising revenue. There are connections here with the romantic notion of the artist in the garret and with the editor as a lone voice or highly individualistic hero. This may be contradicted in practice when, for example, Mark Higham maintained that 'a lot is kind of instinctive. . . . there isn't a science', while later in the same interview he referred to a brainstorming meeting in Brighton prior to the magazine's launch, to the magazine's two-year plan, to the significance of readers' letters and 'all the surveys we've done so far'. He also felt that most of the recent launches had been 'driven by the fact that *FHM* is selling half a million copies'.

Gill Hudson was similarly pragmatic about the role of market research: 'Research is quite useful to show to your boss and say, "Look, we're right". But basically you can't run a magazine on [focus groups].' Jerome Smail (*Xtreme*) described all such research as 'marketing bullshit', while Adam Porter (who edits *Loaded*'s website) was equally dismissive:

> We just go on instinct really. . . . I mean we have a tendency here to, like, shy away from all that market research. . . . We could go on dissecting every single journalistic nicety but basically *Loaded* is addressing a section of the populace that hasn't had a magazine directed at it before.

The only significant exception to this apparent general suspicion of focus groups and market research came from Andy Clerkson, who described the detailed planning that preceded the launch of *Stuff for Men*:

> Stuff came from a one line idea from my Editor-in-chief, Gill Hudson, who is the editor of *Maxim*. We were on a new projects kind of committee – I'm sure every company kind of does this you know, has a regular team that meets every three or four weeks to look at new ideas pitched in from

outside, you know, from third parties as to launching their magazines and you have to come up with your own ideas.

In this case, the idea of a consumer magazine for men appealed to the publisher, Felix Dennis, because of the company's existing expertise in computer magazines, bought overwhelmingly by men, and because of the current success of its men's lifestyle title, *Maxim*. Dennis gave the go-ahead for research to be done nine months prior to the magazine's launch. Clerkson continues:

I took a three- or four-week sabbatical to look into producing dummy pages. We thought the initial thing to do with it would be to go to focus groups with dummy pages. I mean there are a number of ways you can launch these days. At first we thought we would just produce a thinned-down magazine and put it on the back of *Maxim* so we would just sell it as a free supplement. . . . But in the end we decided it would be . . . easier in a way and probably quicker . . . to produce dummy pages, and take those to focus groups . . . which we did. So it took us about four weeks to dummy up what would be about 30 or 40 pages with possible sections, headings with boards saying what the magazine was about, mission statements, and then saying what each section would do and how we would do it. But really the pages were there just as a visual link and to show a bit of attitude and try and get it across. Mostly it was the magazine described in little paragraphs on boards and we took that to focus groups, various focus groups of men aged from I think we had 18–24, we kind of had 25–30 and then 30+.

PJ: So do you recruit those through a market research agency or . . .?

Yeah we use a market research agency that basically sorts all those out for us. And in there we just had a varying degree, because at first we just tried to look at age groups and age ranges. That was one of our first intentions, so amongst that we just had varying people, some people who read magazines a lot, some people who only read specialist mags and some people who only read general interest men's mags and some people who just never read magazines really, you know or hardly read anything other than TV listings titles. Um, and that probably took until May – yeah it was early May when we did the focus groups, and the results of those came back and we had a board meeting at the end of May . . . which said yes go ahead with the project. But they then had to take the boards out to advertisers, or to potential advertisers – people that they obviously knew in the company. That would have been quite a hush-hush thing, that wouldn't have been ringing up people cold and saying come and have a look at our new magazine. That would have been head managers here who knew major buyers in media buying agencies who would say, 'Do me a favour, have a look at this and tell me what you think'. Um, and obviously people would come out and see so they could judge our potential. That probably took until June, so there was a few weeks doing that really, leading to the end of June and then you've got the go ahead. I mean that came up very positive, the reader research came out positive, so we said we'll launch it and that was July and we actually started working – I started working kind of on my own on the first issue in the middle of July. So I think it was fast . . . from the original kind of concept to the actual launching and getting a magazine out in November.

It may be that other magazines have equally rigorous market research programmes and pre-launch routines but that editors wished to stress their independence and creativity to us as interviewers. It is certainly part of a particular kind of journalistic myth to de-emphasize the more rational quasi-scientific aspects of marketing in order to emphasize the scope for editorial flair and imagination. For example, Adam Black (*Loaded*'s commissioning editor) attributes their success to the fact that the magazine continues to read as if it is 'driven by instinct rather than market research' (*Observer*, 20 October 1996). The ideal magazine is represented as an 'organic' product rather than as something that has been laboriously con-structed from careful research and the relentless pursuit of advertis-ing. As we argued previously, such codings potentially have as much to do with the culture of the magazines as the culture of fast-moving capitalism. That is the languages of gut instinct actually signify the need to respond to new market opportunities and cultural shifts. The editors then simultaneously need to plan magazine futures coupled with the requirement of responding quickly to changing market conditions. The new rapid-action capitalism needs to be able to respond to cultural shifts while simultaneously stimulating them.

The 'necessary evil' of advertising

A magazine's marketing department may, of course, have quite different views from its creative and editorial team, with a fair degree of antagonism acknowledged to exist between them. Editors tended to regard advertising as a 'necessary evil' – or what Mike Cones (*GQ*) called 'a marriage of dubious convenience' – rather than as an intrinsic part of what the magazine was trying to achieve editorially. Emphasizing their personal creativity, editors were quick to accuse one another of being in the thrall of advertising. Before she left *Esquire*, for example, Rosie Boycott claimed that *GQ* has 'sold its soul in pursuit of advertising' and that Michael VerMeulen, its current editor, was 'editing an advertising vehicle' (*Guardian*, 8 November 1993). In some cases, of course, the distinction between advertising and editorial has become quite blurred, as with *Stuff for Men* where the concept of magazine-as-product has merged with the idea of magazine-as-a-showcase-for-products.

Several of our interviewees reported a backlash from advertisers regarding the sexual content of the magazines. Mark Higham reports that *Escape* and *Loaded* had both experienced 'a bit of a backlash from advertisers' but that increasing sales had silenced their critics: 'Readers loved the sex content and it doesn't really matter what advertisers say, if you've got the numbers reading your mag then you can get the advertisers no matter what.' Others were more circumspect about the power of advertisers in relation to editorial freedom. Mike Cones told an anecdote about the now-defunct style magazine *Blitz*, which he regarded as having acted as a warning to other magazines:

> There was a very famous incident several years ago with a magazine called *Blitz* which was a unisex, younger person's style magazine. It was pretty good. . . . Anyway, what this woman did was a story whereby she took a load of very high-profile perfumes out into the street and got people to smell them and then quoted their responses verbatim. And some people said: 'It smells like drain cleaner', 'I wouldn't be seen dead anywhere near it'. And of course the people who make these fragrances spend a vast fortune on their advertising in magazines like *Blitz*, and overnight they said 'Fuck you' and withdrew their advertising. The magazine folded almost immediately because no one would advertise in it because they thought, 'Why am I spending all this money if you're just going to slag me off?' And that was it: a very painful, short, sharp lesson in the power of the advertiser. And so we, to some degree, preserve some editorial integrity. But, in the end, if the advertiser looks at what we've put in the magazine and says 'Well, this doesn't interest me. I can't see how this is going to enhance my product by being associated with whatever page it happens to be', then they may start looking elsewhere.

Several magazines, including *FHM* and *Loaded*, have had hostile reactions from advertisers, including Chanel and Calvin Klein, both of which were reported to be concerned that the magazines' sexual content could give their products a bad image ('Backlash against lads' mags', *Guardian*, 28 August 1997).[5] According to Chanel's marketing director: 'We are judged by the company we keep' (*Daily Mail*, 28 August 1997). Again, there is a tension between appealing to readers as an acceptable alternative to socially stigmatized pornography while not antagonizing potentially lucrative advertisers. In Peter Howarth's words (as editor of *Esquire*): 'It is embarrassing to admit to buying a top-shelf magazine and perhaps even more embarrassing to admit to buying a dedicated fashion or style magazine. So we are all engaged in this process of saying that we are news- or editorial-based' (*Independent on Sunday*, 25 May 1997).

Like several other editors, Gill Hudson is highly critical of the advertising industry ('The whole advertising world is just up its own bottom . . . they're very, very precious'), but she acknowledges their power. Restricting the 'pornographic' content of the magazines is, she argues, 'nothing to do with what the reader would or wouldn't want. It's the advertisers who have the real control because they just won't advertise in anything smutty. . . . We could all be a lot dirtier than we are but you wouldn't get the advertisers in, so the advertisers . . . are in control.' The level of sales is, however, clearly relevant, redressing the balance in favour of editorial independence. Andy Clerkson (editor of *Stuff*) felt that *Loaded* and *FHM* had redefined the men's magazines' relationship to the advertising industry:

> I think that early on [in the 1980s] men's magazines weren't interested in the readership, they were approaching as much the advertisers as they were [their readers] because ultimately magazines will make more money out of their advertisers. . . . So magazines like *Esquire*, *Arena*, *GQ* were there to attract advertising to get maybe 80–90,000 men to buy into a lifestyle. . . . *Maxim* still has a tough time trying to pull in some of the Chanels and Guccis of this world. . . . A lot of the traditional advertisers in the men's press don't want to go near the kind of, the naked flesh and the attitude that the magazines portray. . . . I think if you have *FHM*'s levels of sales . . . then you've got to advertise with them.

The concept of 'attitude' alluded to here is clearly a key editorial concern, reflected in the title of one of the magazines (*Attitude*) and in the description of another magazine (*Stuff for Men*) by its editor as 'Which? – with-attitude'. 'Attitude' refers to the way that different magazines attempt to find a distinctive voice in which to address their readers, conscious of the process of market segmentation: 'Consumers will become more discerning and demanding so there will be a lot of . . . general magazines, each with a slightly different attitude, each of which is trying to say "We represent you"' (Mike Cones, *GQ*). Editors reject some articles because 'they just aren't good enough, or they're too "laddish" or too serious, too woman's magaziney, too much psychobabble, or haven't got enough attitude' (Gill Hudson, *Maxim*). Others speak about 'getting some attitude in there' (Mark Higham, *Escape*) or (as quoted above) using dummy pages with advertisers 'to show a bit of attitude' (Andy Clerkson, *Stuff*). The term clearly condenses a lot of what the magazines are aiming to achieve, also functioning in opposition to the idea of an overly-commodified 'aspirational' lifestyle: 'the [early magazines] were extremely upmarket, very aspirational, dread word' (Gill Hudson, *Maxim*). To have attitude in the context of magazine publishing means to create a stylistic sense of your own product. It means to contribute to the house style of a magazine which is simultaneously seeking to create a sense of its own distinctiveness while trying to cash in on the popularity of men's lifestyle magazines more generally.

Another way of thinking about attitude might be through what Bourdieu (1984) calls 'distinction'. In this sense, attitude signifies a particular form of laddishness that can be defined through what it is not or what is its 'other'.[6] That is, in certain readings, to have attitude defines a certain *masculine* lifestyle quality which involves being fashionable, hanging out with your mates, and not being under the thumb of your girlfriend. Having attitude in this respect means being stylish and masculine as well as not being defined as uncool or feminine. In magazines like *Loaded*, attitude also clearly stands in opposition to the values of a more determined and serious-minded, career-driven upward mobility. Yet it can also embrace the values of a more aspirational lifestyle, associated with the more hedonistic forms of consumerism.[7] As a leader-writer in the *Independent* put it:

[M]en's magazines are largely a fantasy, the glossy pornography of aspiration. . . . Leaf through the latest bumper editions and what you will find is essentially a hymn to autumn fashions, as the men's monthlies sing their love songs to the likes of Armani, Hugo Boss, Paul Smith, Nike and Calvin Klein.

According to this anonymous leader-writer, 'the publishing phenomenon of the Nineties' amounted to little more than 'a celebration of selfishness . . . a rather narrow and particular lifestyle that has consumerism as its guiding principle'. As a result:

the new media ultimately fails to satisfy. There is a brittle, surface feel about men's magazines that springs from their superficiality, their obsession with appearances, their preoccupation with the mechanics of sex, as though eroticism was no more than genital rubbing. What's missing is emotion, depth, the sense that they are about real lives. They promise much, but often feel hollow. (15 August 1997)

The hedonistic values of a consumerist lifestyle were enthusiastically embraced in *Attitude*, the only men's magazine designed specifically for a gay readership. As its editor, James Collard explained, his readers had become disenchanted with the more po-faced, campaigning style of the gay press. His own readers, he insisted, 'had more in common with a club-going *Loaded* reader than . . . with a dull old Nelly' (*Guardian*, 12 January 1998). Collard's ability to define his readers in terms of their brand-label consumer preferences epitomizes David Chaney's (1996: ix) definition of lifestyle as 'embedded in a culture of consumerism':

> 44 per cent of *Attitude*'s readers go to the gym twice a week. Now, they are not going to strut around in a feather boa at the weekend – they're more likely to wear Nordica sports or Adidas snowboarding trousers. . . . Modern life has done us such huge favours. We love products which signal modernity, brands that are strong. We never drink Vladivar, only black-label Smirnoff. It's like we've escaped from the suburbs – if we see anything that looks like 'Asda price' we'll run a mile back to our Alessi kettle and our Clerkenwell loft. (*Guardian*, 12 January 1998)

Other magazines, like Wagadon's short-lived men's title *Deluxe*, also attempted to embody the values of 'lifestyle shopping' for men (cf. Nixon, 1992).

Responding to the market or creating a niche?

Partly because of their association with the style press, including magazines such as *i-D*, *The Face* and *Arena*, the main publishing houses (EMAP, NMC, Condé Nast and IPC) were hesitant to enter the men's magazine market until a mass readership could be guaranteed. Even in the late 1980s, the industry was still reacting cautiously: 'The so-called style magazines appeal only to certain types of men. *GQ* is a specialist interest. It's a lovely market but it's just not important yet. As yet the whole thing is still embryonic' (*Campaign*, 7 July 1989, quoted in Nixon, 1996: 142).

A similar tension ran throughout our interviews, where editors appeared unclear as to whether they were setting a trend within the publishing industry or following changes taking place elsewhere. Some of the editors had responded to changes in the marketplace following the growth of the internet or the increasing popularity of club culture. Others characterized men's magazines as more innovative, driving the market. This contradiction is present even within a single interview. So, for example, according to Mark Higham (*Escape*): '*Loaded* got men looking at news-stands', suggesting that the magazine was instrumental in carving out its own market. But, he also suggested, if *Loaded* had come along five years earlier, 'blokes would still have been into it', implying that the market existed prior to the magazine. Once *Loaded* and *FHM* began to demonstrate their mass appeal, the industry responded in predictable fashion, as Mike Cones (*GQ*) recognized: 'there's obviously a market here [which] we've got to get a slice of'. More recent launches, such as IPC's *Later*, are clearly targeted at perceived gaps in an existing market, in this case for older men, aged 25–40, who have out-grown the more 'laddish' and youthful appeal of *Loaded*, so 'out goes lager, four letter words, B-list celebrity chicks in skimpy underwear [and] in comes money, success, nostalgia, keeping fit . . . and relationships, replacing one-night stands' (*Guardian*, 27 April 1999).

While some editors cheerfully admitted their willingness to 'cannibalize' existing markets, attracting readers from other magazines or launching specialist titles on the back of successful general interest magazines, others insisted on their independence from rival magazines. Mike Higham (*Escape*) represents the former position:

> When we launched we were going for the *Loaded* reader and the *FHM* reader. . . . The market has become so big now that people are looking for sections of those big magazines to turn into magazines themselves. . . . Because the men's market is so big, those small sections are fracturing off into whole magazines.

By contrast, the whole ethos of *Loaded* represents the latter position of 'doing its own thing', irrespective of changes taking place elsewhere in the market. According to Adam Porter, for example, while they 'take note of what the punters [readers] say':

> we don't really concern ourselves with other people who produce mags. . . . I can honestly say I've looked at that magazine [*FHM*] only a couple of times in my life, you know. . . . We know we're alright. . . . We have a laugh . . . chuck ideas around. . . . We cobble it together like that really.

This kind of editorial braggadocio presents a very different picture from the business of magazine publishing as represented by painstaking market research, readership surveys, analysis of circulation figures and demographic trends. It also runs counter to the promotion of a culture of laddism as part of a more manipulative mass culture thesis in the sense implied by Adorno and Horkheimer (1973). Rather than originating from a single source or being imposed from above, the magazines' content and style has emerged from several different sources in a relatively fractured and haphazard way. The market was, initially at least, extremely unstable, with little sense of the size and composition of the target audience. As we go on to show (in chapter 5), the magazines are subject to a similarly fractured and pluralistic variety of readings rather than to a single decoding of the editors' hegemonic message.

The editors' constant uncertainty about adopting the right tone for addressing their readers is clearly revealed in their approach to the encoding of advice and information. While some of the magazines claimed to provide knowledge and advice to their readers ('as a magazine we try to turn information into knowledge': Mark Higham, *Escape*), most were aware of the need to be entertaining rather than didactic. Several editors spoke of the importance of 'being able to relate to your reader' (Gill Hudson, *Maxim*), 'representing' the reader (Mike Cones, *GQ*) or being the reader's friend (Mark Higham, *Escape*). This is particularly true of consumer magazines like *Stuff*, whose editor, Andy Clerkson, described 'the biggest battle we have is the entertainment versus useful nature of the magazine'. He addressed this dilemma by adopting a fairly downbeat tone, comparing the style in which information was presented in the magazine with the kind of advice you get at the local pub:

> If you're down the pub . . . you know someone'll say 'I've just bought a mobile phone' or, erm, 'Jesus Christ, have you seen they've got helicopters that fly to the moon'. . . . We do try to bring it down to that level . . . [rewriting expert reviews] into something that could've been your mate telling you in a kind of more relaxed environment.

Clerkson went on to espouse a kind of 'blokeishness' that contrasted markedly with the characteristics of both the new man and the lad: 'it's quite earthy, it's kind of a sensible person, you're not poncey but you're not some outrageous looney kind of beer-drinking, lager-swilling, get your tits out kind of lad'. A similar dilemma exists, especially for the more popular, downmarket titles, like *Loaded*, *Maxim* and *FHM*, in how to present sexy images without being accused of downright sexism.

Sexy or pornographic?

Gill Hudson argued that the use of irony was vital in making readers feel comfortable about the magazine's sexual content:

> I don't want to produce a magazine that is sheerly pornographic because porn is not ironic or funny [but] if we ignore the fact that sex sells . . . we're just stupid. . . . I think the humour is very important and it's also a way of making men feel comfortable with something that men are going to do anyway and not beat yourself up about it.

Referring to readers who are married with kids looking at 'pictures of girls with their tits out', she argued: 'that is totally compatible with being a good guy. . . . What's wrong with that?'[8]

A similar argument was made by the editor of *Arena* when it published its first swimsuit special, claiming that their readers 'are sophisticated enough to see that it's handled in an intelligent and amusing way . . . [with] a degree of irony' (*Guardian*, 13 July 1998). Adam Porter (editor of *Loaded*'s website) appeared to share this philosophy, feeling no need to defend the magazine's representation of women:

> I could quite happily sit here and justify what we do but I don't personally feel that we need to. *Loaded*'s not a sexist magazine, like *Loaded*'s strictly into sex, it's sexual, like into sex, but there's a difference between being sexual and being sexist. . . . I mean, we don't use degrading language and we don't use like bad attitude towards women in any respect anywhere. . . . I don't believe we're sexist in the slightest, I really don't. . . . I think that people who read *Loaded* worship women. . . . Our publisher, our boss is a woman and we don't have a problem, no-one here has a problem with that.

The defensiveness with which these remarks are expressed, though no doubt influenced by our obvious scepticism as interviewers, suggests that there is more of a tension here than Porter is willing to admit. Another way of understanding these remarks is through the prism of what Ulrich Beck (1997) calls 'constructed certitude'.[9] Understood simply, constructed certitude is the attempt to shield tradition from criticism by excluding certain questions. In this case, magazines like *Loaded* ('for men who should know better') offer a celebration of laddishness (a more assertive reinvention of heterosexual masculinity) that is widely accused of being sexist. In Beck's terms, the magazine's response is to claim that they are not sexist but sexual, taking refuge in their readers' natural sexuality. This not only dismisses certain questions as to how heterosexual masculinity might be being reformulated at the present time, but also evades the charge of sexism as irrelevant. The process of naturalizing sexuality also obscures the extent to which lad culture in general and magazines like *Loaded* in particular are not merely reflecting a 'natural' masculinity but helping to construct it. That is, in a world where gender and sexuality are increasingly plastic and open to question, some (at least) of the magazines deal with this ambiguity by treating their representations as above criticism (simply stating the obvious). Those who seek to challenge their views are readily dismissed as having failed to grasp the magazine's point ('we worship women').

Conclusion

In the introduction to this chapter we suggested that editors were walking a fine line, balancing various conflicting demands including the desire to entertain their readers without alienating advertisers.[10] Here, we suggest that the way these editorial tensions are discussed reflects the anxieties and contradictions of contemporary masculinities (which are dealt with in greater depth in our analysis of the focus group transcripts). Several of our interviewees were conscious of these dilemmas, including Mike Cones (*GQ*), who offered the following analysis:

> [T]he reason that men's magazines have begun to be more successful these days is that men are . . . almost like headless chickens in as much as it's very difficult to know what to believe in. . . . Boys in school are constantly being told that girls are smarter than they are . . . it's almost as if they need permission to behave in a certain way, to think a certain way. They need some kind of validation for the way they actually do feel, even if they have no opinions at all. . . . It's like there's nothing gone on, their whole life is dominated by sport, alcohol and sex and that in my opinion is why magazines like *FHM* and *Loaded* have become as successful as they have. It's because they appeal to the absolute base instincts in most men, but they glorify it so that guys think that it's OK. Before they might not have been embarrassed as such but a little bit self-conscious about being so boorish but now it's being celebrated in print so therefore we have permission to behave this way. It's OK, it's legitimate.

Cones went on to suggest that the magazines are 'pandering to a perceived need':

Men tend to talk about anything but themselves or their problems. . . . So I think [the magazines are] a substitute to some degree for talking. It's almost like having a one-way conversation if that's possible. . . . The onus is on the man to be the strong provider, as it were, and you have to maintain the veneer of impenetrability and invincibility and I think that's what men's magazines almost encourage, not specifically perhaps but they do. . . . It's all the kinds of things that you need to know or you might need to know to lead some kind of meaningful life. . . . A lot of the time men don't feel empowered or qualified to make particular decisions, they're not sure whether it's the right decision.

This particular discussion concluded with a contradiction: men are worried about 'being useless in bed, not being very good at sport and losing their hair', while, as consumers, they are becoming increasingly sophisticated: 'more discerning and more demanding'. This hints at another tension for editors between the desire to address their readers as 'regular guys' or 'ordinary blokes' and the recognition (encouraged by their advertisers) that the magazines are an important vehicle for those with more aspirational lifestyles. While Andy Clerkson (*Stuff*) was quite open about the aspirational nature of his target market ('men in their late 20s, early 30s . . . who are, you know, probably single and aspirational . . . who've got some cash to spend and are quite aspirational about how they spend it'), other editors were much more hesitant to describe their readers in these terms.[11]

Several of the editors thought of their target readers as people like themselves ('People in the office, really'), with the magazine covering 'what we do in our social lives, go down the pub, go to the cinema, what I would term "regular guys", that's ultimately the lifestyle we're targeting . . . professional people who have got a life' (Mike Higham, *Escape*). *Loaded*'s editorial team also espoused this 'democratic' ideal, epitomized in James Brown's frequent claims to be editing a magazine that is written for people who like the things he does and had previously been ignored by publishers (*Independent*, 7 February 1995). But this egalitarian impulse is undermined by Brown's high-profile 'celebrity' lifestyle, including his boast, on moving from *Loaded* to *GQ*: 'I don't know about the others, but I'm a fucking star' ('Mags and megastars', *Guardian*, 30 June 1997). Similarly Mark Higham argues that his readers are aspiring to the lifestyle of those who write for magazines like *Escape*: 'I think our readers are probably aspiring to be like many of us on the team . . . professional people who have got a life.' Jerome Smail also emphasized the 'adrenaline-fuelled active lifestyle' portrayed in *Xtreme*, but claimed his magazine had 'the least marketing-type bullshit'. It was 'aspirational, but in a less pretentious way' than the other magazines.

Gill Hudson pursued a similar theme, insisting that *Maxim* readers are 'like the kind of men I know, regular guys, full of all sorts of contradictions, whose main priorities in their lives are to have a good job, a good relationship, maybe kids, they worry about their money, their health, their holidays – like ordinary life'. As an editor, she insists that every story concludes by 'bringing it back to the reader': 'discussing real issues in a non-worthy way. I think we're actually very useful . . . there's lots of really good information in there.' While she describes the magazine as 'a manual for life', her desire to avoid appearing 'worthy' hints at another tension for editors. Addressing this dilemma, she insists that *Maxim* is not a 'lad mag':

> It's much more complex than that . . . most of our readers are both 'new lad' and 'new men', capable of getting blind drunk on a Saturday night but equally capable of holding a door open for a woman and being at the birth, the whole lot in one person.

The very idea of the new lad, she claims, 'got in the way' of what *Maxim* was trying to do.

This refusal to be pigeon-holed was characteristic of all the interviewees. Like Hudson, Adam Porter (at *Loaded*) disowned the 'new lad' label: 'I don't know what people mean by it to be frank.' He felt that the media were keen to classify people and that *Loaded* wanted to avoid the kind of restrictions that this entailed. As a group, the editors were keen to distance themselves from any kind of academic analysis, reacting with frustration to those who they felt missed the point that magazines were designed to be entertaining, not to contribute to a political or academic agenda. Alan Lewis (Editor-in-chief at *Loaded*) denied any complexity in explaining the magazine's commercial success: 'All we did is get back to basics and acknowledge that men are pretty simple souls' ('Now it's lads on top', *Guardian*, 5 September 1996), while Gill Hudson expressed her dismay at those who forget that the prime purpose of magazines like *Maxim* is to entertain:

> A lot of academic people come along and berate me and other editors, 'Why don't we run poetry?' – because people are buying these magazines for entertainment. Primarily it's enjoyment. You have to remember that we are in an entertainments industry, we're not out to benefit mankind.[12]

Hudson expressed the same reservations about recent media coverage of the magazines:

NS: What do you think of some of the press that you've got?

Gill Hudson: Well I just get . . . I'm bored by it, I mean I just kind of think 'Come on, say something new about it'. They all keep making the same points, the same tedious points about women. Keep calling us a 'lad's mag'. It's just boring, it makes me depressed about journalism generally. I think when you look at what's going on underneath that, get off the 'new lads' bandwagon. The trouble is the press at the moment are so driven by kind of two-dimensional pen portraits, you know: 'new lads', right let's find something else. It was yuppies a few years ago, new men and new lad, and they're all . . . it's much more complex than that and I just wish someone would write an intelligent piece about what's really going on and don't just trot out the same old platitudes.

As all of the previous quotations suggest, editors are pulled in several different directions simultaneously, trying to address men as a group of 'regular guys' while targeting specific market segments; aiming to be the 'reader's friend', while providing advertisers with access to a large market of aspirational consumers; giving useful advice without being dull; and providing sexy content that entertains readers without antagonizing respectable advertisers. The knowing tone of the magazines and the frequent use of irony is a clear response to these editorial pressures and a key to their commercial success. It is therefore to questions of content that we now turn in the next chapter.

4

Questions of Content

The appearance of men's lifestyle magazines has (as we saw in chapter 2) raised a torrid discussion in the media in respect of their content and alleged effects. In this chapter we look more closely at some aspects of their content in terms of the constructions of masculinity that they represent. We focus on the content of the magazines as they appeared to us in the mid- to late 1990s, a period dominated by the commercial success of *Loaded* which was to have a significant impact on the style and content of many of the other magazines. While our focus in this chapter is principally on questions of sexual politics, personal relations and men's health issues, we also address the ironic tone of the more laddish or downmarket magazines (where serious discussion of relationships and health issues is notable by its absence). We might, of course, have chosen other features such as readers' letters, editorials or food and drink, sport and money. We decided to focus upon questions related to relationships and health because this coincided with much of the recent writing on gender transformations and embodied identities, and because these issues represented some of the genuinely 'new' aspects of the magazines. Given the popularity of the magazines and the fact that many of the features concern men's behaviour and relationships it seemed possible that the magazines represented an acceptable vehicle for exploring the more intimate aspects of masculinity for which few alternative spaces currently exist (cf. Morley's (1992) work on men's reported avoidance of soap opera because of their apparent wish to avoid discussions of intimacy and domestic responsibility). We also decided to focus upon health magazines because they seemed to be aimed at slightly older men, were not as laddish as the market leaders and were connected with the increasing concern over issues related to the body and fitness discernible within other arenas of contemporary consumer society.

This chapter forms something of a bridge between our analysis of the editorial process involved in the production of the magazines (discussed in the preceding chapter) and issues surrounding their consumption (covered in the next chapter on the magazines' readers). We focus on verbal content since so much of the existing research on men's magazines, including that by Mort (1996) and Nixon (1992, 1996, 1997), has focused on their visual content. In this, our research parallels much of the earlier work on women's magazines, concerned with questions of textual content and stylistics (e.g. Frazer, 1992; McRobbie, 1991a, 1991b; Winship, 1978, 1987). Our focus on content also allows us to identify the discourses that are available within the magazines concerning gender identities, men's health and sexual politics, which readers can then 'rework' in their attempts to 'make sense' of the magazines and their implications for changing masculinities (the focus of chapter 5). The chapter also allows us to draw some preliminary inferences concerning constructions of authenticity and the (potentially subversive) use of irony in undermining such constructions – issues to which we return, again, in the following chapter on readers' discourses and dispositions.

We decided that we could provide a better feel for the available discourses within the magazines by discussing certain articles at length rather than via a more quantitative overview of magazine content. We did, however, undertake a short quantitative analysis of *FHM* and *Men's Health* (January–June 1997). This revealed that *FHM* devotes approximately 45 per cent of its content to advertising compared to less than 28 per cent in *Men's Health*. In quantitative terms, the largest category in *FHM* was not sexual relationships, comprising only 3 per cent of content, but pictures of women (7.5 per cent) and fashion (12.3 per cent). By comparison, *Men's Health* ran very few pictures of glamorous women, devoting about 10 per cent of its pages to sex and relationships and only 2.7 per cent to fashion coverage.[1] This tells us something about the different identities of the magazines although of course it also misses a great deal.

For example, our own experience of reading the magazines (as well as the focus groups and editorial interviews) points to the cover being the most important feature. In this respect, a crude content analysis tells us very little about how different magazines seek to position themselves in relation to their rivals. For example, the emphasis upon sex and relationships in *FHM* might score poorly in terms of overall content, but these issues were often positioned towards the front and middle of the magazines (fashion is usually towards the back), as well as being highlighted on the cover. Despite our emphasis on the magazines' verbal content, we do not wish to downplay the importance of their visual appeal and, especially, the choice of cover images. In this respect we concur with David Chaney's (1996) suggestion that visualization has become the central source of meaning within contemporary urban and consumer cultures. The changing spectacle of the magazine covers (made even more dramatic by the rapid expansion of titles) and their linkage into other visual forms such as television is a key feature of their appeal. What McRobbie (1982: 269) says about *Jackie* could also be said about men's magazines, in that 'the dominance of the visual level, which is maintained throughout the magazine, reinforces the notion of leisure. It is to be glanced through, looked at and only finally read.'

Our particular focus is, however, on the magazines' *stylistic* and *narrative* construction: how they look and how they adopt a particular storytelling approach, including the provision of lists and snippets of advice as devices for the discussion of sexuality (Pfeil, 1995). In particular, we shall explore the different discourses and fantasies that the magazines make available to their readers. Without making assumptions about how they are read, this chapter explores the horizons, contradictions and codings offered by the magazines, showing how the texts capture certain pleasures and identifications in being young and male. We attempt to give a reading of the magazines that recognizes the way they construct the subject through both conscious and unconscious dimensions (Walkerdine, 1990).

In general, the magazines address the reader as a 'mate'. They attempt to become the 'reader's friend' by offering handy hints, pointing out obvious pitfalls and providing useful advice, all in the language of common sense, with irony being used as a warning against taking anything that is said too seriously. In this sense, the magazines are careful to avoid talking down to their readers. For example, *Loaded* maintains an interactive website and regularly publishes the phone numbers of the production staff at the front of the magazine. The language used is, then, familiar, in an attempt to produce a sense of mediated intimacy between the lads who run the magazine and their (equally laddish) readers. Similarly, *FHM* also publishes the phone numbers of its staff, runs a regular section on bar room jokes, letters to the editor (where they invite ugly readers to write in to be fixed up with a shag), various sections offering advice (from sex to how to fix your own motor) to flirtatious interviews with fashion models. Despite the fact that men's magazines have a disjointed narrative flow, the overall form of address used is friendly, ironic and laddish.

On the other hand, *Men's Health* has incorporated many of these features but is much more concerned with technical detail. In this respect, there is a clear divide between the 'expert' (the magazine) and the person in need of advice (the 'reader'). It is assumed that the flow of knowledge is overwhelmingly one way (from the magazine to the reader), but that the magazine can be trusted (like a good doctor) not to mislead the reader. Consequently, the set of social relations presumed by *Men's Health* is both hierarchical and invites a believing rather than an ironic disposition.

This distinction should help us draw some conclusions as to how we might understand the magazines politically. In particular, we would like to emphasize the impact that *Loaded* made on the visual style and content of the other men's magazines. *Loaded*'s arrival in 1994 radically reshaped the field of men's magazine journalism. According to Tim Southwell (the magazine's second-in-command):

> For issue one we played to what we believed were our strengths. We went on tour with Paul Weller, Deeson wrote about how great hotel sex was and I'd gone skydiving in California. We also had the famous pictures of Liz Hurley in *that* pair of pants – the pair that showed a little too much of what it should have been concealing. Plus Rod Stewart, George Best, Dave from *Minder*, Beavis & Butthead, Vic Reeves, *Withnail & I*, Gary Oldman, Eric Cantona and the first-ever UK magazine interview with Tiger Woods. All for an introductory price of £1. (Southwell 1998: 55–6)

To mark the magazine's distinctiveness from the other (then more upmarket) men's titles, *Loaded* deliberately focused on football, cars, drinking and music. In an early editorial, James Brown comments: '*Loaded* should be rammed full of the things that people go on about in the pub and that stuff like health and perfume should be left to the adult mags. Remember, grooming is for horses' (July, 1995). The use of laddish irony which became common currency within *Loaded* changed the face of men's magazine publishing. Both *Maxim* and *FHM* borrowed from and reinvented the magazine's visual and verbal economy, blurring the distinction between such lad's mags and more upmarket titles like *GQ* and *Esquire*.

We have argued that the general distinction between upmarket magazines aimed at slightly older men (*GQ*, *Esquire*, *Arena*) and downmarket magazines (*FHM*, *Maxim*, *Loaded*) has become increasingly blurred (with James Brown's editorial move from *Loaded* to *GQ* acting as a key signifier in this respect). So, for example, Peter Howarth (as editor of *Esquire*) sought to defend his magazine's reliance on a diet of 'babes and boobs' by arguing against the idea that there had been a recent dumbing down of men's magazines. Yet he went on to say that 'any good magazine must offer a balance of content, and part of that balance, if it is to reflect the interests of men, will inevitably be articles on beautiful women' (*Guardian*, 25 November 1996).

The popularity and commercial success of *Loaded* undoubtedly had an impact on the other magazines, with the softer, more caring versions of masculinity (associated with the new man) being displaced by another image whereby other aspects of masculine behaviour, such as drinking to excess, adopting a predatory attitude towards women and obsessive forms of independence (read: fear of commitment and connection), have become the new focal point. As Sean Nixon (1996) has pointed out, the emergence of the 'new lad' signifies the difficulty of reinventing heterosexual scripts, with irony being used to distance the reader from these difficulties. However, we would argue that whereas the function of irony in relation to the 'new man' was to provide a safe distance between the reader and less traditional scripts, with the current wave of new laddism irony now operates to subvert political critique. To offer a political critique of the magazines is to miss the point of the joke and place yourself outside a mediated laddish community. However, irony in men's magazines also functions in a similar way to the new wave of women's magazines (discussed by McRobbie, 1999) in that it allows men to experience the contradictory nature of the magazines (and masculinity) at a safe distance.

We also wish to suggest that the public appearance of the magazines has brought into the open a number of anxieties and fantasies about men and masculinity in a changing society. As Peter Middleton has argued in relation to another form of popular culture:

> [Comic books] offer powerful fantasies in a graphic mode which does not intrude too much disruptive reality either in the storyline or in the sketchy visual representation. . . . Above all, comics offer the inside story on the adult world. Hyper masculine action comics are offered to boys as the inside information on men's lives, information they find hard to get from anywhere else. (1992: 25)

The 'knowing' sexism of the magazines also operates within a wider culture which has introduced the idea of relationships as a central concern for both sexes. The changing sociological context within which the magazines have appeared means that they are a far more complex phenomenon than arguments that are concerned with backlash imply. The magazines, then, are caught between an attempt to construct masculinity as a form of fundamentalist certitude, while simultaneously responding to a world where gender relations are rapidly changing. In sociological terms the magazines can be made sense of by identifying the social and cultural contradictions that they are trying to handle, caught between an awareness that old-style patriarchal relations are crumbling and the desire to reinscribe power relations between different genders and sexualities.

While the expansion of the men's magazine market attracted widespread media attention as a result of the emergence of 'lad mags' such as *Loaded*, *Maxim* and *FHM*, other more niche-marketed magazines were also becoming commercially successful. *Men's Health*, for example, witnessed a steady expansion of sales from 130,000 in the first half of 1996 to more than 280,000 by the second half of 1998. Unlike most of the other men's magazines, *Men's Health* has continued to feature the naked torsos of well-built young men on their covers, resisting, to some degree, the culture of new laddism. The magazine's target market is also distinctive, aimed at slightly older men, with an overt focus on health, exercise and diet.[2]

Arguably, then, a different version of masculinity is opened up by the health magazines as they focus overtly upon the healthy body. Indeed, what was noticeable from our focus group interviews was how rarely health was actually mentioned as a topic for discussion. This was particularly marked, as most of the men's titles carry health sections, although they are usually positioned towards the back of the magazine. In this respect, the magazines could be said to occupy a terrain where certain issues in respect of the body are given increased visibility, but in such a way that they do not contradict dominant constructions of heterosexual masculinity.

In order to sharpen our analysis we begin by focusing on questions of sexual politics, presenting a critique of the ways that the magazines specifically handle questions connected with intimate personal relationships between men and women. As we shall see, the magazines reflect a concern with the private and intimate spheres of the life-world which more traditional versions of masculinity have foregone. An emphasis on previously repressed areas of masculine experience, including men's appreciation of other men's bodies, fashion and health, mean that reading the magazines is part of an ambivalent social experience. While the magazines are undoubtedly a celebration of white male heterosexuality, they are also deserving of a more critical response. In this respect, we argue, the magazines signal a shifting terrain of concerns related to intersubjective relations between men and women that should be read politically.

In what follows, we argue that the magazines have opened up a discursive space in which some of the ambiguities and contradictions of contemporary masculinity can be explored. In particular, we use our analysis of the magazines' content to ask a number of theoretical questions: to what extent are the magazines simply a forum for the reassertion of a hegemonic masculinity? How, if at all, are contemporary masculinities problematized in the magazines? Do they provide a critical forum where new sexual identities can be experimented with and inclusive forms of cultural citizenship promoted? How does the ironic and instrumental framing of the articles impact upon their construction? And what possibilities do they open out for new heterosexual scripts?

Boys love their girls

The breakdown of the nuclear family is normally told in terms of an irresistible force (women and feminism) meeting a resistant object (men and power). Barbara Ehrenreich (1983) takes a slightly different tack through this narrative by arguing that contemporary post-traditional society has been equally shaped by the agency of men. In telling this story she points to the precursors of contemporary men's lifestyle magazines (such as *Playboy*) which were advocating a strategy of consumptive fun and sexual liberation away from the normative constraints of the nuclear family as far back as the 1960s. Magazines like *Playboy* were essential in promoting the belief that well-adjusted heterosexual men could avoid the commitments of conventional marriage for reasons other than homosexuality. Further, the development of beatnik lifestyles, human potential movements and concern about male heart disease all helped develop a discourse of critique around the idea of male sacrifice in the workplace and in the home. Hence, just at the point that women were asserting their right to autonomy in terms of work, sexuality and other social relations, men were also fleeing from the rigidities of the breadwinner role. The new self was given a purpose through the accumulation of personal pleasures, and valued individual choice above anything else (Featherstone, 1991; Rose, 1989). Such a view heralded the possibility of a masculine or feminine self realizing its deepest desires not through sacrifice and duty but through the tragedies and triumphs of love and sex.

Many of the articles in contemporary men's magazines reconfirm this social pattern. This is done in two main ways. The first is to stress the virtues and dangers of a 'singles' lifestyle that is orientated around pleasurable consumption. The other emphasizes the constraints and traps of conventional heterosexual marriage (namely, domestic responsibilities and children). These discourses and repertoires are obviously two different sides of the same coin and are linked through a celebration of autonomy and a fear of dependence. *XL* magazine (July 1997) offers a typical article in this respect under the headings 'Are you better off single? Meet the eternal bachelor, footloose and fancy-free for the foreseeable. Not for him the relentless grind of domestic life or the style-cramping mire of monogamy. No way, mate'. The article offers an ironic, up-beat narrative about a professional man who, on turning 35, realizes that the pleasures outweigh the 'pains' of being single. The article's overwhelmingly ironic tone makes plain that, despite pressures from your immediate family to get married and produce children and despite losing contact with married friends, a modern bachelor can expect emotional support from other single people (mostly women), nights out with their mates (mostly men), the time and money to indulge their hobbies and a string of casual affairs with younger women. The great prize of batchelorhood is represented as a life where one has little responsibility for others and where one is truly free to do as one chooses.

Similarly, an article in *Maxim* ('Better Dead Than Wed', May 1997) comments on the growing number of single men who have either chosen to postpone marriage or avoid it altogether. Marriage is again viewed as a form of social constraint preventing young men in their early thirties from living a life of consumptive and sexual freedom. That marriage is ultimately seen as a way of feminizing and castrating men is evident in the subtitle, which suggests *'modern marriage is about as friendly as a set of nutcrackers'*.

What is obviously missing from this celebration of one-night stands, obsessive consumerism and male bonding is how men's needs for reciprocity and emotional warmth are to be met. If the modern self emphasizes autonomy, it also places an extreme premium upon intimacy. The articles offer an unproblematic view of freedom and independence without the connected need for security and belonging. At a time when relationships are crumbling, with increasing male long-term unemployment and new demands being made by women of their male partners, the culture of the magazines suggests a form of masculine disavowal and social release through consumptive hedonism. (Indeed, one of the magazines in our study appropriately enough calls itself *Escape*.)

There are, undoubtedly, new opportunities for men in a society in which the traditional track to heterosexual monogamy is increasingly open to question, and the magazines obviously play some part in making new identity formations publicly available. However, it is not so much convivial love or old-style patriarchy that is being offered but a desperate defence of masculine independence. Read more sociologically, the way of avoiding the complex chaos of modern relationships is to find a secure identity in phallic certitude. The gratifying fantasy being offered here is one of omnipotence, whereby single heterosexual males (with access to material resources or a 'worn smooth credit-card') cruise through an edifying social world.

However, the magazines are also representative of more ambiguous locations of sexual anxiety. For example, *XL* (October 1997) ran a more troubled article called 'Diving back into the Datingpool'. The article outlines some of the pitfalls of being single when you are past the age of 30, the concluding point being that meeting sexually available women is a far more complex and difficult process than it is for men in their late teens. The narrative flow of the article is structured around initial feelings of optimism after being released from a long-term relationship, only to be followed by crushing disappointment. The disappointment is connected to the mourning of the loss of masculine agency. 'The brave new world of pussy galore' turns out to be the one where you are dependent upon your friends for dates, older women expect commitment and younger women recognize you as 'a sad old lech'. The more ambivalent tropes here powerfully articulate a sense that in terms of the negotiation of love and sex older single men face an anxiety-producing social world. Despite the article's cultural conservatism (apparently only sad people over 30 still go to clubs), it also prefigures a more 'realistic' concern with the shifting terrain of relationships than was absent from the articles analysed this far. Yet the overwhelming sense is a form of masculine mourning for a loss of phallic certitude, having been plunged into a world of complex social arrangements.

We should, however, be careful not to assume that the articles actually represent what men really want. Such a supposition would both offer an overly simplified connection between what is in the media and how it is interpreted, and those feelings that are consciously expressed and those that are too painful to articulate. Nonetheless, the predictable and repetitive nature of the articles reveals a desperate (if not manic) attempt to shore up a rigid cultural identity devoid of intersubjective tension. For example, marriage is not to be avoided due to its connection to old-style patriarchy, but because it represents a restriction on masculine forms of self-definition. Further, despite the evidence of more ambiguous frames, even depressive features centre on the sense of a lost world where more ambivalent feelings have to be kept at bay. Whereas the new man welded together narcissism and nurturance, the new lad offers a rather different cocktail of staunch independence, masculine nostalgia and (as we shall see) misogyny.

Don't you want me?

In order to emphasize the extent to which the magazines – in part at least – symbolically represent a fundamentalist attempt to reinscribe male dominance just at the point of its passing, we focus here on some of the articles that deal directly with relationships. Many such articles – although, as we shall see, there are exceptions – mix irony, handy hints, calculative reason and a playful misogyny to entertain their readers when discussing sexual relations between men and women. Of the available examples, we have chosen three articles. Two are from the current market leader: 'Whip Her Into Shape' (*FHM*, June 1997) and 'The Seven Shag Itch' (*FHM*, February 1997), and the other is from *Maxim*, which has a similar tone and style: ('This Woman Can Seriously Damage Your Health' (April 1997). All three articles can be read as offering advice to men in a world where the negotiation of sexual relations has seemingly become increasingly problematic. In this respect, the articles warn readers of possible danger signs, situations to be avoided and easily learnt strategies which will enable them to negotiate what they want. It is noticeable that more recent men's lifestyle magazines have continued to run very similar articles in respect of those analysed below. For example, *FHM* (November 1999) has recently featured articles like 'Extreme Sex: The missionary position losing its appeal', 'How lucky is your girlfriend?: She may moan, but your lady does not know she's born', 'Slavery: sampled' (accompanied by a photograph of a naked woman on a lead) and 'Lesbian sex therapy' all in the same issue. The continuity and prominence of articles in respect of male sexuality all point to the fact that they continue to be a central feature of the appeal of men's magazines.

The narratives offered by the articles under review are neither fully modern nor postmodern. Their dominant trope recognizes the more uncertain contexts within which contemporary sexuality is negotiated, but this is framed within a context that offers instrumental solutions to such problems. For example, the *FHM* article (June 1997) starts with the proposition that many men find it difficult to ask their sexual partners for what they want in the bedroom. However, more troubling topics that can be related to whether men actually know what they want are avoided, and the article's cynical and manipulative tone encourages men to be more open about the way they negotiate sex. This could be by returning sexual favours, doing the cleaning or taking her out for a meal (however, the article insists that this should always stop short of the promise of marriage). The dominant flow of the narrative recognizes that men are 'hopelessly inept' when it comes to negotiating sex, and encourages them 'to take charge in the bedroom'. Female sexuality is crudely represented as something which needs to be mastered and controlled, and that men and women are polar opposites in terms of their sexual identities and desires. The magazine suggests that men always want to take women roughly, whereas she would always prefer a candlelit bath. There is little point discussing what men and women want because this is self-evident and their sexual imaginations are driven apart through the operation of gender polarities.

The use of binary oppositions in terms of men's and women's sexuality is most pronounced in the second article (*FHM*, February 1997), which sets out to ease men's guilt about wanting shallow relationships with women that are over in a matter of weeks if not days. The narrative traces through a series of different types of sexual intercourse, which begins with the 'drunken shag' and ends with a final 'good-bye shag'. The hero of the story avoids commitment, becomes bored very quickly and has a flagging libido which is only revived once a male rival appears on the scene. Women, on the other hand, want commitment, to plan a future together, weekends away and nice surprises. The modern man seemingly falls so short of women's expectations there is little to be gained in trying. Much better to take what you can while holding women at a distance. The narrator comments: 'The idea of this being a serious affair shocks you to the core. After all, where did she get the idea that a freewheeling stud like you was up for anything permanent? Especially as she's not exactly as fit as you thought' (*FHM*, February 1997).

Jessica Benjamin (1995) and John Forrester (1992) argue that fantasies such as the one demonstrated here are actually an aggressive and retaliatory response to feelings of helplessness. Earlier repressed feelings of being dependent on their mother and of being absorbed into their mother are fended off through aggression and power. Men therefore need to feel powerful in order to become like their fathers and to reverse feelings of dependency. The next step towards misogyny is to become fearful of what you were originally dependent upon, while preserving more nurturant feelings evident in early relationships. Psychically, this is how the split between virgin and whore, or wife and mistress, is born. Processes of psychic splitting are also evident in the preservation of the idea of phallic control and omnipotence. Such is men's need to forget the early trauma of feeling at the mercy of the mother's love and care that the infant learns to invest heavily in desires associated with self-sufficient omnipotence (Sayers, 1995). Indeed one of the most powerful messages that comes across in the magazines (despite the mournful tone of the *XL* article discussed earlier) is that the modern man should be able to act in any way he pleases free of feelings of guilt, depression, anxiety, doubt or ethical complexity.

This feeling was most cogently expressed by one of the men in our focus groups when he said (about men):

> [T]hey have more freedom now than ever before, much much more. They're earning more, they can have as much sex as they want. They can go out and do what they want. You don't need to have a little wifey at home to darn the socks, you just throw the socks away and buy a new pair. That's really it, there is not the same kind of social pressure on men to have a family, to have a wife . . . you can do what you want. (London journalists)

Arguably, there is a very neat fit between what is expressed above and the culture of the magazines. In the face of a more chaotic and complex world emerging between the sexes, the magazines are picking up on certain aspects of a rapidly detraditionalizing society, while ignoring others. Indeed, it is probably their unacceptable, anti-politically correct, overtly laddish sense which is part of their appeal. The cynicism of the articles accepts that there is no real defence of extreme forms of masculine behaviour, but that there is also little alternative. Laddishness here is marking what it means to be 'authentically' male. In this respect, the new lad simply defines himself as a reaction to the new man that went before. If the new man believed it was important to develop a more nurturing role (no matter how synthetic this might have been), the new lad would probably ridicule such notions before falling back on the idea that masculinity is after all fixed by biology. The ideology would be that men are now authentically speaking up for themselves, refusing to be bullied by others into being anything other than what they truly are. The new man was what women wanted men to be, whereas the new lad is men throwing off this synthetic media image for something more in tune with reality. Obviously what is missing from this view is the extent to which the 'lad' is as much of a social construction as the new man. Further, that both the new man and the new lad share a concern with the presentation of self through a range of products, including hair gel, deodorant, fashion and other lifestyle accessories – laddishness no longer signifying an absence of concern with bodily maintenance. Moreover, the cultural construction of new lad acts as a means of enforcing boundaries between men and women (Sibley, 1995). The accompanying fear seems to be that unless men and women are rigidly rendered apart, this would then introduce a small grain of uncertainty within the representation of masculine identity, thereby threatening to undermine it altogether.

The new lad, then, acts as a kind of counter-modernity, or what Beck (1997) has called 'constructed certitude'. New laddism, as we have seen, leaves no room for doubt, questioning, ambiguity or uncertainty. To ask questions as to what it is that men actually want from their relations with women is to ignore the most obvious facts of what everybody already knows. It is to engage in a lot of pseudo intellectual meandering which ultimately leads nowhere. However, as we outline in chapter 5, focus groups participants' reactions to the magazines both reaffirmed these patterns while also presenting a more ambivalent set of responses.

Our third article (*Maxim*, April 1997) demonstrates how much 'new lad' culture is based upon a fear of the feminine. This article is the most overtly psychological in that it seeks to define, categorize and mark out distinctive features of a new breed of girlfriend. In Foucault's (1977) sense, power operates through discourse to pro-duce a particular personality type so that it might be judged, observed and subjected to the male gaze. Expert opinion is marshalled to warn readers about a particular kind of '90s woman who is overly emotionally accommodating and compromising, until she eventually snaps. Male readers are warned not to fall for the superficial charms of 'elastic band woman'. According to the article, it is women (not men) in the mid-'90s who 'can't bear what comes from being dependent upon another person's love and approval'. Again, by making the woman the focus of the narrative the article positions men as being completely autonomous without any emotional needs of their own. However, the piece spends more time cataloguing outrageous acts of revenge than it does outlining a personality profile. In a sense, then, the article is less about the surveillance of women (although this is certainly present) and more concerned with the pain that can often surround close emotional relationships. To offer up women's inability to recognize their emotional lack within a celebration of masculine agency is surely a crude act of displacement. Due to the increasingly breakable nature of social relationships, modern social life is increasingly intercut with feelings of loss. The very impermanence of intimate relations will mean that over the course of a lifetime both men and women will have to deal with feelings of rejection, self-doubt and other troubling anxieties involved with separation possibly on numerous occasions. This is seemingly difficult to square with the dominant ideology of the magazines, which is to provide images of self-sufficient successful men who adopt a more strategic approach in respect of sexual relations. As Martin Buber (1958) argues an I–thou relationship is based upon an openness to the other which is curtailed in relations which are more instrumentally defined. Within I–it relations, the relationship is rigid, ordered, reliably structured and ultimately cold. Buber insists that love relationships depend upon more related and ultimately unpredictable webs of involvement. That this could inevitably lead to an acceptance of the risks that are involved in any relationship is what is being avoided here. Relationships that are alive to the possibility of transformation inevitably run the risk of disappointment and failure. It seems to us that it is the very possibility of personal pain that is being displaced by the magazines' attempt to provide their readers with an identikit of potentially vengeful partners.

Lexicons of love or operator's manual?

Despite the predominant impression that has been given so far, the magazines also offer tips and advice, similar to those that might be found in self-help books and women's magazines. This kind of information is normally organized into lists, depends upon advice from psychological experts and suggests easily learnt rules and procedures that, if followed, offer the possibility of a more fulfilling relationship. As is well known, self-help books are overwhelmingly targeted at and read by women. In this respect, we could perhaps read their emergence with some ambivalance. On the one hand, their evident popularity can be tied into the transformation that is evident in the 'unfreezing' of gender relations and the subsequent discourses tied into the idea of developing a relationship that have accompanied this transformation. On the other hand, they might also be read less as guides to a more unstable intimate sphere and more as a way of bureaucratizing the self. That is, while lists of rules offering advice to heterosexual couples could be seen in terms of the creation of increasingly plastic relations between the sexes, in other respects they signify a form of technocratic consciousness (Habermas, 1971). Ian Craib (1994) argues that as late capitalism becomes more frag-mented, it has opened the way for the introduction of new social scripts promoted by a lifestyle industry. However, many of these new scripts, for men and for women, have sought to foster an illusory powerful self. This self embodies a desperate form of wish-fulfilment that desires to break out of the messiness of life. Lists like the ones under investigation usually judge relationships in terms of their ability to deliver care, emotional intimacy and respectful relations. Craib's point is that these elements are all important but that successful relations are also about the negotiation of other more destructive, fragile and less controllable feelings.

For example, the January–February 1997 issue of *Arena* carried an article called 'How to have a better relationship'. The article is organized in terms of ten easily understood bullet points, with number 9 reading:

SHOW RESPECT   Research suggests that couples who have more than one put-down to every seven positive statements are heading for break up. Don't disrespect your partner, if she's so hopeless how come you're with her? Either sort out what is between you or get out.

In terms of the cultural frames that are being suggested here, it is evident that articles such as the above are simultaneously a response to the reformation of intimate relations and a continuation of some of modernity's more instrumental frames. While the generation of respect presumes a modicum of equality between the sexes, it is hard to escape the impression that a good relationship is a quantifiable phenomenon. Viewed purely instrumentally, a good relationship can be determined by providing a balance sheet of positive as opposed to negative statements. Unless the correct level of emotional satisfaction is reached at any given time readers are advised to make a clean break.

Articles of this kind, which are most likely to be seen in magazines such as *GQ*, *Esquire* and *Arena* (the so-called upmarket end of the men's magazine market), are similar to those found in women's glossy titles such as *Cosmopolitan*, *Marie Claire* and *Company*. Notably, several of the other magazines, in particular *Loaded* and *Attitude*, both run problem pages which aim at ironizing standardized forms of advice such as that offered above. For instance, *Loaded*'s readers are invited to send their problems to 'Dr Mick' (featured on the penultimate page), a cigar-smoking psychiatrist often pictured holding a gun (May 1997, August 1997, September 1997). Similar to the rest of the magazine, the page adopts an irreverent, cynical tone where pointless answers are given to pointless questions amidst a backdrop of chuckling blokeishness. This is seemingly underlined by the fact that Dr Mick's readers are informed that he can't answer all the letters because he's a 'lazy bastard. Besides he over charges.' Conversely, *Attitude*'s (June 1997, July 1997, August 1997) 'Dear Jools' column is aimed like the rest of the magazine at gay men, with this particular section adopting an overtly camp disposition ('If you really want to turn your life around, then you might find moving out of Wolverhampton will work wonders for your self-respect'). A camp sensibility is described by Susan Sontag (1966: 287) as the 'sensibility of failed seriousness, of the theatrical-isation of experience'. Camp refuses the harmonies of traditional seriousness and the risks of fully identifying with extreme states of feeling. Camp privileges irony, style and aesthetics over tragedy, content and morality. Richard Dyer (1992) argues that a camp sensibility and the gay community continue to be profoundly inter-connected. This has arisen historically because gay men in particular have gained a sense of status and personal self-esteem through their mastery of style and artifice. According to Dyer, gay men have historically developed an acute sociological sense for surfaces, appearances and forms due to the need to be good at disguise, requiring that they appear to be the same as everyone else. *Attitude*'s Dear Jools column specializes in comic exaggeration, making fun of heterosexuals via exaggeration and irony. However, Dyer also points out that camp has its blind spots in that it can lead to an inability to read social relations politically and can often be seen as championing emotional shallowness.

Our argument, then, is not that we should moralistically reject the interventions made by the magazines into questions of intimacy. Such a strategy would be drawn into the position of arguing that there was a set of discoverable truths about personal relations that the magazines should be conveying. This would inevitably end with the suggestion that some of the consumptive pleasures involved in read-ing these magazines could and should be replaced by something as didactic as a government information leaflet. Rather, the magazines can be viewed (within certain limits) as a source of pleasure and amusement, but they can also be seen to include certain absences and ideological strategies. Magazines are largely cruised and flicked through rather than being the subject of ideological scrutiny. In this respect, they might be assumed to work precisely because they are able to occupy a field that is ultimately contradictory. As we have shown, they are simultaneously a response to changing gender relations, a form of masculine escape and involve the promotion of an omnipotent self that (even if it is in the short term) can be experienced as providing a source of emotional satisfaction. In this sense, the magazines can be read as offering temporary solutions to contemporary anxieties connected to the reformation of masculine identities.

It is notable, for instance, that the magazines carry many features on dangerous sports and leisure pursuits. For example, two of them (*Xtreme* and *XL*) are almost entirely devoted to outdoor pursuits and 'extreme' sports. These activities often involve a high level of risk, including white-water rafting, mountain biking, parachute jumping and climbing. Arguably, these features are representative of the externalization of risk away from more dialogic emotional encounters that are involved in interpersonal relations. Contemporary masculinity is more attuned to imagining and projecting itself through visual and discursive figurations of bodily risk than emotional engagement. In this respect, what the magazines offer can be interpreted as short-term resolutions of more systemic anxieties and contradictions. However, and this is a point we return to in chapter 5, the magazines do make public an interrelated set of male anxieties and pleasures. Their widespread availability enables men to work through a complex set of male fantasies. Indeed, as we shall see, it is the magazines' ability to bring certain aspects of masculinity into the public domain that partially accounts for their success. Our concern is not to censor these new aspects of masculinity (reconfining them to the closet) nor to celebrate their appeal in an uncritical or unambiguous way. Rather, we seek to ask political questions as regards their construction (also pointing to certain omissions), while respecting the contradictory nature of the features they inevitably draw upon. Before investigating these features further, we want to look at the emphasis placed upon the body by men's health magazines.

Consumption and the sociology of the body

The body has become one of the central topics for debate within sociological theory. Arguably, the refocusing of attention upon the body has been mainly prompted by the emergence of a consumer society and the changing relationships between the sexes (Turner, 1991). Capitalism is no longer dependent upon the condemnation of sexual and physical pleasure and the maintenance of strictly disciplined forms of manual labour. Instead, the body in a consumer culture is both disciplined and hedonistic. In such a culture the body becomes the vehicle for pleasure, youth, health and fitness; that is, it is increasingly viewed as a passport to the good life. In this respect, the body does not signify the site of an uncontrolled hedonism, but the need for a calculating attitude towards the body (Featherstone, 1991). It is seen as a project that can only become completed once we have made certain lifestyle choices. How we choose to regulate and present our bodies becomes increasingly open to question in a culture where it is read as an expression of individual identity (Schilling, 1993). The body, then, is viewed as an unfinished project that has a certain historically and geographically determined malleability (Harvey, 1998). Similarly, Pasi Falk (1996) suggests that we should understand the increased consumption of vitamins amongst the educated middle classes as an attempt to control the future of the body. Falk argues that it only makes sense to link health and longevity if we connect it to the view that life itself is a project within modernity. Health then becomes connected with the idea of an 'open future'. Good health and a strong body are a way of preventing future ills. The reason that men's health magazines emphasize constant exercise, taking vitamin pills and regulating diet is a way of dealing with the uncertainty of what our bodies may have in store for us. The culture of the health magazines can be seen as a form of magical thinking that involves a narcissistic fight for life against a time-related future. Falk writes:

> The mental image of individual life in the form of a graph does not have the form of a cycle or parable intertwined with the ones to come. Rather it is conceived of as a line, first ascending (growth) and then continuing horizontally towards an end point out of sight (embalming). The Narcissistic 'fight for life' is not a confrontation with the actual threats here and now but rather a fight against time related to the future per se as a threat. (1996: 193)

The argument presented here is that, within a consumer culture, the body is increasingly experienced as the responsibility of individuals and as having an uncertain future. The body becomes individuated and broken down into an assemblage of parts. The magazines, in particular, encourage their readers to think of bodies as being made up of 'six-pack' stomachs, piston-like arms and legs and cosmetically improvable skin (cf. Radner (1995) on the Jane Fonda Workout).

However, the problem with the discussion so far is that it does not take enough account of the gendered nature of the body. As Connell (1995) argues, our bodies are addressed by contemporary cultures as having a particular materiality and in terms of specific metaphors that have a different resonance for different genders. That is, the idea of the male body being a machine or whose aggression is dependent upon a genetic disposition is a metaphoric and symbolic way of representing sexual difference. In a different context, Naomi Wolf (1990) has explored the ways in which women in a commercial culture are judged and attributed status through the ways in which they maintain and present their bodies. Here, we want to explore the ways in which the body is represented in terms of specific masculine codes within the content of men's health magazines.

How is the 'reader' of men's health magazines addressed by the text? As we shall see, what is evident in this respect is the continued importance of paid employment (work) for men's sense of identity and a shared context where masculinity is increasingly open to question. Men's health magazines encode new sets of social contra-dictions whereby men continue to seek their identity through work, but combine this with more equal relationships with their partners, more affective relations with children and a more 'concerned' relationship with their health generally. In this respect, the magazines prepare men for the atomized world of late capitalism, providing them with crucial ammunition in helping them gain a competitive advantage over other men and looking good to get/keep the girl. The hyper-competitive social relations of late capitalism manifest them-selves in male relations at work, in friendships and in relations with women. Often this serves to mask other ambivalent feelings con-nected with men's own emotional needs. The need for intimate human relations that men have found so difficult to recognize within themselves are displaced through myths of self-sufficiency and independence.

Men's health magazines, anxiety and the body

The social and cultural picture that develops from the previous analysis is one where certain features of masculine behaviour are open to critical scrutiny while others continue to be shielded from such criticism. For example, it is noticeable that the health magazines, rather than seeking to question men's disposition towards work, turn other activities into new forms of compulsion and discipline, while simultaneously maintaining the fantasy of 'having it all'. By fantasy we do not mean something that is opposed to reality, but an imaginary space through which we see and project ourselves (Elliott, 1996). This particular social fantasy is the complex outcome of the ties between modernity, masculinity and the need to keep more ambivalent frames at bay. Modern men, according to the magazines, can work really long hours, develop new and satisfying relations with women and children, while preserving their bodies against ageing and decay more generally. What is important in this respect is the specific shape that this fantasy takes, given the restructuring of the workplace and the new sets of social relations with women it has also helped to bring onto the agenda. That is, the idea of 'having it all' takes a particular form and has a specific resonance for professional men at this point within the history of modernity. However, within our focus groups there was also evidence of a considerable amount of scepticism of the idealized images of masculinity promoted by titles such as *Men's Health*: '[T]hese people are gods, these people have never been rejected, don't have to work for a living, they don't have normal human relations' (Bristol students). Here, we want to draw attention to the gendered and instrumental nature of men's health magazines. While it is true that women's health magazines such as *Zest* (Britain's no. 1), also display some of these features, they are encoded differently, given that their target is women. As we shall see, *Men's Health*'s obsession with work, machine-like metaphors and building muscle all point to the gendered nature of men's health magazines.

In terms of locating this specific set of social anxieties and fantasies, we shall see that they are positioned within a variety of discourses and social practices that interconnect the body and society. In this respect, we shall explore: (i) the idea of an uncertain future in respect of employment and the body; (ii) the notion of the body as a machine to be disciplined; (iii) the value placed upon speed and performance; and (iv) the displacement of questions related to mortality and death. Throughout the analysis we shall seek to link the domains of work and consumption paying particular attention to issues related to time and the body.

An uncertain future

Here, we argue that much of the health advice that is offered in the magazines is meant to preserve the body against decline. Just as men face an increasingly uncertain future in the workplace, so their bodies become places of intense anxiety and scrutiny in terms of their inevitable decline. In order for this decline to be halted or at least temporarily arrested, the body becomes something that needs to be invested in and worked upon. In short, we are seeking to explore the way that anxieties about work or employment are both represented through and displaced onto the body. The body in this argument becomes a new site of social discipline. By discipline, we mean that the masculine body needs to be trained, regulated and more generally consciously moulded into shape (Foucault, 1977). Nearly all of the health magazines outline programmes that offer 'the unexpectedly simple way to burn fat' (*Men's Health*, January–February 1998) or the chance to 'build muscle . . . a better body in four weeks' (*Men's Health*, November 1998). These are fitness programmes, the primary aim of which is to tone muscle on the body. This is usually achieved through a series of exercises that are organized into a number of carefully timed schedules and routines. For instance, 'the skinny man's build-up plan' offers a series of muscle enhancing exercises and a dietary regime that will improve the body in 28 days. This article is backed up with a 'real-life success story' which tells the tale of how 'one man gained 36lbs of muscle' (*Men's Health*, November 1998).

The tie between work and masculinity has historically proved to be a strong one. The advent of capitalism saw the progressive separation of the worlds of men and women in respect of public and private domains. Men's sense of self and identity was largely secured through their ability to perform paid employment outside of the home. The development of 'informational' capitalism has, however, broadly changed the associated patterns of work and culture. While, globally, the emancipation of capital from labour has had uneven effects, it has helped produce a world whereby the vast majority of new jobs that are created are part time, based upon temporary contracts and team work (Castells, 1996). This new economic set of determinants can be linked into less stable patterns of employment, the entry of women into the labour market and more niche-marketed forms of culture. There is also evidence that amongst the increasingly hard-pressed, career-obsessed professional classes time has become an ever more scarce resource. An overworked society, at least in certain sectors, means that it is difficult for people to balance a diverse number of social roles and duties (Castells 1996: 367).[3] Further, Richard Sennett (1998) has argued that the partial abandonment of relatively stable and routinized forms of work in favour of more risk-laden and flexible work practices has certain destructive implications in terms of our shared abilities to maintain a relatively stable sense of self. In the new world of flexible employment, the rules are made up as we go along, the ability to adapt and change is the most prized of possessions and the act of departure valued above that of reaching the destination. In other words, it is our ability to embark upon risky ventures, respond to new opportunities and the requirements of an increasingly deregulated labour market that is at the heart of contemporary capitalism. The fragmentation of common communities of fate has delivered an individualized world where to stay put is to be left out. The weakening of social bonds and the lack of certainty in terms of employment more generally means that feelings of connection, attachment and belonging are only ever achieved with greatest difficulty in the modern world. The fear of disposability, firms downsizing and the idea that our skills may well become redundant in the future mean that the workplace can only offer the most insecure of identities. This argument, as should by now be clear, has particular implications for men, given that work has historically been the place where a sense of masculine worth has been sought.

What, then, do new regimes of repetitive discipline offer men in terms of the body? First, rather than seeking to develop a more ethical relationship with work and the body, the culture of the health magazines is involved in the extension of regulatory disciplines to the body. The body, then, becomes a domain to be 'worked upon' and regulated. The body requires finely itemized forms of labour in order that it might produce certain measurable effects. This process of physical transformation grants the masculine subject a sense of security and continuity denied him within the workplace. It is not that the workplace is given up as a place of masculine striving, rather that its very uncertainty converts the body into a new project of identity. While the future of the body, like that of work, is clouded in uncertainty, the magazines suggest that the body can be 'worked upon' to produce measurable results. Whereas good performance in the workplace does not necessarily guarantee job stability, the body at least seems to offer rewards in respect of the amount of effort that is undertaken on its behalf. This is prefigured in articles that promise the possibility of a great body 'at nearly 40 years old' or, more directly, the ability to 'stay young' (*Men's Health*, January–February 1998).

Arguably, the new disciplines and regimes of performance that come through regularized forms of exercise and diet are the 'return of the repressed' in terms of the attempt to provide a relatively stable narrative of self. Another way of saying this would be to argue that as the world of work (and indeed the same could be said for heterosexual relations in general) becomes increasingly risky, a new sense of security is sought within the body. That is, through the 'measurable effects' of exercise, the body not only becomes instrumentalized but also the place where hard work seems to reap benefits. By this, we do not mean that all men who read the magazine will experience their bodies in the way being described here. Rather, our argument is that one of the dominant fantasies in respect of the male body is that it visibly responds to regimes of self-mastery and control. The focusing of men's agency upon the body indicates an increasingly narcissistic culture, and a world where the body becomes a new locus of control.

This can only be partially explained through changes in the labour market and the extension of disciplinary mechanisms more generally. As Giddens (1991) points out, we could equally argue that the magazines provide guidebooks in reflexive forms of self actualization. However, the obsessive bodily cultures of men's health magazines might be better represented as a 'pathology of reflexive self-control, operating around an axis of self-identity and bodily appearance' (Giddens 1991: 105). In this respect, *Men's Health* articulates an ideal subject who is constantly monitoring the body and seeking opportunities, often in unusual locations, to exercise. For example, an article headed 'Room For Improvement' (*Men's Health*, July–August 1997) lists exercises that can be done in hotel rooms.[4] Another, called 'the best exercise', argues that 'modern life is packed with things that don't deliver what they promise: heavyweight title fights, and women in Wonder Bras' (*Men's Health*, December 1997). What is offered is something more reliable and solid (knowledge you can trust) in the form of 'exercises that really work'. In the face of cultural uncertainty, the social fantasy is of knowledges that have calculable returns. It is an attempt to gain a sense of masculine autonomy over a private world in a public culture which is increasingly fraught with risk and uncertainty. Men are encouraged to 'work the body' (in private) in order to be able to succeed in the (public) world of relationships and work.

Our other point is that the link between the body and work is also maintained if we consider the volume of articles that involve a discussion of stress and time. The magazines juxtapose the fantasy of 'having it all' with some of the difficulties involved in trying to hang onto this particular conception of self. The men's magazines are full of advice and handy hints as to how you can 'beat the stresses of the day' (*Men's Health*, March 1997) or 'ditch stress in less than five minutes' (*Men's Health*, November 1998). The connection here is that stress has to be cured quickly because men's lives are increasingly overcrowded. This assumption is made explicit in the men's health magazine, *ZM*. In the first issue the editor writes:

> It's not that life's bad. Far from it. I drink beer, I see bands, I fall over. I even get the occasional lie in. I had one in March. I just suspect there could be a load more things I could find time to do, if only I could organise everything more efficiently. Particularly all those bits that are supposed to make life healthier and easier – like eating more fruit, taking zinc, and sorting out my finances. Great ideas, but when, and why, and what difference will it make to all the other minutes of the day? Which is where *ZM* comes in. (Winter 1998)

This particular aspect of modern professional men's lives is also evident in much of the advertising carried within the men's health magazines. A fairly typical example is an advert for a vitamin supplement called 'Wellman', which pictures a well-dressed man with six arms holding a pager, exercise weight, mobile phone, degree certificate, pint of lager and tennis racket. Underneath the reader is confronted with the question 'Wellmanaged?' which is used to refer to the busy and stressful lives many men are currently leading. Much of the advertising in this respect is seamless with the magazines' editorial content. This creates an interesting paradox, in that, in a life of constant activity where we have to keep constantly moving, it makes our lives both more fulfilling as well as more stressful. Rather than proposing that men need reflexively to decouple their sense of self from that of the workplace, what is offered is a host of articles and advertisements showing how men can deal with stress quickly and avoid wasting time. Advice of this kind can range from '50 ways to make your life easier' (*ZM*, Winter 1998) to 'how to squeeze every last drop of fun and ounce of value from 60 minutes' (*Men's Health*, November 1998). In the world of leisure, just as in the world of work, time has become 'a scarce commodity' (*Men's Health*, November 1998). Again, the point here is to promote a certain version of masculinity that can 'deal with' or 'cope with' the pressures of modern life, rather than asking political/ethical questions as to how some of these connections need to be rethought at the level of the individual and the community.

The body as machine

Within modern culture, men's relationship with their bodies is often represented as being purely instrumental. Feminist psychoanalytic thinkers such as Chodorow (1978) and Benjamin (1990) have argued at some length how this can be connected to the maintenance of gender polarities and an unconscious fear of the feminine amongst men more generally. In a similar vein, Seidler argues:

> Within modernity we have learnt to treat the body as a machine that functions according to its own laws and principles. We learn to treat it something like a car. If it breaks down it needs to be taken to the garage. Similarly it is doctors who have professional knowledge about male bodies. This sustains an external relationship with our bodies that allows us to continue using our bodies as instruments for proving ourselves as men. (Seidler 1997: 186)

The two elements outlined by Seidler (the body as a machine and the body as governed by experts) are particularly evident within the magazines. The application of instrumental logics and easily learnt tips and advice is meant to keep the body 'running along smoothly'. The most often used metaphor in relation to the body and sources of food and energy is that of 'refuelling', which is used in conjunction with definite 'expert' knowledge as to how to recharge the body. A fairly common way of representing this is:

> The phone has rung incessantly for three-and-a-half hours and your computer has crashed a record eight times in a morning. With things only likely to get worse, you're forced to treat lunch time like a pit-stop in the Grand Prix that is your working day. . . . A sandwich made with large chunks of brown bread is great fuel as it provides plenty of carbohydrate which will break down the glucose to feed the brain and muscles throughout the day. (*Men's Health*, November 1998)

The social world we are being asked to envisage is one of the overworked male professional who needs to regenerate his body in the shortest possible time. Such a disposition reinforces hegemonic constructions of masculinity, while linking them to some of the more instrumental features evident within modernity. Such cultures seek to convert the body into something that can be controlled by scientific forms of rationality protecting the self from having to develop a more vulnerable relation with the body's own needs. It could also be argued (as we have seen) that one of the reasons for the popularity of men's health magazines is because men find it so difficult to talk to one another about bodily matters. In such a culture, writes Tracey (1997: 197), masculinity 'strives to overcome the feminine in inner and outer worlds'. In this respect, the body can be seen as crucial, as it occupies the frontier between the social and the unconscious. The tough masculine body must keep at bay unconscious needs for feelings of emotion, care and Eros. That is, such representations and feelings are interpreted as failing to embody thrusting forms of heterosexual masculinity. To instrumentalize the body is to deaden the self in terms of the more reciprocal relations that heterosexual men might form with their unconscious, with women and with men of different sexualities. The attempt to govern the body through such a culture serves the interests of certain forms of masculinity that seek to hold in check the development of less certain and more reciprocal relations within the self and between the self and others.

Speed and performance

All of the health magazines view speed and performance as positive social goods. As we have seen, men's work and personal lives are currently under strain as a result of the broadening of the masculine role more generally and the perceived need to work long hours under conditions of economic insecurity. Under such social conditions, the magazines emphasize the importance of performing tasks, activities and social practices both efficiently and quickly. Perhaps not surprisingly, many of the articles are concerned with the pleasures of speeded up sex or the quick workout. In terms of sexuality, articles instruct men to 'target sex lines on the areas of the skin where the nerves are closest to the surface' or suggest that touching is a 'warm-up' with the end result being her 'dragging you into the bedroom quicker than you can say stubborn stain remover' (*Men's Health*, January–February 1998). A feature called 'The Art of the Quickie' confirms that 'there's a time and a place for a frenzied quickie' (*Men's Health*, March 1997). The danger here is that sex becomes connected to a form of means–ends logic, thereby draining the activity of meaning, intimacy and a sense of connection. Further, other leisure pursuits become valued if they can be mastered quickly: 'Learn to sail – in just 2 days'; and a joint ad between Austin Reed (clothes) and Mitsubishi (cars) offers 'Life in the fast lane' (*Men's Health*, June 1997).

Viewed hermeneutically, we can argue that capitalism as a social system places a heavy emphasis upon speed and performance.

Whether this is through the capacity of corporations to make money quickly or through maxims like 'time is money', the economic system has a definite temporal dimension (Adam, 1995). However, the extent to which we see our emotional ties, intimate relations and sexuality through this prism has potentially negative consequences. Lorenzo Simpson (1995) argues that it is specific to technological forms of rationality to value ends over means. This converts a concern with experience into questions over resources. In this respect, technological rationality is a 'result-anticipating activity' (Simpson 1995: 48). The meaningfulness of the social expression of sexuality under the schema of speed is converted into a desire to achieve penetrative sex as quickly as possible. What this brackets off or displaces is a host of concerns that cannot be understood within thinking driven by functionality or efficiency. A concern with the end result of erotic engagements not only reaffirms more traditional, less vulnerable features of masculinity, but reduces sexual practice to pleasure in search of an ultimate end. This again neatly ties certain aspects of masculinity and modernity together, while keeping at bay more ambiguous feelings and representations. An obsession with the speed of sexual performance can be simultaneously linked to professional men's overcrowded leisure time, the desire to reaffirm less uncertain models of sexuality, and the spread of instrumental reason through popular culture – hence the concern about not using time efficiently and productively. This is well illustrated by an article called 'More sex, sir?' in which Greg Gutfeld writes: 'You're wasting time sitting around. It's Friday night: you meet some friends after work, go to a pub, sit down, munch on a bar snack, listen to another band mangle *Addicted to Love*, then you go home. You meet no one but the overworked barmaids. Then you repeat the whole thing next week' (*Men's Health*, June 1997).

The displacement of death

The representation of time as a scarce resource can also be related to the displacement of a number of ethical questions concerning human mortality. In this respect, the magazines promote a modernist culture of health and fitness in order to avoid questions of bodily decline and, finally, death. The health magazines we have focused on are all targeted at men from their late twenties and early thirties onwards. There are other magazines concerned with health and fitness which are intended for a younger audience (such as *XL* and *GQ Active*) which do not have the same obsession with maintaining the body against ageing and decline. According to the magazines, concern about bodily decline only seems to become a preoccupation once young men enter a certain phase in the life-cycle. A fairly typical example in this respect is a *Men's Health* article called 'Stay Young' (January–February 1998). Through the application of science, technology and advice from experts (suggestions which include staying out of the sun and the use of face cream), the impression is given that, while ageing cannot be finally defeated, it can be slowed down. Even more overtly, the possibility of making the body immortal is suggested through 'How to make your back last forever' (*Men's Health*, September 1997), although the connections between the magazines and mortality is usually more subtle than this might suggest. Our concern here is to argue that the culture of bodily fitness and exercise is bound up with a fear of death and mortality.

Elias (1985) and Giddens (1991) have both commented upon how death within modernity has been sequestrated from everyday life through its confinement in institutions and through processes of individualization more generally. What Elias (1985) calls the 'loneliness of the dying' is the loss of the living community before the moment of death. The tragedy here is that in the face of death we often go silent, because we lack a common language in which to frame the experience, and that the person facing death does so in isolation from significant others and the wider community. Death is something to be hidden away and privatized within modernity. This being the case we have to search for the trace of death where we would not expect to find it. Death, to follow Baudrillard (1991: 185), 'is no longer where we think that it is'. Fear of death becomes not the fear of being bodily killed, but the fear, as Castoriadis argues, 'that everything, even meaning, will dissolve' (Castoriadis 1997: 136). This might enable us to understand the obsessive and repetitious nature of much of the magazines' content in respect of the culture of bodily fitness. As we have already pointed out, the magazines display an excessive concern with the body's physique, to the extent that men are encouraged to exercise in a variety of social spaces. This, as we have seen, is often linked to a concern with time (time as a resource is always short), which is perceived to be literally running out. The excessive nature of this concern over bodily decline signifies (no matter how repressed) a recognition that the attempt to keep the body youthful and vital will ultimately end in defeat. Hence it is the repetitiousness of images of the active body which signal its relation to its own other.

Death represents not only the end of time, but also the end of the body. What modernity offers is not so much a language and understanding of death but an instrumental language of survival. Bauman (1992) argues that since we have lost the collective sense that death opens out another stage of being, it has become reduced to exit. The only language that is widely available to all is an instrumental language of survival which aims to keep death at bay for as long as possible. For Bauman, death acts as 'a specific and avoidable cause: an event which enters the vision, the realm of the meaningful, only through the task of promoting or preventing it, of making it happen or not allowing it to happen' (1992: 137). What Bauman terms the language of survival is precisely what is offered by the culture of the magazines. It is one of monitoring your diet, taking vitamins, avoiding stress, building muscle and keeping fit more generally. Altering Elias's terms somewhat, Bauman argues that it is not so much that we die in loneliness as in silence. Death becomes something to be ashamed of in a world where instrumental reason stresses the effective and efficient body. Death is that which cannot be mastered and controlled, despite all our efforts to mould and shape the body. These concerns can be forgotten about, or at least this is the expectation, through daily regimes that invite us to keep an ever-watchful eye on our health. The anxiety and concern that initially become attached to an ageing body are managed by spending more and more time and money keeping death and decline in check.

These features outline a concern with preserving the body, or 'keeping it', as opposed to *Loaded*'s focus on 'losing it'. Whereas *Men's Health* articulates a concerned subject, constantly monitoring his body to 'keep' or 'improve' what he has got, *Loaded* celebrates a culture of disregarding the body by focusing on different kinds of 'excessive' behaviour. Another way of explaining this divide is to argue that men's magazines symbolize different cultures and discourses of risk. That is, *Men's Health* encourages an instrumental and calculative attitude towards the body which is used to hold in check and reverse bodily decline. It is a risk culture whereby hazards are defined in terms of tips, advice and fitness programmes drawn up by experts. This sets up, as we argued earlier, a hierarchical relation between the magazine and the reader where 'definite knowledges' are passed on. As Beck (1992) argues in respect of the environment and science, attempts to define risk instrumentally almost certainly leave many questions unanswered. For example, what are the consequences of over-exercise, and do magazines such as *Men's Health* strengthen rather than ease anxiety in relation to the body? The appeal to definite knowledge may indeed be a way of 'keeping it', but what are the unintended consequences of attempts to instrumentalize the body? By contrast, *Loaded* offers a different kind of risk culture, one that says men should risk drinking to excess, drug-taking, being unfaithful/avoiding commitment. In this respect, then, new laddism is a high-risk culture of carefree consumption and sexual hedonism regardless of the personal consequences. That there may also be unpleasant side-effects to such a culture of risk was hinted at by James Brown when he said on his move from *Loaded* to *GQ*: 'I'm not a 25 year old loafer any more, I'm confronting new things in my life now' (*Independent on Sunday*, 19 April 1997). While social and physical risks connected to the body are instrumentalized by *Men's Health* they are mostly displaced by *Loaded*.

Irony and the cultural politics of masculinity

To conclude this chapter, we wish to draw some political conclusions concerning the cultures of commodified laddism and men's health magazines. We do this by asking what kinds of cultural politics are opened up by the magazines. In particular, we are concerned to link issues related to irony and cynicism (most evident in the lads' mags) and an instrumental relation to the body (mostly relevant to the health magazines) through an attempt to politicize mediated masculinities in late-modernity.

As we have seen, one of the defining features of the 'new' men's lifestyle magazines is the pervasive use of irony. Irony allows you to have your cake and eat it. It allows you to express an unpalatable truth in a disguised form, while claiming it is not what you actually meant. To render an ironic claim harmful – that is to claim that language can hurt – is, in this reading, to miss the point. However, as Freud points out, irony, perhaps like dreams, might give us clues to some of the unconscious motivations of the speaker/writer. In this respect, irony operates as a form of self-distancing or illusion whereby the speaker/writer wishes to conceal from themselves as well as from the listener/reader what is being articulated. For Freud, irony is a particularly interesting site for the investigation of unconscious motivations (Stringfellow, 1994). While we have followed this particular line of argument, what is missing here is an understanding of what might be called the 'excessive' nature of irony. By this we mean that in some of the magazines (*Loaded* and *FHM* being the prime examples) irony is not used as it might in everyday conversation as an occasional twist or departure from an ongoing discussion that works through a number of linguistic tropes. Irony, in these magazines, is mostly not subtle but excessive. According to Timothy Bewes (1997: 37), irony in the 1990s has become the 'capital-lettered watchword of the Zeitgeist journalism'.

Yet, in another sense, we might wonder whether the magazines can be described as ironic at all. Richard Rorty (1989) claims that ironists have to fulfil three different categories including: (i) a form of radical self-doubt concerning the vocabularies they are currently using (because they could equally use others); (ii) realizing these doubts are unlikely to be replaced by certainty; and (iii) not thinking that their current vocabularies are any closer to 'reality' than others. If we accept Rorty's description of (radical) irony then the current crop of men's lifestyle magazines come closer to the ironist's opposite – that is, common sense. It is precisely the lack of awareness of the constructed nature of masculine identity that seems so pervasive. Yet to argue that the magazines reflect the return of a form of masculine common sense is to treat the texts as less problematic than we believe them to be. Our argument is, rather, that irony is used as an ideological defence against external attack (only the most humourless do not get the joke) and an internal defence against more ambivalent feelings that render masculine experience less omnipotent and less certain than it is represented here.

In terms of the magazines, irony can be said to have a dual function. The first is that it allows readers to receive advice in respect of sexuality, indulge in the fantasies of successful manhood and consume representations of beautiful women in a relatively comfortable and guilt-free way. That is, the unstable nature of the content carves out a space for the magazines to be experienced as pleasurable. This provides a horizontal zone of communication which enables many of the readers to explore mediated forms of masculinity in a period of social change (as discussed in the next chapter regarding readers' discourses and dispositions). However, we can equally read the excessive irony of the magazines as a form of cynicism that seeks to dismiss more political forms of critique that may become aimed at the magazines.

Cynicism has been described by Peter Sloterdijk (1988) as 'enlightened false consciousness'. By this, Sloterdijk means that cynicism is a form of unhappy consciousness which has already been enlightened in terms of its unacceptability. Cynical reason does not ask for or expect to meet the criteria of universal justification. Hence traditional forms of ideology critique would not work with the magazines as there is no truth behind the illusion to be discovered. This is because both the readers and producers of the magazines are joined together in a cynical game whereby no one any longer takes the actual content of the magazines seriously, while simultaneously recognizing that they promote a masculinist culture.

Zizek (1989) has taken this argument a stage further by suggesting that, because cynical reason dispenses with the idea of unmasking (both the readers and producers of the magazine fully realize that the irony is a defence of male dominance), we need to point to the extent to which the magazines are cultural constructs built upon unconscious fantasies. Irony then becomes a conservative political force in that it is a refusal to engage with a variety of political and ethical engagements (cf. Bewes, 1997). For Zizek, there is little purpose in pointing to the fact that such magazines deliver a 'patriarchal dividend' because they already accept this. Yet such an analysis bends the stick too far. While it is the case that the magazines have a cynical component, this could arguably work as a way of fostering ideological strategies that are not in themselves ironic. The content of the magazines could be said to provide ideological reinforcement for ideas concerning men and women being constructed as binary categories, and the promotion of narcissistic illusions within men. Indeed, what is more pertinent to our aim is the connection between the magazines' cynicism and the appeals to authenticity evident within the construction of the new lad. The ideological join in these overlapping discourses is the idea that, despite experiments in sexual identity brought through by feminism and social movements orientated around sexuality, for heterosexual men, the lad is what we are left with. Cynicism and authenticity are connected through the mutual recognition that men are not for changing. The contradictoriness of the magazines does not come from their irony, but their ability to commodify an unstable dialectic that opens out certain questions while closing others down. Part of the pleasurable nature of the magazines comes in exploring this very divide.

This was also a consistent feature of the focus groups (explored in more detail in the next chapter): 'You know, whether I want to start screwing around or whatever . . . it's okay to be this, this is actually who I am' (Islington professionals); and 'it's sort of allowing you to say and think and talk about things you may have thought' (Manchester lecturers). Hence, what is being argued here is not that the magazines have structural effects, nor that they are blank screens upon which readers simply project their fantasies. Rather, we have argued that they are part of a wider social context that provides a means for handling social contradictions and unconscious motivations. In this way, therefore, the magazines are neither part of an ideological prison house nor are they simply consumptive fun.

One of the most interesting things about men's health magazines is that, for the most part, they are rarely ironic when it comes to the possibility of bodily transformation. Irony in the magazines is usually reserved for some of the articles about relationships or male competitors in the workplace. Men's health magazines are better read as an attempt to commodify new levels of concern and anxiety about the body amongst professional men while maintaining certain hegemonic notions of masculinity and technical reason. As Anthony Giddens (1994) argues, in a detraditionalizing society the main threat to 'well-being' comes from what he calls 'productivism'. Productivism is derived from a society within which work becomes a form of compulsion, and where economic development is valued above human well-being. In seeking to promote a reflexive citizenship that questions these trends, we need to decouple rampant industrialism and commodity capitalism from how we define human needs and happiness. In terms of health, we cannot expect our common needs to be met by either economic growth or new 'social' rights being fostered by public health systems. This is because the new globalized economy both produces massive structural inequalities and diminishes the state's capacity to deliver health services. In terms of citizenship what needs to be recognized are the common obligations we all share in respect of taking responsibility for our individual well-being and the development of a reflexive culture in respect of the body. Giddens suggests we view health 'generatively' by promoting greater levels of awareness of the complex dimensions of risk evident within contemporary civil society. Positive welfare in this respect would involve the widespread critique of certain widely held stereotypes of macho behaviour and certain destructive lifestyle pursuits which can be linked to ill health. Indeed, given that Giddens (1994: 248) argues that he is centrally concerned with the 'generative encouragement of lifestyle change', we might expect such new dimensions to be opened by the recent wave of men's lifestyle magazines. However, and in this sense the magazines remain paradoxical, their ability to make public a number of dominant fantasies in respect of masculinity continues to contribute to their ambiguity. This aspect is explored further in chapter 5.

Conclusion

In this chapter we have analysed the content of men's lifestyle magazines through a particular focus on their coverage of sexual politics and men's health issues. Drawing on a range of sociological and psychoanalytic theories, we have argued that the culture of masculine instrumentalism advanced by the magazines promotes the increased visibility of men's health issues while offering readers a form of 'constructed certitude' in respect of the body (Beck, 1997). Our analysis suggests that in their coverage of men's intimate relationships and health issues, the magazines offer definite forms of knowledge that prevent more ambivalent and troubling questions and anxieties from emerging. Men's relationships with their bodies take on new forms of compulsion as they enter into an increasingly risky world in respect of formal employment, gender relations and their own bodies. Thus the appeal of the magazines might be viewed in terms of their ability to deal with some of the contradictions that are making themselves felt within men's lives while keeping more troubling and anxiety-provoking features at bay.

A more critical sexual and cultural politics would therefore need to practise what Laclau (1977) has called the 'politics of interruption'. This ultimately holds out the possibility of agencies within civil society deconstructing and circumventing the seemingly coherent identities pressed by ideological forms of closure. The revelation that masculine identities are constructed (rather than natural or authentic) could then be linked to wider efforts to provide alternative political spaces for the critical discussion of what it means to be a young, heterosexual man today.

A re-engaged feminist sexual politics and new forms of cultural citizenship would need to accept that the construction of masculinity and femininity is at any given point likely to be constituted by a number of overlapping and competing discourses. In the next chapter, we explore how readers themselves attempt to 'make sense' of these competing discourses, whether they derive from the magazines themselves, from associated media commentaries or from wider social changes that are impacting on contemporary masculinities.

What a cultural politics may have to learn from the new men's lifestyle magazines is that contemporary mediated masculinities are pleasurable, ironic and less fixed in their cultural construction than might initially appear to be the case. Furthermore, attempts to equalize gender relations are likely to be interrupted and defeated by failures of the social imagination and more unconscious processes. As Chantal Mouffe (1993) argues, we need to develop a sense of a common good in respect of gender relations while recognizing the impossibility of it being realized. Such a view should be both anti-essentialist (men are not, after all, a stable category) and utopian (holding out the possibility of effecting new cultural and psychic dimensions which may provide imaginative suggestions to current masculine ambiguities). Read politically, therefore, the most evident 'truth' about the magazines (accepting their ambivalences) is that they simultaneously contribute to and detract from this agenda.

5

Readings

Drawing on focus group discussions with a wide range of men (and a smaller number of women), this chapter seeks to understand what the recent dramatic growth of the men's magazine market signifies in terms of men's changing identities and gender relations. In particular, we explore how our focus group participants attempt to 'make sense' of recent changes in masculinity and consumer culture through their reactions to the magazines, including their coverage of previously neglected topics such as fashion, health and relationships.

The chapter examines a variety of different readings of men's lifestyle magazines, exploring the way that different individuals and groups of men attempt to make sense of what they read and of related changes in contemporary masculinities, particularly as they are reflected in recent developments in commercial culture (cf. Jackson et al., 1999). To clarify our methodological approach (discussed at greater length in the Appendix), the focus group participants were not selected according to their readership status, contrasting *Loaded* or *FHM* readers, for example, with readers of *Arena* or *Esquire*. We did not set out, in the market research tradition, to characterize the readership profile of particular magazines. Nor have we sought to compare committed readers of specific magazines with those who had little or no investment in the magazines. Instead, focus group participants were chosen for their social diversity in terms of age, class, ethnicity and other personal attributes. By this means we have identified a wide range of readings of the magazines and of the masculinities that are represented in the magazines. Although our respondents included some with relatively little direct knowledge of the content of particular magazines, all were sufficiently aware of the magazines as a genre to have an opinion about their place in popular culture and what they might signal in terms of changes in contemporary masculinities. A full list of the focus groups follows:

Bristol: media studies students
Bristol: middle-class lecturers
Bristol: musicians and artists
Derby: middle-class professional men
Derby: 30-something middle-class public sector women
Islington: public sector professionals, Asian/Jewish Londoners
London: art college students
London: 30-something middle-class counsellors
London: journalists (professionals and students)
London: unemployed men (with care worker)
Manchester: middle-class lecturers
Pimlico: 25–35-year-old graduates
Sheffield: 18-year-olds, unskilled working class/unemployed
Sheffield: 40-something gay men
Sheffield: men's clothes shop assistants
Sheffield: postgraduate students
Sheffield: working-class disabled men
Stoke Newington: media professionals
Taunton: 30-something working-class bikers (motorcyclists)
Turnpike Lane: 25–40-year-old graduates

Discourses and dispositions

Our interpretation of these diverse readings rests upon an analytical distinction which we draw between discourses and dispositions. The analysis begins by identifying the range of *discursive repertoires* ('discourses', for short) that different individuals and groups of men draw on in order to 'make sense' of the magazines. As we did in chapter 4, we then use Ulrich Beck's (1997) notion of *constructed certitude* to help explain the magazines' varying appeal to different groups of readers. Next, we attempt to identify the different *discursive dispositions* ('dispositions', for short) that are adopted towards the previously identified discourses, including attempts to read the magazines 'against the grain' of the culturally more dominant discourses. The identification of these dispositions allows us to describe the degree to which each of the discourses is adopted, rejected, ironized and so on by different individuals and groups of men. We conclude the chapter by indicating how the various discourses and dispositions are distributed among our focus groups, drawing on the work of Pierre Bourdieu (1984) to highlight the variable *cultural capital* available to different individuals and groups of readers. We also highlight the ambivalent discursive space that the magazines have come to occupy in both material and symbolic terms.

The chapter focuses on the 'consumption' phase of the circuit of magazine culture, but not in isolation from other aspects of magazine production and content. It differs from most of the previous research on masculinity and the media, which focuses on visual and verbal representations of masculinity in magazine content.[1] In contrast to most previous studies, our research attempts to access the more mundane level of magazine consumption as represented in 'men's talk' about the magazines' content, style and wider cultural significance. Though our analysis focuses on men's talk, the inclusion of some mixed gender focus groups and one all-women group provided additional insights into contemporary constructions of masculinity and gender relations. Indeed, the group that was most openly hostile to the magazines and most critical of the resurgence of laddish forms of masculinity was the only all-female group (Derby women). When voicing their disapproval, the group's apologetic tone suggests that they constructed our research (and us as researchers) as generally supportive of the magazines. While this chapter focuses on men's talk as providing access to everyday discursive constructions of masculinity, our analysis certainly does not exclude women's voices. The analysis is based on what respondents said about the magazines (and how they said it) rather than how the magazines are actually read, which would have required a different (more ethnographic) methodology.[2] In this respect, our approach is similar to Hermes's (1995) identification of the various 'interpretive repertoires' through which women's magazines are made meaningful, though (for reasons we outline in the Appendix) we do not follow her approach in its entirety.[3]

In making a distinction between discourses and dispositions, we acknowledge Bourdieu's insight that the discourses and practices of culture (attending a football match, looking at a painting, reading a book) are clearly distinguished from our dispositions towards culture or what Bourdieu calls the *habitus*. According to Bourdieu, the *habitus* is a class-specific set of dispositions whose content is determined by the dominant class relationships in a social field. It is a learnt bodily disposition which promotes feelings of in-group solidarity and serves primarily to mark out distinctions and boundaries between different social groups. Following Bourdieu (1990), we argue that an analysis of dispositions allows us to account for a link between culture and agency, which avoids more overtly structuralist concerns that have shown little regard for the creativity evident within everyday life (Giddens, 1984). Where our analysis differs from Bourdieu is that, by concentrating on group differences, he obscures the reflexive capacity of individuals within groups to be able to adopt a range of dispositions during an ongoing conversation. Whereas Bourdieu is primarily concerned with dispositions that are relatively durable within the domain of social class, we are concerned to map personally held dispositions onto more public categories in a way that respects both macro- and micro-levels of analysis.

Discourses (or what we have termed 'discursive repertoires') are the *public forms of talk* that enable individuals and social groups to make the magazines meaningful. Dispositions, on the other hand, are more personal and open the possibility of less ordered and more ambiguous meanings. To talk of dispositions in terms of our project enables us to break with popular media perceptions of a homogeneous and unrelenting laddishness without adopting the language of outright refusal suggested by notions of resistance that were evident in earlier strains of cultural studies (e.g. Hall and Jefferson, 1976). The emphasis we place in what follows on ambivalence and ambiguity raises the question of how far the dominant meanings and discourses of masculinity go in imprinting themselves upon the subjectivity of the 'audience'. It also points beyond a desire to map the conversations held about the magazines onto more stable categories suggested by terms such as 'reader response' (cf. Tompkins, 1980).[4] Our understanding of this process is more dialogical, in that the dispositions which readers adopt towards the discursive repertoires are a product of the relation between members of a particular group and the wider social context, and between individual participants and publicly sanctioned discourses concerning the magazines, including our influence as researchers. Our analysis suggests that a notion of ambivalence, rather than ideological indoctrination or refusal, most clearly helps us to understand the ways that different dispositions are mobilized by different groups and individuals (cf. Stevenson et al., 2000b).[5]

Discursive repertoires

We start with an analysis of the discursive repertoires identified through our reading of the focus group transcripts. We have already discussed in some detail how the transcripts were analysed (see the

Appendix and Jackson, in press). To recapitulate briefly, the process involved all three researchers listening to the tapes and reading the transcripts repeatedly, independently noting key phrases, ways of talking, patterns of response, reading practices, uses and pleasures of the text. We met regularly to discuss each transcript in turn. We then began to distil the major themes, waiting until all the transcripts had been individually coded in order to avoid reaching premature conclusions (cf. Stewart and Shamdasani, 1990; Strauss, 1983). At the end of this process, we identified a range of discursive repertoires through which our respondents attempted to 'make sense' of the magazines, as listed:

- surface and depth (including 'trash');
- honesty;
- naturalness;
- openness (including 'visibility');
- harmless fun;
- change (including 'backlash');
- seriousness;
- women as Other.

We start by taking each discourse in turn before beginning to theorize their connections in terms of the 'opening up' and 'closing down' of new discursive spaces. All of the discourses, we suggest, can be understood in terms of the ambiguities of contemporary masculinities, which are resolved (discursively at least) through notions of 'constructed certitude'. We then move on to discuss the dispositions that different groups and individuals took towards each of the discourses, understood in terms of their differential access to cultural capital. We recognize that the distinction between discourses and dispositions is a somewhat arbitrary one since it is not possible to voice a discourse without simultaneously adopting a disposition towards it. We employ the distinction here, however, to improve the clarity of our presentation. Since our aim was to identify the discursive repertoires that are drawn on by different groups of men, most of the quotations in the following discussion are attributed to the focus group from which they derive (e.g. Islington professionals, Manchester lecturers, etc.) rather than to individual members of each group.[6]

'Surface and depth'

Many of the focus group participants drew on a discourse of 'surface and depth' in their reflections on the magazines. Those who were most critical of the magazines argued that they were 'too shallow . . . lacking in depth' (Islington professionals). While they might be 'nicely packaged', with an attractive 'glossy format', they were criticized for their lack of substance. Some participants made a connection between the magazines' glossiness and the superficiality of the new forms of masculinity with which they are sometimes associated. For example, the idea of the new man was described as a 'glossy image' of men who 'pretend to be nice', a caricature that doesn't exist in reality (Pimlico graduates). Others described the magazines as only superficial, a trend 'like Lacoste shirts' (Sheffield clothes shop assistants). While men may have changed superficially, in that it is now 'acceptable to wear perfume' and 'flourish your way of dressing', men's core interests (in 'sport and fucking') were said to have remained the same. Even those who championed the magazines stressed their external appearance: 'They're lovely, they're glossies, they're like a box of chocolates' (London journalists).

A frequent metaphor for the perceived lack of depth or substance was the notion that the magazines were highly disposable: 'crap' or 'rubbish'. One of the 18-year-olds described the magazines as 'excellent toilet literature. They're trash though.' Another felt that 'there's nothing really new in them, is there, it's all been done before . . . this is just recycling the whole thing over and over again . . . it's all repackaged and regurgitated' (Sheffield gay men). Others described *Loaded* as 'full of rubbish . . . most of it's pap' (Sheffield disabled men). A member of the London counsellors' group described *Loaded* as 'quite trashy', while the Manchester lecturers described the magazines as 'full of all sorts of rubbish . . . just shit . . . vacuous . . . silly and superficial'. So, too, for the Sheffield postgraduates, the magazines were 'a waste of time . . . crap . . . a waste of money'; 'they're just so disposable . . . rubbish'. Whereas you might treasure a special interest magazine on photography or film; 'these, you'd stand your coffee on . . . do you know what I mean? . . . you read it, then you chuck it', 'they're not treasured things'.[7]

The magazines' disposability can be linked to Hermes's (1995) argument about the mundanity of magazine reading but may also represent a way for participants to distance themselves from those, like us, who were engaged in what many of the participants clearly regarded as a futile search for cultural meaning or political significance: 'It's just a laugh in the pub sort of thing . . . something you can't take too seriously . . . nothing too heavy . . . not in depth' (Derby men).

The disabled group criticized the glamourousness of the cover photos ('these gorgeous bodies on the front'), arguing that a magazine's contents were more important ('because beauty's only skin deep . . . it's what's inside that counts').[8] For others, the magazines' value lay in their very disposability: 'I know it's rubbish and I think that's what I value'; 'I think it's their disposability that I like about them' (Sheffield postgraduates).

Related to the idea of disposability, only a few participants were prepared to describe themselves as committed readers (though the Turnpike Lane and Islington groups included some subscribers). Most men described themselves as 'casual' readers and were keen to distance themselves from any sense of commitment to a particular title. This may reflect the notion that magazine reading is a fairly mundane activity; that magazines are 'easily put down' (Hermes, 1995). Indeed, several participants were keen that we did not over-interpret the magazines, exaggerating their cultural or political significance, as in the following exchange:

> *Andy*: Well, you could get all theoretical, couldn't you, and talk about postmodernism and all that kind of stuff and maybe that's it, maybe you know, now identities are a lot more complex . . .
> *George*: I think we're being far too theoretical about it. . . . I mean, buying *Loaded*'s not a political act in any shape or form. (Sheffield postgraduates)[9]

For some readers, the magazines offered a 'dream' or an 'image' that was acknowledged to be quite seductive but which shouldn't be taken 'at face value . . . it's all about image, isn't it?' (Bristol lecturers). The magazines were for 'flicking through' and 'dipping into', not to be taken seriously: 'It's a bit like *Eurotrash* [a Friday night TV programme aimed at the post-pub 'youth' market]. You know where you are, it just turns out to be a bit thin' (London unemployed men). Those (including academics like us, it was implied) who exaggerated the magazines' significance, simply missed the point that they were only intended to be read 'for a laugh' (part of the discourse of harmless fun discussed below).

Those who saw the magazines as an extension of previous media creations such as the 'new man' were quick to reject them as 'just a fashion accessory really'. They were equally dismissive of their readers, who 'haven't got a true bone in their body', 'they're all shallow' (Taunton bikers). Men who were more sympathetic to new forms of masculinity might still regard the magazines as 'a lot of crap', valuable only as 'a kind of escape' (Bristol lecturers). Even those who saw the potential for the magazines to evolve into a forum for men to discuss 'interior things about masculinity or [alternative] ways of being masculine', criticized their superficiality: 'It's just skin deep, you know . . . there's nothing substantial there' (Stoke Newington media professionals).

'Honesty'

Several groups distinguished *Loaded* from the rest of the magazines, claiming that, while the others pretended to be sophisticated, cultured and intelligent, *Loaded* was 'more blatant', with 'no pretensions' (Islington professionals). Magazines like *GQ* were described as 'arty' or 'aspirational' (for people with 'lashings of dosh'), presenting a superficial or glossy image of the 'new man'. By contrast, *Loaded* was more 'honest': 'a celebration of the unacceptable face of men' (Pimlico graduates). Even among those who preferred 'classier' magazines such as *Arena*, with 'more cultural integrity', a contrast could still be drawn between magazines such as *GQ* and *Esquire*, 'dressing themselves up in a glossy cover', and *Loaded*, which was 'a bit more basic' (London journalists). Similarly, those who found *Arena* too highbrow ('pseudo-arty'), like the Sunday broadsheets, would read *Loaded* 'just for a laugh', as they did the tabloids (Turnpike Lane graduates).

Some groups were sceptical about *Loaded*'s way of addressing its readers, seeing it as 'manipulative' (Stoke Newington media professionals) or as appealing to the 'lowest common denominator' (London counsellors). For the majority of respondents, however, *Loaded*'s blatant emphasis on women, sport and entertainment was a welcome contrast to the 'airs and graces' of the more style-conscious magazines: 'They make no qualms about it . . . they're not hypocritical' (Bristol students). Other groups also spoke about the 'honest and open view' of 'shameless' magazines like *Loaded* which don't feel any need to justify themselves (Manchester lecturers), celebrating 'a kind of freedom to . . . shout and be kind of loud and get pissed' (Stoke Newington media professionals).[10]

Loaded's founding editor James Brown was singled out for praise by many readers. Unlike the other magazines, whose editors had to strive for success in a calculated manner, James Brown was said to embody the magazine's values in a more natural way (recalling our discussion of 'authenticity' in chapter 3). Although he studiously cultivated this image (via biographical material on the UpLoaded website and in media interviews, for example), many readers appeared to take the image at face value: 'He seemed to live and breathe it . . . in an honest way' (Bristol musicians and artists). Whether Brown's popular reputation has survived his latest business exploits remains to be seen: in May 2000, he successfully floated his own publishing company ('I Feel Good Holdings plc') on the Alternative Investment Market at a valuation of £10 million. Describing his publishing philosophy as 'trying to unite the disciplines I learned at Condé Nast with the editorial freedom of *Loaded*', he realized a £5 million profit before the first issue of his latest magazine *Hot Dog* had reached the news-stands (*Guardian*, 22 May 2000).

'Naturalness'

Many of our focus group participants argued that the image of the lad was a more natural form of masculinity than the contrived image of the new man which it replaced as a dominant media construction during the 1990s. The magazines were welcomed as promoting an image of masculinity that was more natural in at least two senses: more authentic (true to men's real selves) and less contrived (unlike images of the new man). The idea that the new man was a media fiction was widely shared: 'The new man went too far . . . [he was] unrealistic [and] didn't exist except on television' (Sheffield 18-year-olds); he was 'a fiction created by Richard and Judy [day-time TV presenters]' (London journalists); 'all about image' (Bristol lecturers); 'a mythical creation . . . completely unrealistic and artificial . . . I think the media makes a lot of it up' (London counsellors).[11]

Unlike the rather diffuse image of the new man, none of our respondents had any difficulty in identifying the characteristics of the new lad, reeling off a familiar list of traits and consumer goods: 'beer, shoes, cars, stereos and women' (Sheffield 18-year-olds); 'big chunky watches, suits, haircuts' (Bristol lecturers); 'beer, football, women, clothes, music and films' and, later, 'football, booze, women, films, what was the other one?' (Sheffield postgraduates). The list of characteristics (which is clearly mirrored in media accounts of laddish masculinity, as discussed in chapter 2) was sometimes qualified, as in the following discussion:

> *Eddie*: I think [the magazines] are aimed at the average lad . . . have a few beers, watch the footie, trying to, er, pull girls [laughs] . . .
> *Tom*: It's like getting away from the 'new man' image.

Eddie: But at the same time it's not going back to like the . . .
Tom: It's like you've got to look good, but you've still got to have your
traditional attitudes, like having beers and watching footie . . . you can go
out and have a good laugh, a few beers, but you can also, like, be civil you
know, like sensitive (Sheffield 18-year-olds).

The apparent ambiguity of contemporary masculinities was taken up
by several other groups, describing forms of masculinity that were
'not sexist, not racist but interested in drinking, getting drunk'
(Sheffield disabled men) or 'being a boy, liking your beer, but also
being quite aware, do you know what I mean? It's OK to be a bit of
a lad . . . [but] you can have your politics and respect women'
(Sheffield postgraduates).

If laddish masculinity was only too 'natural' for some men, others
were grateful for the support that the men's magazines gave them in
legitimizing behaviour that might previously have been criticized.
Whereas, previously, men had been in constant danger of 'slipping
up and making some mistake' (Derby men), there was now more
cultural approval for 'being yourself'. The magazines have played a
crucial role in this: 'giving you permission . . . to be the man you
want to be . . . you know, whether I want to start screwing around
or whatever . . . it's OK to be actually who I am' (Islington professionals); 'it's sort of allowing you to say and talk about things that
you might have thought but you didn't really talk about too much
and you might feel slightly embarrassed about' (Manchester lecturers). In response to this widely felt sense of insecurity, the magazines
were seen to offer 'like a palliative for all the things that you're
unsure about' (Pimlico graduates). The magazines were there 'to
assure your identity . . . how you're supposed to look' (Sheffield
disabled men); their success 'plays upon those things that you're
going to feel inadequate about . . . because you want to make up the
deficit' (Stoke Newington media professionals); 'you need that kind
of support' (Bristol musicians and artists).

The repertoires of 'honesty' and 'naturalness' are also significant
in that they imply the existence of a more balanced form of masculinity – in between the extremes of the new man and the new lad –
neither a traditional form of masculinity nor a simple response to the
alleged extremes of feminism and political correctness (discussed
below). This more 'authentic' form of masculinity was felt by some
groups (e.g. the Bristol students) to be most closely approximated in
Loaded (in terms of its 'honesty' and lack of pretentiousness). Other
groups felt that such balance was potentially available in new and
more open forms of masculinity, an opportunity that had failed to

materialize or a moment that had been lost (e.g. the Stoke Newington media professionals).

As discussed in chapter 2, media constructions of laddishness have come to seem so 'natural' that for many respondents there was no need to defend them or to consider alternative forms of masculinity. While some participants were critical of the magazines' celebration of laddish masculinities, many more revelled in the lack of restraint implied by what they construed as a return to more 'natural' expressions of masculinity, including, for example, the opportunity to look at pictures of sexy women in an unselfconscious and relatively guilt-free way. The Sheffield postgraduates argued that *Loaded* 'does something dead simple', reflecting 'how blokes are'. While images of the new man were commonly recognized as a cultural construction, laddish forms of masculinity were generally regarded as more 'honest' and 'natural'. As one of the Manchester lecturers suggested: 'New Laddism is a sort of honest and open view about blokes between the ages of 17 and 35.' By the late 1990s, then, laddishness had become so taken-for-granted as a form of masculinity that it was widely regarded as 'natural', in contrast to other versions of masculinity, such as the new man, which were commonly perceived to be a media construction.

'Openness'

Returning to a more 'honest' or 'natural' expression of men's true selves is partly contradicted by some of the magazines' encouragement of a greater sense of 'openness' to new forms of masculinity. Magazines such as *Men's Health*, for example, encourage men to be more open about themselves (to talk about their feelings, for example), while bringing out into the open certain (previously repressed) aspects of masculinity, including more public discussion of men's relationships, fashion and health. However, the magazines constantly monitor this process, using humour and other devices to help distance their readers from any embarrassment that they might feel at being seen to take these issues too seriously.

Expressing 'openness' about sexuality raised particular problems for the magazines and for the men in our focus groups. While the magazines are dominated by images of sexy young women, their fashion pages also provide readers with a publicly acceptable way of looking at images of beautiful young men without the stigma that attaches to reading or viewing more explicitly homoerotic images: 'most gay magazines you couldn't read [in public, but] I wouldn't feel embarrassed reading this on the train'; 'there's lots of gorgeous blokes in it and perhaps they appeal to both [gay and straight] markets, you know' (Sheffield gay men).[12] While, for some readers, the magazines might open up a space to desire differently, in other respects they simply reinscribed traditional notions of gender and sexual difference ('Who's gay, who's straight?' *Maxim*, January 1997). Apart from the sheer predominance of female models in the magazines, the fashion sections that feature male models are usually relegated to the back pages. Even there, male models tend to be shot in very active, sporting poses (doing kung fu or judo kicks, for example) or alongside female models, apparently confirming their heterosexuality. As one reader argued:

> [T]hey've managed very subtly to avoid the gay . . . because there is a hetero and gay distinction here . . . but it's absolutely [clear], you know, these are guys' guys, this is about a hetero guy. It's quite interesting the way that that's been stressed and a lot of taboos have been very very carefully scooted around. (Stoke Newington media professionals)

Other readers were more ambivalent about representations of sexuality in the magazines, talking about having 'a sneaky glance' and referring to their 'illicit aspect' (Pimlico graduates). One participant worried about reading *Men's Health* on the bus while travelling through Manchester's gay village, fearing that people would assume he was gay. More common, however, was the suggestion that 'gay people have led fashion in our lifetimes and we can see that the gap between the straight scene and the gay scene has sort of closed' (Sheffield gay men). Nor was this view restricted to gay men. Whereas men were previously 'very coy', now they were 'opening up' (London art college students); 'I think people are more open, it's socially more acceptable to say that you are different, you can sort of desire openly as a man' (Bristol lecturers).

One of the key ways in which the magazines handle the tension between the need for men to be more open while maintaining their traditional (gendered and sexually stereotyped) notions of masculinity is through the use of humour. So, too, in our focus groups, humour was often used to return the conversation to safer ground following a discussion of emotional relationships, personal problems or sexuality – a point we elaborate upon further below. A similar argument applies to the repertoire of 'harmless fun' which is mobilized in opposition to those who take the magazines too seriously, rather than reading them for a laugh. This same repertoire can also be deployed against those who find the magazines offensive, verging on pornography.

'Harmless fun'

Those who read the magazines in an instrumental fashion – in search of serious advice on personal or emotional problems, for example – were frequently ridiculed by those who saw them primarily as a source of entertainment, with little or no serious content. Readers' letters and problem pages, in particular, were generally regarded humorously as the domain of 'sad losers' (Bristol lecturers) rather than as a source of practical information or serious advice. Even those groups (Sheffield 18-year-olds; London art college students) who regarded the problem pages favourably saw their value in discouraging people from taking themselves too seriously. Rather than offering 'serious advice [which] is just bollocks isn't it', the tone of these pages is characteristically satirical: 'sending itself up as you read it' (Islington professionals). Those who studied the consumer reports in *Stuff for Men* were also regarded as 'a bit sad' (London counsellors), likened by some respondents to the 'sad bastards' who bragged about their achievements: their friends, computers, fashionable clothes and good jobs (London unemployed men).

The construction of the magazines (and particularly the humorous style of *Loaded* and *FHM*) as 'harmless fun' is clearly contestable, though at the risk of being regarded as humourless or sad. The insistence by many participants on reading the magazines just for a laugh can be seen as a convenient way of denying their wider political significance.[13] The same tone has been adopted in several recent British television series, including quiz shows such as *They Think It's All Over* and *Never Mind the Buzzcocks* and situation comedies such as *Men Behaving Badly* and *Game On*. Like the magazines, these programmes adopt an exaggerated, ironic and over the top sense of laddish humour that defies political critique.[14]

Many of our focus group participants recognized these same cultural reference points, defending *Loaded*'s supposed sexism as ironic: 'It's a bit like *Viz*, because *Viz* started off being . . . ironic . . . then I stopped getting it because I either grew out of it or it didn't get too good . . . and with *Loaded* it had irony in it' (Manchester lecturers). *Viz* has also been accused of sexism, notably for its extremist feminist character Millie Tant and the contrasting characters of the 'fat slags' ('don't fancy yours much'), an accusation it counters with its slimy character Sid the Sexist and ironizes with the misguidedly right-on Modern Parents. Respondents even ironized their transition from one magazine to the other: 'It's just a natural progression . . . I mean I'll probably buy *Viz* every now and again but I've progressed'; 'You'll be on *Esquire* soon mate' (Bristol students).

An alternative reading therefore opposes 'harmless fun' with potentially offensive material bordering on pornography: 'My wife just thinks *Loaded*'s rubbish; she thinks it's soft porn, vulgar' (Sheffield postgraduates). While some participants expressed themselves 'amazed' and 'deeply shocked' at the 'demeaning' way the magazines depict women, 'verging on porn' (London journalists), this was a comparatively rare response. Others found them 'a bit dodgy' (Sheffield 18-year-olds) or 'a bit offensive', but concluded that 'it doesn't bother me', 'it's just a bit of fun' (Turnpike Lane graduates).[15] While the magazines were described by one group as 'the acceptable face of porn' (London unemployed men), they were more commonly regarded as 'a bit of escapism' or as a simple commercial response to the 'massive gap in the market between the top shelf and the motoring magazines' (Derby men). The distinction between men's magazines and top-shelf pornography was frequently insisted upon:

> *Charles*: It's different from getting a porn magazine, isn't it really . . .
> *Alan*: You obviously wouldn't classify it as pornography or they wouldn't be selling it at Safeways. I mean, it's on the top shelf . . . but it's not classified as pornography. (Manchester lecturers)

Similarly, one of the Sheffield 18-year-olds repeated his mother's mockery of his decision to buy *Loaded*: 'She goes, like, couldn't you reach the top shelf?' Far from being offended, most participants argued that the magazines were 'just entertainment', 'not very harmful . . . just a bit of fun' (Manchester lecturers). Occasionally, readers admitted to a sense of embarrassment, as the following exchange suggests:

> *Sean*: I wouldn't buy *Loaded*. I'd be embarrassed to buy it . . . I certainly wouldn't take my copy home.
> *John*: I wouldn't read it in public.
> *Nick*: I wouldn't be embarrassed about reading it on a train . . . because they are acceptable . . .
> *John*: Yeah but . . . it obviously isn't hard core porn and yet it's blurring the boundaries . . . (Manchester lecturers)

Others readers shared this sense of disquiet, feeling 'a sense of shame about them . . . it's a kind of softened pornography', though they argued that we have all become 'desensitized to those images' (Bristol musicians and artists).

The magazines attempt to defuse this potentially damaging issue through the use of ironic humour.[16] As has been recognized within literary criticism, however, irony is characteristically two-edged: potentially subversive but politically suspect (Hutcheon, 1994), rein-scribing the very thing it claims to ironize. This ambivalence explains how *Loaded* can be said to be both the most 'honest' and the most 'ironic' of the magazines: 'like two excuses to different audiences' (Bristol musicians and artists). While some readers acknowledge that irony may implicate the reader in what is being ironized – 'the irony was just a bit of a cover up. . . . It can cut both ways. . . . By the end I felt implicated in it' (Manchester lecturers); 'Irony only works once or twice, after that it doesn't become ironic any more does it' (Bristol musicians and artists) – this is a fairly rare position. Generally, readers celebrated the magazines' sense of humour, contrasting it with the more 'po-faced' tone that they attribute to women's maga-zines – 'women's magazines don't have that wink, wink, nudge, nudge kind of irony' (Stoke Newington media professionals) – and to the more 'style-conscious' of the men's magazines – 'Does the word "poncey" mean anything to you? *Esquire*'s poncey' (Sheffield postgraduates).

'Change'

As the preceding discussion suggests, men's magazines are character-ized by numerous contradictions.[17] Through the magazines, men are being called on to be more 'natural', 'open' and 'honest', while simultaneously seeking reassurance for their insecurities, needing permission to be a particular kind of man, and searching for ways of legitimizing behaviour that others may find offensive. This sense of contradiction also pervades readers' explanations of the social changes that are thought to underlie the magazines' commercial success. Some readers spoke of the magazines as a response or backlash to feminism (always defined as 'extreme' or 'ultra-feminism', in one case even as 'femi-nazism'), helping men feel easier about themselves, 'releasing' them from the 'kicking' one man felt he had received from feminism (Islington professionals). Others thought that there had been an opening up of the very narrow definition of acceptable roles for men, but that the gap had soon narrowed down again (London counsellors). Another man reflected that: 'There was a moment there actually which I think was lost . . . but [the magazines] started to run in the opposite direction, towards consumerism which works by conforming, dumbing down' (Stoke Newington media professionals).

Even those who didn't read the magazines were aware of their current popularity, though they found it difficult to explain their longer-term cultural significance:

> I go to Safeways about twice a week and there's no way I'm going to buy [*Loaded*] but I keep clocking it . . . because I can't believe that qualitative shift. . . . But whether it's here to stay, it just depends why it's come out as it has done now. I mean, I read in the papers and . . . like this could either be the last gasp of men . . . in a sort of semi-ironic way [but] maybe boundaries are breaking down and it's like . . . whether it's taking the piss or whether it's actually reinforcing them . . . I don't know. (Manchester lecturers)

While some participants regarded the magazines as 'a reaction against political correctness' (Bristol lecturers) or a response to feminism which had simply 'gone too far' (Taunton bikers), others saw them in purely commercial terms, comparing their success to the rise of club culture (Malbon, 1999). Several groups identified this possibility, arguing that 'it's industry-driven, it's all manufactured isn't it . . . a cynical attempt by IPC' which owns 'a frightening amount of magazines' (Sheffield postgraduates). Other groups also referred to the magazines as a kind of parallel to the commercialization of drug and club culture, denying any deeper change in gender relations: 'I don't think there's been a change in new men to new lad . . . they've always been there but they have come about now . . . due to the massive commercialization in the dance music culture and the drug culture' (Bristol students). Asked whether men have changed and whether that might be why the magazines have appeared at this point, one woman simply replied 'Not really, it's the market isn't it' (Derby women).

Several participants spoke about the wider social changes that they felt were reflected in the magazines, though this often only occurred as a result of our prompting. The most common changes were referred to in terms of a backlash against feminism and the alleged excesses of political correctness. However, several participants totally rejected the idea that the magazines could be interpreted in these terms. One of the Manchester lecturers reacted angrily to the suggestion that the magazines were 'some sort of backlash against feminism: I think that's just crap'. More unusually, laddish masculinity was itself described as a kind of backlash to the broadening of masculinities implied by images of the new man. In this reading, the magazines could be seen as embodying 'some kind of backlash ... from roles being expanded' (London counsellors). Others saw the magazines as part of a general media-manipulated shift in culture, 'like Britpop and the big thing with Oasis and Blur' (Sheffield postgraduates).

One or two participants related the magazines' success to wider social changes such as 'the decline in this country of traditional industry ... a job for life. ... It's a compensatory effort isn't it? If you don't have the status, the security, the self-confidence and everything else, that goes with the job for life, then you've got all these other sources of comfort and security, your car, clothes' (Bristol lecturers). Others interpreted the magazines as a reflection of changing gender relations where 'the whole culture is shifting ... lads are sticking together ... building a group identity' in response to changes in the workplace which are forcing men to adapt (Turnpike Lane graduates).

'Seriousness'

As might be anticipated from the earlier discussion of 'harmless fun', the discourse of 'seriousness' was generally regarded as something to be avoided, engaged in by those 'sad losers' (feminists, academics) who misunderstood the primary purpose of the magazines (having a laugh, purely for entertainment). A common way of avoiding being seen to take the magazines too seriously was to adopt an ironic tone of voice. One of the Manchester lecturers recognized this strategy within the magazines themselves, arguing that social changes such as the decline of heavy manual labour and the feminization of the workforce had led to the 'last gasp' of traditional masculinity being expressed (as quoted above) 'in a sort of semi-ironic way'. For this respondent, 'talking in italics' was a convenient way of circumventing criticism for a lack of political correctness. More generally, however, while many readers commented on the use of irony in the magazines – 'very tongue in cheek' (Bristol students) – relatively few participants adopted an ironic mode of address themselves. Irony was more commonly adopted as a disposition than as a discourse in its own right (see below).

As we were frequently reminded, the magazines should not be taken too seriously: 'I tend not to bother ... I sometimes read them like round at other people's houses ... anything that happens to be lying around'; 'you're not going to sit down and read, back to back ... like cover to cover, you just pick it up now and again ... if

you've got a spare half hour' (Sheffield 18-year-olds). Others agreed:
'I read them at work when I've got a bit of time to kill. You know,
if you're going on a train journey' (Bristol musicians and artists). Or,
as one member of the Taunton bikers' group put it:

> [N]ormally I read in bed but that's more likely to be a novel or something
> like that. I find that magazines are too . . ., you can't really get into them,
> the articles aren't long enough, it's over before you've started, so I generally
> read when I'm eating or something like that, sort of eating and flicking
> through them and stuff . . . if there's nothing on telly and I'm bored and I
> don't want to read a book.

Similarly, for one of the Sheffield postgraduates, reading *Loaded* was
something to do when 'now't else was happening'. Those who took
the magazines too seriously were dismissed as 'sad, single [and]
lonely' (Bristol lecturers).

'Women as Other'

The discourse of 'women as Other' can be interpreted in a number
of ways. In several cases, men drew a distinction between the way
they approached the magazines as readers and the way they constructed women as readers. Men described themselves as casual
readers ('browsing' or 'flicking through') compared to the almost
religious way they felt women read magazines:

> *Dave*: A friend of mine, she was really addicted to, like magazines. I mean
> she bought for England kind of thing. She'd buy things like *Marie Claire*,
> *Cosmo*, the lot you know . . . and I mean I used to quite regularly at
> weekends, you know, flick through them . . .
> *Steve*: . . . with *Cosmopolitan* and *Marie Claire*, she'll read them . . . and
> she takes something serious from them.
> *Dave*: While we'll take it for what it is.
> *George*: Well, Sharon [his wife] tends to read magazines, you know like
> *Elle*, religiously, you know she reads every article religiously, whereas I'll
> flick through: 'that's shit, that's shit. I'll read that, the rest is rubbish, in the
> bin'. (Sheffield postgraduates)

This exaggerated sense of gender difference is clearly contradicted by
research on women's magazines which shows that they are read in a
very similar way to how reading men's magazines is described here,
with relatively little attention, leafed through and put down as more
pressing commitments arise (cf. Hermes, 1995). The point to be

emphasized here, however, is the ideological construction of gender difference, whether or not it is borne out in practice.

Very few participants saw gender differences other than in binary terms (constructing women as 'the opposite sex'). One of the few exceptions argued that 'A lot of what I want to read is also within women's magazines. You know, there's a false dichotomy' (Bristol lecturers). Another respondent felt that 'a lot of that macho stuff was dropped in the last few years; it's like this whole gay thing and everything; it's a lot more open now than it used to be [with] more femininity coming out in the male thing' (Taunton bikers). Others recognized that 'there's a cross-fertilization with a lot of women's magazines as well, so, you know, the same company, has a male version and a female version, 'cos a lot of things like the structure is very similar as well [to] a lot of the female orientated magazines' (Sheffield postgraduates). For most readers, however, men's magazines were strongly differentiated from women's magazines: 'It's all love and shite [in women's mags] . . . There's not much about love in men's mags' (Sheffield 18-year-olds).

The discourse of 'women as Other' also applies to the ways in which women were represented in the magazines, as objects, simultaneously to be desired and dreaded. While most readers argued that the sexy images of women in the magazines showed how much they 'love women', others felt that the magazines portrayed women in a much more hostile fashion: 'Women are the enemy. Women are this peculiar thing that you fancy and you want to shag . . . but the bad thing is, they want to have a relationship' (Manchester lecturers). A member of this same group wondered aloud if the magazines were 'written by men who are afraid of women'. He went on, cautiously, to explain: 'When I was at university . . . there were sort of women [who were] feminists of an ultra sort and you couldn't say things, not even in a jokey way.'[18] Other participants referred to the magazines as providing 'an insight into female psychology' (London unemployed men) or, more prosaically (in response to Kate), 'how you lot work' (Sheffield clothes shop assistants). One member of the Derby women's group expressed a similar view in relation to men's interest in women's magazines: 'Men are a bit secretly excited by women's magazines. . . . Blokes can't get enough of them. . . . They think it's going to be secrets, you know, women are mysterious to men.' She concluded: 'maybe that's why they need things like men's magazines, to sort of educate themselves, because women do talk more [than men]' (Derby women).

Constructed certitude

The preceding analysis of our focus group transcripts has identified a range of discursive repertoires through which men attempt to 'make sense' of the magazines in terms of their understanding of the changes taking place in contemporary masculinities. How, though, can we make sense of this material analytically? We wish to suggest that most, if not all, of the discursive repertoires identified above can be seen as variants of the ambiguities facing men, referred to popularly as a 'crisis of masculinity' or, in more theoretical terms, as 'gender trouble'. Men are being asked to be more open about their feelings while treating change with a lack of seriousness, as something that can be dismissed as largely superficial rather than calling for more profound personal changes in their social relations. They have therefore come to rely on natural or honest representations of masculinity, rejecting appeals to 'softer' forms of masculinity as dishonest and unnatural media constructions. The popularity of more laddish forms of masculinity which continue to treat women as Other, is defended as harmless fun, handled with an ironic sense of humour in the magazines and with a general lack of seriousness by our focus group participants.

How, then, might these ambivalences and contradictions be resolved, discursively, at least in terms of men's everyday lives? Much of the current literature on identity articulates a sense of the self as caught between chaos and certitude. The breakdown of tradition, the globalization of culture and the refashioning of sexual identities have all been represented as having had a marked impact upon the construction of the gendered self. While much postmodern discourse has pointed towards the fragmentation and commodification of modern identities, other currents have referred to the preservation of older social divisions that have come to be associated with modernity (e.g. Giddens, 1991; Lash and Friedman, 1992).

The modern self is seemingly caught between a more uncertain and reflexive disposition and more stable social markers. Taking the example of changing masculinities, many of these features soon become apparent. Reviewing the sociological literature, Segal (1990) points towards the 'slow change' of masculine identities in respect of participation in childcare, the declining importance of the 'breadwin-ner' role and adherence to heterosexual norms and practices. Yet it is undoubtedly the case that the commodification of masculine anxieties, growth in awareness of health issues and a more reflexive

disposition towards fashion and the body (all evident in the magazines) articulate more ambivalent frames.

As in our previous discussion of editorial work and magazine
content (in chapters 3 and 4), however, we would wish to place our
understanding of these ambivalences in a wider context. We refer, in
particular, to the destabilizing effects of the fast-moving world of
late-capitalism on traditional forms of masculinity. In understanding
this process, we have found Ulrich Beck's (1997) discussion of
'constructed certitude' helpful. For Beck, the construction of certitude
represents a form of counter-modernity. If modernity has meant
increased questioning of tradition, doubt, reflexivity and the unfreezing of gender relations, counter-modernity attempts to dismiss such
issues or to render them more manageable. The attempt to replace
questioning and doubt with more certain frames of reference can be
related to a number of fundamentalist currents which are articulated
in terms of certainty rather than risk. Beck writes:

> Certitude arises from and with the prevalence of a 'magic of feelings'
> (to use a modern term), an emotional praxis that sweeps away the
> trembling and hesitation of questioning and doubting with the instinc-
> tive and reflex-like security of becoming effective and making things
> effective in action. (1997: 65)

According to Beck, the construction of certitude offers a 'magical'
solution to questions of identity, eradicating doubt and the need to
orientate oneself in a world that is increasingly perceived as being
fragile and uncertain. In terms of masculinity, the more 'certain'
world of patriarchal relations is not only part of a wider nostalgia
for a social order that protected men's material interests, but one
that offered more straightforward codes in terms of what passed as
acceptable masculine behaviour. However, wider economic changes,
the questioning of sexuality by lesbian and gay groups, the undermining of traditional notions of public and private, and the political role
played by feminism more generally have all served to destabilize
modern masculine identities. Hence, in a situation where certainties
and tradition are being progressively undermined, they have (somewhat paradoxically) to be 'constructed'.

The construction of certitude in cultural forms need not, however,
be read simply as a backlash against feminism. Instead, we suggest
that, while such formations have political implications, they may be
understood as a more complex response to changing gender relations.
Arguably, the construction of certitude gives both men and women a
sense that the social world is more stable than it actually is. That is,

images of phallic masculinity promote a cultural 'comfort zone', giving the self (however temporarily) a sense of fixity and psychic security.

How, then, might this analysis be applied to our understanding of men's lifestyle magazines? It is most apparent in the profusion of 'how to' sections that are carried in many of the magazines, offering advice (often in a semi-ironic tone) so that readers can brush up on a variety of techniques from the monitoring of sexual performance to changing a car tyre. For example, *Maxim* (July 1997) carries a typical section called 'How to be better than her last lover'. In many respects the article reaffirms binary divisions between men and women: whereas she needs to feel relaxed, intimate and that she can trust her partner, he simply wants to have sex. However, the article stops some way short of simply reaffirming old-style patriarchal relations, as the reader is made aware that he is likely to be compared to his partner's former lovers. Unless he 'proves himself' a good lover, the relationship may founder. In stories like these the magazines can be read as offering a space of both certitude and reflexivity, as simultaneously a material force seeking to rework gender relations and a cultural fantasy with few if any practical implications. These constructions are politically important, as such cultural practices continue to mark contemporary culture's 'distance' from modern feminism, while remaining pertinent as fantasies, allowing temporary forms of closure from men's current gender troubles.

In many respects, the magazines provide a meeting point between the new culture of reflexivity and a way of granting masculinity a more ontological definition. Many of the reflexive spaces first noticed within the magazines' content by earlier commentators such as Mort (1988), as offering the potential for progressive social change, have been colonized by a culture of laddism. On the other hand, we maintain that ambivalence can still be detected in terms of the magazines' content (spaces of anxiety, medical and emotional advice, etc.) but more importantly in terms of the ways in which the magazines are read and talked about. That the magazines' advice to readers is often expressed in a semi-humorous, ironic tone suggests that the magazines occupy an ambivalent space for many of their readers rather than offering ready-made solutions to their perceived problems. We shall return to this sense of ambivalence and ambiguity later, once we have discussed the range of discursive dispositions adopted by our focus group participants towards the magazines.

Discursive dispositions

Having outlined the discursive repertoires that characterize men's talk about the magazines, we now wish to outline the range of discursive dispositions that were taken towards each of these discourses. To avoid repetition, we shall not take each discourse in turn, illustrating which dispositions were most prevalent in each case. Instead, we will treat this part of the analysis as a separate set of dispositions, though we reiterate that it is, in practice, impossible to articulate a discourse without simultaneously adopting a disposition towards it.

While we found little evidence of directly 'oppositional' readings, actively resisting the laddish ethos of the magazines, we found considerable ambivalence in the way they are read, suggesting a pervasive disquiet with more hegemonic forms of masculinity.[19] Without focusing on dispositions, our analysis might have obscured readings that go against the grain of dominant discourses, where a particular discursive repertoire was identified by a focus group participant ('harmless fun', 'naturalness', etc.) but where that individual did not personally endorse such a view. Restricting the analysis to the level of discourse may have exaggerated the pervasiveness of dominant discourses, or even implied our own complicity with them. To address this problem, we have in this section attempted to identify a range of discursive dispositions that individuals took towards each of the repertoires, allowing for 'refusal' or 'rejection', for example, as well as dispositions that endorse a particular discourse, such as 'celebration' or 'compliance', as in the list below:

- celebratory;
- compliant;
- hostile;
- apologetic;
- deferential;
- defensive;
- vulnerable;
- distanced;
- refusing/rejecting;
- analytical;
- dismissive;
- ironic.

Tactics, such as silence and humour, are also considered alongside more explicitly oppositional strategies (cf. de Certeau, 1984). Some of these dispositions appear to be rooted in aesthetic or political attitudes that are more or less independent from the group context in which they were articulated. Others are clearly shaped by the context of interaction (with other members of the group and with ourselves as moderators). As such, we would agree with Pearce's remarks about the politics of reading, when she argues that: 'why we end up approving or disapproving of a work will often depend on the (*interactive*) processes at work in the reading as well as on the ostensible frames of reference, aesthetic and political, to which we refer' (1997: 217).[20] In the following section we identify a number of examples of such ambivalences, returning to one of the initial aims of our research: the possibility that the magazines might be seen as opening up a discursive space for their readers, offering ways of 'doing masculinity' differently, while simultaneously reinscribing its more hegemonic forms.

The predominant tone in many of our focus groups was *celebratory*, championing the honesty and lack of pretension of magazines such as *Loaded* (hailed by a member of the Pimlico group as promoting 'the unacceptable face of men'). According to the Bristol students, *Loaded* 'makes no qualms about it . . . they're not hypo-critical'. Even for those with some personal reservations about the magazines, there was a general sense of *compliance*: 'they don't feel the need to justify having women with very few clothes in them any more . . . it's shameless' (Manchester lecturers).

Occasionally, however, our focus group participants expressed a different view, including several cases where readers were outrightly *hostile* towards the magazines: 'I'm just amazed at the way they depict women. . . . I'm deeply shocked' (London journalists); 'I'm sorry but . . . it just gets a bit boring after a while, just treating people like sex objects' (Derby men).[21]

As these examples suggest, such views were often expressed in a (semi)-*apologetic* tone. Several participants appeared to be monitoring their conduct for our benefit as researchers. To give a couple of examples: 'I mean, you've got a pretty bird on the front [cover], er woman, sorry' (London unemployed men), and 'No offence, but women are interested in things like that [relationships], aren't they' (Sheffield postgraduates). In other cases, however, men appeared to be making very little effort to monitor their comments, suggesting that feminist critique has made relatively little impact on masculinist discourse (even among media studies and social science students who have clearly been exposed to such debates). Laddish talk, it would appear, has become so naturalized as not to require any defensiveness in its articulation.

This was also apparent in the *deferential* tone that participants took towards one another, ensuring the (re)production of a laddish group consensus. In the Taunton bikers' group, for example, there was a general disdain for the readers of men's magazines, described contemptuously as 'muppets'. Though all of the group appeared to share this view, it later became clear that one group member regularly bought *Men's Health*, while another spoke openly about his changing taste in clothes:

> *Hal*: You know how you can get stuck in your ways?
> *Billy*: I think so.
> *Hal*: Like, for instance I got a load of *Next* vouchers for Christmas so I went in there and I got a load of stuff and I waited a couple of months and then got a bit more. So, I'm thinking, why not?
> *KB*: Do they do biker things in *Next*?
> *Hal*: No. I was nearly wearing the same tee shirt that I'd been wearing for the past five years. We were going out for a meal, you know, and wearing the same old tee shirt and jeans.

After some laughter from the rest of the group, he went on:

> *Hal*: I do like to dress up now and again, smart and um . . .
> *Kate*: So the magazines would help in that respect?
> *Hal*: Um, yeah, maybe . . . just to see what was, what people are wearing and, um, I wouldn't look completely stupid when I went out.

In other cases, the conversation would open out into a hesitant critique of the magazines before being rapidly closed down again in a rather *defensive* manner, frequently through the use of humour or consensual references to sport:

> *John*: But I think if you want to think about it, [the magazines] sort of legitimize laddishness, you know, whereas before, you'd be a bit quiet about that. You wouldn't be sort of upfront about talking about women like that . . . you know it's a bit of a group thing where you can have a bit of a chin-wag and a laugh, you know.
> *NS*: Right, and do you think that's a good thing or . . .
> *Larry*: No I don't like it . . . it does offend me slightly.
> *Mick* [closing this line of conversation down]: It doesn't bother me one way or the other. It's a bit of fun really isn't it.

Or later on:

Larry: I mean personally, I'm quite interested in men's health and problems, you know, and fitness and whatever, I think it's quite important. And it always niggled me that women were catered for in that area . . . you know sort of sexual problems or health problems that men tend not to talk about as much as women may and I think it's good that that sort of opens up as well . . .

John: There's an air of embarrassment, I suppose, you wouldn't discuss it openly and I certainly wouldn't, unless there was something seriously wrong with me, go to the doctors, you know just brush it under the door and hope it will go away. . . . Men just kept those things to themselves. They don't generally talk to each other about them. You'd face ridicule from your friends down the pub if it was dragged up . . .

Larry: So I would say that's quite an important breakthrough [though, he adds, defensively] I could live without any of it, you know, I wouldn't miss any of it.

NS: Right.

John: You know, to be honest with you, if I was going to buy any of these mags one subject it would be football. . . . Health doesn't interest me very much . . . but football's my main thing. (Turnpike Lane graduates)

A similar kind of defensiveness is also evident in discussions of sexuality, when, for example, the Bristol students attempt to defend the magazines' portrayal of women ('I don't think it's sexist at all . . . more of a celebration . . . they don't slag women off. . . . They love women'). Compared to these more predictable responses, one man suggested that 'the roles that men can adopt have widened [from] a very narrow definition of what was acceptable masculine role models. I think it's opened up . . . but now they're being narrowed in again' (London counsellors).

Another participant in this group referred to men's roles 'being expanded, then now being narrowed again', while a member of another group suggested that:

There was a moment there actually which I think was lost. . . . There was a moment about the beginning of the '90s where *Iron John* [Robert Bly's best-selling book on the men's movement] was published and there was suddenly, you know, there was a great concern, there was certainly a focal point for, you know, men who . . . for somebody to talk about masculinity, to talk about father and son relationships and what not, and it, I suppose, it was about the time maybe these things [men's magazines] were a twinkle in somebody's eye. (Stoke Newington media professionals)

But, the same participant continued, things had then started to run in the opposite direction, towards a more rampant 'consumerism' and the moment had passed.

The use of spatial and temporal metaphors in these extracts ('lost moments', 'opening up', 'narrowing down', being 'upfront', etc) is, we argue, highly significant. We want to suggest that the 'new' issues being covered in the magazines – a concern for health, relationships and bodily display – may not be new for individual men. What is new, however, is the sense of an emerging *public discourse* on men's health where new spaces have been opened up in which men can acquire the kind of practical and discursive competencies they may previously have lacked. While this may not be the case for some of the magazines which continue to treat health issues and sexual relationships in a jokingly ironic way, it would certainly be true of *Men's Health* and one or two of the other magazines, which try to provide serious advice in a non-judgemental and informative way.[22] This is an aspect of commercial culture that interests us in more general terms, where new spaces are being opened up for different kinds of social relationships and personal identities to be pursued. Subject to market forces, however, these spaces are always vulnerable to recuperation by more conservative forces. This is another of the ambivalences that we would highlight as characteristic of the emerging market for men's magazines.

Many of our participants were suspicious of the power of the magazines and of the publishing industry more generally: 'it's like industry-driven, it's all manufactured isn't it' (Sheffield postgraduates); 'they suck you in' (Pimlico graduates). In contrast to the magazines' image of an unapologetically laddish masculinity, several participants described men as *vulnerable* and needing reassurance: 'a lot of times it's people aren't confident enough . . . to have their own personalities, people are a bit frightened to be individuals' (Sheffield disabled men). Men's insecurities were mentioned by several groups (Derby men; Stoke Newington media professionals), to be remedied by the purchase of appropriate products, including magazines which 'legitimize a certain way of behaviour' (Bristol musicians and artists).

The blame for men's insecurities is, of course, often laid at the door of women, leading to some interesting reversals of conventional power relations, as when the images of women in men's magazines are described as evidence of women's power over men:

Does she look like a fucking victim to you? She scares the shit out of me. You know what I mean? Going up to her in a bar and asking her for a date, you know, it would take a brave man. . . . These are fucking strong, intelligent women. . . . Fucking sexy women . . . powerful as well.' (Islington professionals)[23]

A process of *distancing* was commonly used by other participants to avoid the charge of taking themselves or the magazines too seriously. Such a disposition was evident in men's descriptions of their reading practices as 'browsing' or 'flicking through', with little or no sense of commitment to a particular title: 'I occasionally buy *Loaded* or *FHM* . . . found it quite amusing' (Sheffield 18-year-olds); 'I guess I must have picked them up and browsed through other people's' (Bristol students); 'I've never actually bought one myself'; 'I used to buy them but . . .' (Sheffield postgraduates); 'It's just the first one I happen to pick up . . .' (Bristol lecturers); 'I've actually not bought a men's magazine for maybe a couple of years now. . . . I often browse on the shelf. . . . I only ever read them in the dentist's' (Stoke Newington media professionals); 'I read them at work if I've got a bit of time to kill . . . or if you're going on a train journey' (Bristol musicians and artists).

Distancing sometimes hardened into outright *refusal* or *rejection*, as when a member of the London counsellors group spoke of 'the funny mish-mash of things' that appear in the magazines which he couldn't actually imagine men reading, refusing the alleged coherence of the lifestyle package that the magazines portray (cf. Chaney, 1996). Likewise, many participants resented the idea that they needed a magazine to tell them what to do: 'what's a magazine going to tell you that you don't already know?' (Bristol students).

Other men adopted a more *analytical* disposition (no doubt partly in response to their perception of our 'academic' interests), referring to processes of commercialization and liberalization: 'I don't think there's been a change in new man to new lad . . . they've always been there but [the magazines] have come about now . . . it's like a general liberalization of society' (Bristol students).

Many other readers rejected such an analytical disposition, declining to theorize the magazines and *dismissing* their political significance (as in the exchange between Andy and George, quoted above on p. 115).[24]

Finally, several of our participants adopted an *ironic* disposition towards the magazines (mirroring the ironic tone of the magazines themselves). As mentioned above, however, in our discussion of the discourse of irony, irony is characteristically double-edged. This is clearly demonstrated in the following remarks on the typical range of products ('toys for men') advertised in the magazines:

[Y]ou have to spend £2,000 on a Rolex and then, you know, oh a nice little Fiat Coupe. You know, buy a nice pair of Armani sunglasses for £400 . . . I mean £3,000 for a bike, you know, or a mobile phone. . . . There's

not, you know, twenty ways to spread your DSS [social security benefit].
(London unemployed men)

In this case, the sense of irony borders on outright cynicism, as the
speaker ironizes the magazines' cynical celebration of consumerism.
Other members of this group referred to the magazines as 'a catalogue of boys' dreams', arguing that 'it's like the working-class
people don't really matter, you know . . . a sort of upper-class yob
magazine'.

To conclude our analysis of specific discourses and dispositions,
we also identified various *silences and absences*, both in terms of the
magazines' content and in terms of what men had to say about them.
One glaring omission was the almost total lack of discussion of
parenting within the magazines and among our participants, whether
in relation to men's personal experience as parents or their relationships with their own parents.[25] Among our respondents, there was
almost no discussion of how their lives differed from their fathers or
of what they had learned from them about 'being a man'. Other
absences included issues of race (apparently invisible to our predominantly white respondents) and domesticity (except as a burden to be
avoided).

Cultural capital

The previous sections of this chapter have presented a reading of our
focus group transcripts, organized around the distinction between
discourses and dispositions. Taken together, this material has demonstrated the range of ways that different individuals and groups of
men attempt to 'make sense' of the magazines and associated changes
in masculinities. We have already suggested that this process may be
better characterized in terms of ambivalence and contradiction than
in terms of hegemony and resistance, and that those ambivalences
may be discursively resolved in terms of a process of constructed
certitude. Here, we wish to take the analysis a stage further, drawing
on Pierre Bourdieu's ideas about cultural capital as a way of theorizing how and why different groups of men adopt different discursive
dispositions towards the magazines.

Having highlighted the range of discursive dispositions adopted by
our focus group participants in their discussion of the magazines, we
now wish to consider whether there is a relationship between these
personal dispositions and more macro-contexts. We have found it

useful to draw on Bourdieu's concept of cultural capital as a way of
arbitrating between different discursive dispositions. The term refers
to the acquisition of social status through cultural practices which
involve the exercise of taste or judgement. Originally applied in the
context of educational research in France (Bourdieu and Passeron,
1977), the concept has been extended to a wider field of social
distinctions where tastes and aesthetic judgements function as markers of class (Bourdieu, 1984). Here, we are not so much concerned
with whether or not cultural or symbolic capital can be converted
into economic capital (or vice versa) as with using the concept as a
way of seeing how different discursive dispositions map on to other
social divisions.

For example, a key distinction among our groups was their access
to further education, a form of cultural capital which served as the
main determinant in mobilizing the dispositions of outright refusal,
processes of distancing and above all the ability to be analytical.[26]
The most obvious example in this respect was the group of upper-
middle-class media professionals who lived in the Stoke Newington
area of London. Throughout the discussion the group employed
'expert' frames of reference in talking about the magazines, such as
the following reference to 'classless laddism':

> KB: Is there a class element in Loaded's appeal?
> Monty: Classless laddism . . . an awful lot of culture has become tied into
> football. Football's become very acceptable for all classes . . . you've got
> David Baddiel with his double First from Oxford, sat down with Frank
> Skinner and it's, that: hey, we're all guys together loving football and big
> breasted women.

Most of the discussion within the media professionals group was
about the culture of the magazines as a social phenomenon that can
be analysed in terms of cultural trends and sociological shifts.
Similarly, members of the London counsellors group were able to
utilize an analytical discourse on masculinity and feminism not
available to many of the other groups:

> NS: What is the New Man?
> Chris: Emotional and caring (or at least pretends to be), a mythical creation,
> completely unrealistic and artificial, an attempt to redefine the masculine
> model if you wish . . . the final product of the women's movement.

The paradox here is that the notion of 'classless laddism' is
employed to demonstrate commercial culture's ability to blur class

boundaries, and yet such distinctions are reaffirmed in the very way they are spoken about. These groups that have access to more critical and analytical modes of discourse can be seen both in Giddens's (1994) description of 'clever people' and also in respect of Bourdieu's (1984) analysis of the circuits of cultural capital. The expansion of a mediated culture within modernity has meant that within certain circles changes in public discourses and image repertoires are debated more intensely than ever before. While participation within further education is perhaps the gateway to discourses of expertise generally, the specific forms they take are determined by access to more specific media and professional discourses.[27] To have an opinion about the magazines is to be included within a rich cosmopolitan culture of consumption, where group membership is determined culturally through the capacity to talk in an open and informed way. In this respect, we were often struck by the fact that many of the groups had picked up on the surrounding media debate and were able to offer an informed discussion on the links between masculinity and consumer culture without being regular readers of the magazines.

This is not to argue that other groups did not have access to an analytic mode of talk or to their own forms of cultural capital. The student groups, for example, were able to articulate an informed and critical view of club culture that eludes many academics. The ability to articulate an analytical mode of talk is, however, clearly affected by differential access to cultural capital and is mobilized quite differently by different groups. The most materially and socially deprived group (the London-based unemployed men) are 'analytical' in the sense that they are surrounded by a culture that is difficult for them to participate fully within:

Martin: You see, the magazines, they're sort of like the upper classes and the middle class but the working class I don't see them as enjoying them you know. Because I think basically, I mean you're not talking, you're talking 'above'. In the magazine you're talking above the poorer class you know. You know, you are talking above them and either way that can be derogatory.
NS: And when you say derogatory . . .?
Martin: Looking down at them.

Martin's comment describes what it feels like to be socially excluded from a commercial culture of consumption. This is not so much a space of reflexivity or certitude but a zone of marginalization that is beyond the confines of contemporary commercial culture. Most pressing in this space is not the 'semiotic' ability to interpret contemporary lifestyle changes, but the ability to raise questions about the link between culture and justice. Hence, questions of masculine identity and ambiguity, which are brought into play by most of the other groups, hardly enter the frame.

Elsewhere, the Sheffield 18-year-olds also recognize certain exclusions, but the culture of the magazines is not so much viewed analytically as in terms of the pleasures of being male:

> *KB*: So if you had to say, then, what would be your ideal type of article, or whatever, what would be your kind of, what would you turn to first?
> *Mike*: . . . for example, on that *FHM* with that Jenny McCarthy, people probably go straight to that article straight away, you know, see it on the front and go, she looks quite nice [laughter] and they start looking at the pictures. Ooh!

The capacity of the group to offer a critical account of the magazines is circumvented by two tropes: the first is connected to questions of masculinity, and the second the ability to give an opinion. This group mainly saw the magazines as reflecting the lifestyle which they most aspired to in terms of the forms of masculinity represented in the magazines and a concern with the consumption of fashionable clothes, style and gadgets. The sense of common identification (or sharing a similar sensibility to the magazines) had the effect of rendering the magazines relatively uncontroversial. As Bourdieu argues, however: 'there are dispositions, which by definition, are not opinion if one means by that . . . something that can be formulated in discourse with some claim to coherence' (1993: 157). For Bourdieu, the ability to formulate an opinion means the subject has access to certain symbolic codes and an educated disposition towards culture. To have an opinion, the disposition we hold towards cultural forms has to be one of scrutiny rather than participation, enjoyment and pleasure. However, there are spaces where this typology breaks down, where access to more evaluative discourses has been arrived at by other means such as political involvement. For example, members of the disabled group, while having little access to formal education, were used to offering opinions through their work on the politics of disability.

> *KB*: What kind of person reads the magazines?
> *Dave*: Somebody that to me is false. That to me is somebody having to go with their flow, you know. I'm not too sure who they really are, so they've picked up on this image and pay £500 just to have this particular jacket, that probably looks stupid, because the magazine said: 'This is in. . . . You look fantastic!' And I'll pay for it just because of the label.

The ability to be analytical is what most clearly distinguished the groups in terms of their dispositions towards the cultural domain. As we have seen, this mostly operated along the lines of social class (confirming Bourdieu's argument about the role of 'taste' as a class marker). However, we also found that the kind of analysis that different groups offered depended upon their access to certain professional codes of expertise, and that, following Bourdieu's critics, other forms of disposition were available dependent upon experiences (in this case political) that are not determined by class relationships. This points to a complex relationship between reflexivity and the ability to hold a more analytical disposition that is mainly determined by class.

These features can be complicated further by arguing that the dispositions necessary to participate in contemporary culture are not only connected to the reproduction of distinctive consumptive relations but can also be derived from changes in production as well. As Scott Lash (1994) has pointed out, the demise of organized capitalism and its replacement with informational capitalism has meant that about a third of our society is excluded at the point of production as well as consumption. The result of being excluded from the labour market is not reflexive individuation but alienation. According to a range of commentators, including Campbell (1993), Lash (1994) and Segal (1990), it is precisely within these zones that lad culture is most likely to make its mark, with gang-bonding replacing the disciplines of work. Such a picture not only suggests that there are structural limits to the ambivalences of masculinity, as represented in the magazines themselves, but also in terms of their cultural spheres of influence.

An ambivalent space

Finally, then, we wish to suggest that the magazines occupy an ambivalent space in terms of contemporary masculinities in both a literal and a symbolic way. Don Slater (1997) has suggested that men's leisure pursuits (particularly their hobbies) are identified with times and spaces that are anomalous with respect to both home and work, occupying a space of 'ambivalent pleasure' for men who, because of recent economic and social change, no longer have a proper place at work or at home. Although there are important differences between men's hobbies – often expressed in terms of near-fanatical commitment – and their approach to magazine reading –

whose cultural significance is consistently downplayed as almost a non-activity ('just browsing', 'flicking through') – our understanding of men's talk about the magazines is certainly consistent with this sense of an ambivalent space of pleasure. From this perspective, the magazines' transience, represented as an essentially meaningless and mundane activity, is a central part of their appeal. Apart from 'sad' readers (including academics like ourselves) who take them too seriously, magazines and magazine reading represent a kind of metaphorical (and sometimes quite literal) space between the worlds of home and work from which many men feel an increasing sense of alienation.

Frequently read on trains and buses, or in some other semi-public space such as a doctor's waiting room or the hairdresser's, the magazines represent a commodification of men's leisure time through which the ambivalences and insecurities of contemporary gender relations and identities can be, at least symbolically, resolved. 'Private' consumption at home was consistently downplayed in our focus groups, with only a few participants describing the magazines as bedside reading: 'I tend not to bother. Unless I'm like at a railway station . . . I sometimes read them like round at other people's houses' (Sheffield 18-year-olds); 'I guess I must have picked them up and browsed through other people's. . . . *Loaded* was something that was passed around . . . I thought it was very funny' (London journalists); 'I used to read it [*Loaded*] just before I go to bed, that's the only time I read it. . . . I can go back and read old ones, the articles are that good. . . . I've got all my old ones' (Bristol students).

Through their emphasis on 'lifestyle', men's magazines implicitly address the tensions between domesticity (culturally encoded as feminine) and men's working lives. Men read the magazines for advice on improving their appearance, looking good and keeping fit, yet they distance themselves from taking such advice too seriously. Like the hobbyist who takes his obsession too far (satirized as an 'anorak' or 'nerd'), our focus group participants were constantly asserting the 'correct' way to read the magazines ('for a laugh', not taking things too seriously). The alternative, to be avoided at all costs, was to risk appearing 'sad' or a 'loser': 'it's just sad because it's about sex and the reason you're buying a magazine about sex is because you're not having sex' (Manchester lecturers).

If hobbies once served to 'domesticate' potentially dangerous masculinities, structuring men's leisure time, assimilating them to the world of consumer goods and maintaining their distance from useful participation in domestic labour (Clarke and Critcher, 1985), their significance is now more complex. The rise of *Playboy* magazine in the USA during the 1950s is often taken as a key moment of 'opposition' within this process, encouraging its readers to express their freedom from their imagined subordination to a (feminized) suburban ideal (cf. Ehrenreich, 1983). In a world where leisure interests of all kinds are increasingly commodified, magazine reading can no longer be represented as a simple escape from the serious worlds of paid work and domestic reproduction. Significantly, however, neither work nor home is treated seriously in the magazines. Work is represented as a semi-comical competitive struggle: 'It's a jungle in there: as in football, office teams have eleven positions to fill. But it's every man for himself' (*Maxim*, March 1997). Similarly, the home is depicted as a potentially dangerous world of female entrapment (as demonstrated in our discussion of magazine content in chapter 4) with consumerism represented as an appealing alternative to domestic responsibility and emotional commitment.

From this perspective, the magazines should be located centrally within the rise of contemporary consumer culture, with its seductive possibility of having 'the best of both worlds' (Sheffield clothes shop assistants), a way of buying yourself out of the contradictions of conventional gender roles and relations. Similarly, men's health problems are reduced to manageable proportions in the magazines, fragmenting the body into its component parts, each of which can be improved by purchasing the appropriate sports goods, fitness product or cosmetic.[28] For those with sufficient economic and cultural capital, one respondent insisted, 'it's the best time ever to be a man' (London journalists).

Besides these literal geographies, men's magazines also provide a way of traversing the ambiguous metaphorical spaces of contemporary masculinity and consumer culture. As the editor of *Stuff for Men* put it: 'small planet, loads of ideas, frequently churned out – what does it all mean? A planet chocka with stuff. And that's why *Stuff* is here: to help you navigate through a maelstrom of new things, sifting through the quantity to highlight the quality' (February 1997). The use of an ambivalent (ironic) mode of address here suggests a parallel between the men's magazines and earlier interpretations of the contradictory appeal of women's magazines where it has been suggested that:

[P]erhaps the women's magazine does a better job of speaking for women, of empowering their voices, than does the feminist scholar who has set this as her task. I am not suggesting that we see women's magazines as some emancipatory institution, as the site of authentic resistance to the patriarchal norm [but that] . . . as feminists we might

> learn from the women's magazine as a pedagogical model, one that
> meanders yet remains contained, that offers information within a
> heteroglossia of narratives rather than from a univocal position, that
> accumulates rather than replaces, that permits contradiction and frag-
> mentation, that offers choice rather than conversion as its message.
> (Radner, 1995: 135)

While there are few signs of 'authentic resistance' to the patriarchal
norm in the men's magazines or in the transcripts of our focus
groups, we would suggest that the 'heteroglossia of narratives'
revealed in our focus groups and in the magazines can be thought of
in terms of a number of contradictions and ambivalences whose
cultural and commercial significance should not be underestimated.

It is also through an analysis of these 'ambivalent spaces' that the
magazines may have their greatest political potential in terms of what
they signal for changing gender relations and identities. To reiterate
our earlier argument: while the call to be more open about their
health, relationships or attitudes to bodily display may not be new
for individual men, the magazines provide a public forum for new
ways of thinking about masculinity. Likewise, the magazines may
not represent a response to a historical shift in masculinities, as is
sometimes implied by the notion of a 'crisis of masculinity' – the
prospects of unemployment, ill health and emotional insecurity have
always troubled individual men. Rather, as we argued above, the
magazines can be said to have played a vital role in shifting the
discursive geography of masculinity into a more public arena, helping
men to develop their practical and discursive competencies in a more
reflexive and publicly mediated way.

The public availability of these new and ambivalent discourses
provides men with an opportunity for greater reflexivity regarding
the array of contemporary masculinities that are available to them.
Though it is hard to document precisely, we experienced several
examples of this process at the end of our focus group discussions,
once the tape recorder had been switched off, when men expressed a
sense of enjoyment at having been given an all-too-rare opportunity
to discuss their mutual concerns as men in a relatively public and
unthreatening forum. This confirms our view that the magazines
should not be interpreted in purely negative terms as a backlash to
feminism or as a crudely commercial response to contemporary
gender anxieties. For some men at least, we would argue, the
magazines have opened up a space for public debate about changing
masculinities in a way that has not previously been available in the
more formal political sphere. Moreover, we would claim that this

discursive space can be occupied in a variety of ways, not all of which are immediately colonized by the market. That these more open and reflexive forms of masculinity are regarded with ambivalence is confirmed by the fact that many of our focus group participants were resistant to the idea of needing 'expert' advice (coded as 'sad' by them). Consistent with the representation of laddish forms of masculinity as entirely natural and unconstructed, participants implied that men should be capable of producing such balanced and natural forms of masculinity for themselves.

Conclusion

The analysis presented in this chapter differs from the predominant tone of recent media commentary on the magazines which projects an unproblematic and undifferentiated image of 'laddish' masculinity (see chapter 2). Our research suggests a less homogeneous view of competing masculinities, characterized by ambivalence and contradiction, which we have attempted to clarify by drawing a distinction between discourses and dispositions. As well as exploring these contradictions and ambivalences as a metaphorical space, indicative of the instabilities of contemporary masculinities, we have also suggested that they may be thought of as occupying a material location in terms of the semi-public spaces in which men's magazines are read and the newly 'public' discourses (about men's health, sexuality and bodily appearance) to which they refer.

The magazines, we conclude, might usefully be thought of as one of the (metaphorical and material) 'spaces' in which different forms of masculinity are emerging and competing for public attention. For, as Slater (1997) suggests, the use of men's leisure time in magazine reading and other pursuits is located at a relatively weak point within masculinity, associated with significant pressures on men's changing roles within the privatized domestic context of the home and in the (increasingly uncertain) public world of work.[29] Located at this intersection, the magazines address their readers' anxieties and aspirations. In turn, as our focus groups suggest, different individuals and groups of men negotiate these ambivalent spaces in contradictory fashion, searching for advice and reassurance while celebrating a return to a more 'natural' form of (laddish) masculinity. These readings of men's magazines therefore have all of the ambiguity that Radway identified for women readers of romantic fiction, including its 'incipiently oppositional character'. To paraphrase Radway (1987:

113): reading men's magazines, though often portrayed in more individualistic terms, also represents a collectively elaborated male ritual through which men explore the consequences of their common social condition.

Finally, we are also aware that men's lifestyle magazines open out certain political questions, which we have discussed at greater length elsewhere (Stevenson et al., 2000a). Here, we would suggest that the political space opened up by the magazines is as ambivalent as the ways that they are talked about and the ideological contradictions that are evident in their content. This chapter has sought to articulate the magazines' ambivalence (rather than their neutrality or dominant ideological effects) when it comes to appreciating the discourses and dispositions with which they are associated. Politically, then, we are able to open up the problem of ambivalence in another sense, resisting the idea that there is anything to be done about the magazines, or hoping that they may eventually be replaced by cultural forms that might more directly meet with our approval.

While, in some readings, the magazines may be linked to the defensive persistence of certain heterosexual norms, they can also be read more ambivalently as embodying a number of fantasies about masculine behaviour and performance that continue to have a deep cultural purchase. For many of our focus group participants, we have argued, the magazines offer a form of constructed certitude, providing a sense of reassurance amid all of men's contemporary uncertainties and anxieties. Given our insistence on multiple meanings and fractured identities, however, we would not wish to exclude other interpretations, such as those advanced by Edwards (1997) and Nixon (1996) in relation to a slightly earlier generation of men's magazines. We return to these competing accounts in chapter 6.

Here, however, we conclude by suggesting that the magazines provide a relatively public zone of communication in which different individuals and groups of men are able to explore the contradictoriness of modern masculinities while simultaneously repressing certain key questions regarding their current construction. Viewed in terms of civil society, we might suggest that the magazines have opened up questions of masculinity for wider political debate than would have been likely had it been left to more 'official' channels of political communication. Following Bauman (1991), however, we accept that the ambivalence and disorder of the magazines and the diversity of 'readings' to which they are subjected, means that their political significance cannot readily be categorized.

6

Conclusion

The study of men's lifestyle magazines raises a number of related questions concerning media studies and cultural power, masculinity, and the study of commercial cultures. In this final chapter we seek to point to the contribution that our study has made to these overlapping areas of analysis. We shall argue that our study has identified a number of contradictions and ambivalences in respect of the study of popular culture. As we have already seen, our analysis seeks to articulate a complex position in between some of the dominant traditions within the sociology of culture and cultural studies. Our viewpoint derives not so much from an inability to make up our minds as from the complexity of our field of study and the messiness of the research process. It is, then, not surprising that terms such as 'ambivalence' and 'ambiguity' rather than, say, 'resistance' or 'ideology' have marked our study. In this concluding section, we seek to emphasize the contribution our research has made to a number of existing theoretical debates and research questions, while marking out our own distinctive contribution.

Mediated cultural power

Our study presents an analysis of men's lifestyle magazines that is not best captured by any one tradition within media and cultural studies. As we saw (in chapters 1 and 2), this study has sought to trace the specific rise of men's magazine cultures, while placing them within wider circuits of information flow. We also saw (in chapters 3 and 4) that the meanings generated by men's lifestyle magazines were both diverse and contradictory, while sharing a number of features in common. Further, as we have just seen (in chapter 5), our analysis of magazine consumption points to a number of key ambivalences and contradictions that made themselves present in the public discourses available to our focus group participants. This points to both continuous and discontinuous circuits of information that are available throughout our study. For example, the idea of laddism (which was widely seen by our respondents as a more 'natural' form of masculinity than more 'artificial' constructions such as the new man) suggested that the magazines were a key influence upon the cultural repertoires available to men in making sense of changing gender relations. Such an analysis enabled us to trace connections between the production of the magazines, their content and consumption by different audiences. The magazines are not trivial, as some critics of popular culture might claim, but a key ideological marker in respect of the reformulation of gendered relations. This is, of course, not to claim that meaning is delivered on a conveyor belt from producers to consumers, or that the magazines are the primary source of these discursive repertoires. It is, however, to suggest that during the course of our study the magazines were an important (if overwhelmingly contradictory) site that contributed towards the visual dimensions and cultural understandings of the changes taking place within British masculinities.

We also argue throughout the text that such an analysis only takes us so far, in that it ignores a number of more discontinuous features about the social production of magazines. Here, we might point to our analysis of the relationship between our position as researchers and the editors and focus group participants (as discussed in the Appendix); to the various contradictions being balanced by the editors (chapter 3); to the ironic content of the magazines, which serves to give men access to powerful male fantasies while subverting political critique (chapter 4); to the fact that hardly any of our focus groups discussed the health magazines (chapter 5); to the difficulty in working out whether the men were commenting on the magazines or wider media debates (chapter 2); and, of course, more generally, to the unstable and mundane nature of contemporary consumption. This list, which could easily be extended, points to the limitations of certain traditions within media and cultural studies which have either privileged processes of ideology and hegemony or the resistant practices of the audience (Stevenson, 1995).

Elsewhere, other commentators have sought to abandon questions of media power and influence, frustrated at the seeming impossibility of connecting up the uses of media and consumer goods with wider frameworks of ideology and power (Carrabine and Longhurst, 1999). Such arguments, while suggestive, discount the possibility of building different theoretical models that are open to the continuities and discontinuities of cultural power. Instead, we would argue for a new definition of cultural power that cannot easily be captured through the language of hegemony and resistance or focused exclusively on the actions and reactions of the audience. In its place we offer an analysis that traces a series of resonances across a wider media debate (chapter 2), in editorial style (chapter 3), magazine content (chapter 4) and in different 'readings' of the magazines which attempt to 'make sense' of the social production of magazine cultures (chapter 5). Our analysis has identified a number of ways in which the magazines can be inserted into wider sociological frameworks that attend to the distinctions that are evident within contemporary consumption, and the naturalization of laddish masculinity through discourses of 'constructed certitude'. These discussions refer to wider frameworks of cultural power that the media in general and men's magazines in particular both work within and help construct. The various dimensions that are evident within the analysis underline the necessity of ambivalence as a concept that helps define a field of research that is both open to the question of media and cultural power, while sceptical of sweeping statements that might be made in respect of media effects. We would argue, then, that the media and cultural industries are caught up in complex circuits of cultural power which need to be traced through empirically, given the instability and variety evident within diverse currents of information.

Masculinity and contemporary gender relations

Our research also provides a critical perspective on current debates about masculinity which appear to be divided as to whether or not we can talk about the end of patriarchy. Walby (1990, 1997) makes a distinction between public and private forms of patriarchy. Whereas private patriarchy is dependent upon the oppression of women by men in the household, public patriarchy is enforced through women's exclusion from public domains (the most important of which are the state and the labour market). As a result of the impact of the first wave of feminism (the struggle for basic citizenship rights granting an alternative to dependence), there has been a shift in orientation from private to public patriarchy. In our terms, masculinity is not so much achieved by having a dependent wife as through the ability to earn a 'decent' wage. Patriarchy is a complex system of social relations which makes itself present in the cultural sphere through, for example, the imposition of norms of sexual attractiveness upon women and the popularity of pornography amongst men, which reinforces their control over women.

Similarly, Connell (1995) argues that, despite the impact of the women's movement, rising divorce rates, the entry of women into the labour market and gay and lesbian movements, men continue to draw a patriarchal dividend. The fact that patriarchy can no longer be assumed but has to be actively defended should not prevent one from looking at the way men's interests continue to be supported through economic, political and cultural institutions. What Connell calls hegemonic masculinity is held in place by productive relations (continued patriarchal control over the distribution of wealth and property and the maintenance of social inequality), relations of cathexis (where certain forms of emotion and attachment continue to be marginalized and prohibited in mainstream society) and relations of power (men's continued dominance within the family and other institutions within civil society). Hegemonic masculinity, however, is not a static phenomenon but is an always contested, historically changeable, social practice that depends upon the continued subordination of other sexual orientations, complicity amongst most heterosexual men and the marginalization of other alternative masculinities.

Such analyses are useful in the present context in that they link the material benefits that men continue to reap from relations of dominance and cultural constructions of masculinity. In this respect, Connell advocates a political strategy involving the degendering of society (deconstructing the rigid polarities between masculinity and femininity) to allow a greater range of available sexual scripts and the promotion of social justice between men and women which recognizes how the gender system interlocks with other institutions that promote relations of inequality. Patriarchy, or what Connell calls hegemonic masculinity, is still firmly in place, despite recent sociological shifts and changes. Walby, on the other hand, gives the cultural dimension a more material and structured reading, arguing that it functions ideologically to enforce unequal social relations. However, other voices have argued much more forcibly that patriarchy is being systematically undermined.

Castells (1997), for example, argues that the patriarchal family, the focal point of patriarchalism, is being progressively challenged at the current time. He suggests, along with Connell, that the combined forces of the increased visibility of different sexual practices, the massive incorporation of women into paid work, growing control over biological reproduction and the new self-definitions offered by new social movements are the social forces that are redefining gendered relations. The shaking of heterosexual norms and the disruption of the patriarchal family (primarily through the emergence of singles lifestyles and households, divorce, the practice of living together without marriage and greater autonomy in reproduction) have meant that there is an increasing diversity of family types on offer. Whereas Connell hopes that patriarchy will be undermined through an alliance politics and Walby by the women's movement, Castells perceives that, despite men's continuing social privilege, a reactive politics is unlikely to serve their long-term interests. Unless men are willing to enter into more equal relationships with their partners, they have only two other options. The first is a deeper investment in male-only gatherings, which are likely, in the absence of women, to become spaces of nostalgic yearning for the more certain edifices of patriarchy, and the other is gayness. Whereas Castells views patriarchalism being torn down and ripped asunder by a multitude of social forces, Connell argues more traditionally that male dominance remains because it is in men's material interests. Yet the main problem with the analyses offered by Walby, Connell and Castells is that they are insufficiently concerned with the cultural dimensions and social construction of the current gender crisis. In this respect, both Walby and Connell reduce culture to the material effects of unequal structural relations, and Castells reduces the symbolic dimension to a number of instrumentally defined choices.

The renegotiations of heterosexual relations have also proved to be an important focus of attention in works by Ulrich Beck (1992, 1997) and Anthony Giddens (1991, 1992). Both point to processes of detraditionalization and individuation as being the key focus for the unfreezing and increasingly open nature of previously established patriarchal relations. Industrial society, they argue, was based upon a strict separation between public and private, with women largely excluded from the public and their identities being shaped by a rigid gender system. However, with women entering into the workforce after the Second World War, we are beginning to witness the break up of the gender system. This also releases men from being the sole supporter of the family and thereby unties the previously close connections between work, family and gender. The partial deconstruction of public and private worlds inevitably means that love becomes a more contingent social arrangement. Love, no longer colonized by economic necessity, becomes an empty sign that has to be filled in by the participants within a relationship. In this process,

Beck and Beck-Gernsheim (1995) argue, love has taken the place of religion as the central way through which modern subjects attribute their lives with meaning. Love relationships, then, are the places where we can be ourselves, gain intimate contact with others and find a place where we can belong. However, affective relations, due to the decline of overt class antagonisms, are also the places where individuals are most likely to experience intense conflict. This is largely because more equal relationships imply more freedom for women, but for men they imply more competition, more housework, less 'control' and more time with their children.

Like Beck and Beck-Gernsheim, Giddens (1992) argues that intimate relations in modernity have become increasingly defined around what he calls the 'pure relationship'. Giddens writes:

> A pure relationship has nothing to do with sexual purity, and is a limiting concept rather than a descriptive one. It refers to a situation where a social relation is entered into for its own sake, for what can be derived by each person from a sustained association with another; and which is continued only in so far as it is thought by both parties to deliver enough satisfactions for each individual to stay with it. (Giddens 1992: 58)

The pure relationship offers new opportunities and dangers for people of different sexual orientation, gender and sex. Yet what is clear is that whereas the pure relationship has been ushered in by women, men remain the 'laggards' in the democratic transformation of intimacy. Giddens argues that whereas men have been the carriers of romantic love (based upon idealization, seduction and conquest), women have largely heralded the emergence of 'confluent love'. Confluent love jars with romantic ideals that can be attached to the 'for-ever' notions often associated with romantic love. Confluent love presumes the messy forms of give and take that are necessarily part of any reasonably egalitarian relationship. However, as Giddens points out, traditional masculine identities are particularly ill-suited to taking up the challenge of confluent love given their desire for separation and independence.

A range of feminist psychoanalytic thinkers have pointed out that masculinity can only be born through crippling emotional repression. As Benjamin (1990) and Chodorow (1978) make plain, in order to become male the boy must repress his first love object (the mother) in order to identify with the father. This entails the rejection of feelings of dependence, vulnerability and intimacy with the mother. The emergence of a mentality of 'them' and 'us' when thinking about gender relations, and a fear of close emotional connections with others, become core features of the masculine psyche. The other, then, may become the object of manipulation and denigration, but not, as confluent love demands, reciprocally. Turning earlier psycho-analytic thinkers such as Freud on their head, it is now masculinity and not femininity which is the more difficult achievement and unstable construction. These formulations, it seems to us, make a substantial contribution to the debate. While Beck and Giddens remain overly distant from the actual formulations and ambivalences being played through in the cultural realm, they at least recognize the more chaotic and uncertain relations that are beginning to emerge between the sexes.

The symbolic and unconscious mobilization of fantasy structures (discussed in chapters 4 and 5) therefore opens out more contested and ambiguous spaces than may at first appear to be the case. Our argument points to a critical space between the cultural construction of sexuality and the reformation of material dimensions of power. Arguably, then, it would be mistaken to treat the magazines as either ideologically poisonous (that is to argue that cultural effects are unambiguous and can be 'read off' from content) or ideologically innocent (given their ironic subversion of political critique). Maga-zine culture opens up certain 'imaginative' responses and contradic-tions in respect of shifting contemporary gender relations that cannot be positioned as either the continuation of patriarchy or the blossom-ing of confluent love. Rather, what our study captures is both the commodification of contemporary gender anxieties (explored below) and an internally contradictory popular culture that offers a response to contemporary social change. The different discourses that are deployed by our focus group participants in respect of the magazines have a bearing on the frameworks of thinking and feeling that different individuals and groups of men used to make sense of the magazines as well as changes in contemporary gender relations and identities. Again, at this point, we neither seek to censor the maga-zines nor uncritically to defend their obviously complex influences. We are sympathetic to a cultural feminism that takes the magazines seriously, while remaining open as to how they may or may not fit into wider frameworks of power. For instance, as we have stressed throughout, the magazines provide men with an ambiguous zone of communication that makes publicly available a diverse set of endur-ing male fantasies about the body, work, women and sexuality. On the other hand, their knowing sexism and ironic reference (or cyni-cism) can be contrasted to attempts to politicize a range of social and cultural domains that underpin a diverse set of male relationships.

These considerations, we would argue, inevitably lead to a gender politics that recognizes the ambiguous pleasures of popular culture, while steering clear of some of the problems that have become associated with an uncritical populism.

Commercial culture

Looking back now on the study, we see that one of its most striking features is the historical and cultural specificity of the period under investigation. The project caught editors and the production process, the magazines, the members of our focus groups and, of course, ourselves as researchers during a particular political and cultural period. During the late 1990s so-called 'lad culture' in Britain was, arguably, at its height. The quality press and the new Labour government were becoming concerned about the excesses of the '*Loaded* generation', the tabloids were more sympathetic and the BBC had recaptured public attention with laddish shows such as *They Think It's All Over*, *Fantasy Football* and *Men Behaving Badly*. It was also a period when Oasis and Blur vied for superiority in the pop charts, England hosted the European soccer championships, Nick Hornby and Helen Fielding published popular novels on thirty-something gender trouble and, most importantly from our perspective, the market for men's lifestyle magazines was rapidly expanding. In this context, it was not difficult to get the conversation going within our focus groups as these magazines clearly connected into wider cultural trends and discourses, and had achieved a high public visibility.

While only a few of our focus group participants admitted to being regular readers, most had at least a surface familiarity with the magazines. This was described through fairly mundane practices such as flicking through the magazines, buying a copy for a train journey or even keeping copies at the side of the bed. While there were few 'committed' readers among our focus groups, nearly everyone to whom we spoke had at least glanced at a men's lifestyle magazine or had an awareness of some of the public debates that surrounded them. In particular, our distinction between discourses and dispositions allowed us to identify the common stock of knowledge that was available to most, if not all, of our focus group participants (their discursive repertoires) while allowing us to distinguish different ways of relating to these discourses (their discursive dispositions). In this respect, a key distinction amongst the readers was found to be social class. Working-class respondents were more likely to view the magazines as a mirror to their own lifestyle practices, or as resolutely not for them. Conversely, our middle-class participants (with some exceptions) tended to want to debate the magazines as an aspect of contemporary cosmopolitan commercial cultures. This marker was, however, overlain by more horizontal forms of communication (or discourses of sociability) that cut across questions of class through the different discourses and dispositions that allowed the magazines to be experienced as meaningful. Along this axis, it was not so much the magazines' ability to promote in-group solidarity and feelings of distinction that we found significant, but their capacity to 'naturalize' particular forms of masculine identity through the 'construction of certitude'. While these sociological markers are important, however, we do not wish to underestimate the specificity of the practices and discourses of consumption we encountered. Here, we would position ourselves with a range of critics who have pointed to a certain sociological reductionism that is evident in the study of consumption (Longhurst and Savage, 1996; Malbon, 1999).

A final consideration concerns the geographical as well as the historical specificity of our study and the possibility that the magazines might signify the emergence of particular place-specific masculinities. Besides the observation that these magazines are specifically British (in their sense of humour and approach to fashion, for example, as indicated by GQ's determination to distance itself from its sister magazine Vogue), our editorial interviews and content analyses confirmed the highly metropolitan nature of the magazines. Almost without exception, the editors celebrated the vibrancy of London's West End as a source of editorial and commercial stimulation. So, too, the list of stockists for fashion and other consumer items featured in the magazines rarely went beyond London and a few other metropolitan centres (Leeds and Manchester, for example, but rarely Birmingham or Sheffield). As one of our focus group participants declared: 'It's hard to be a new man in Rotherham' (Sheffield postgraduates). Other places featured as the focus of tongue-in-cheek travel guides (such as Stuff for Men's satirical guides to Bolton and Leicester), as venues for a weekend break from the metropolis, or as places to be avoided at all costs (such as the reference to Wolverhampton in Attitude's Dear Jools column, quoted in chapter 4). As Frank Mort's (1996) research suggests, the metropolitan nature of these new masculine consumer cultures may be as important as the liminal spaces in which the magazines are read or the new discursive spaces that the magazines have opened up (to which we have drawn particular attention in chapter 5).

How to research men's lifestyle magazines within the context of modern commercial cultures has been a question that has received increasing attention lately. Recent analyses (e.g. Nixon, 1996; Edwards, 1997) have attempted to establish whether the growth of the men's magazine market is better explained as a response to the rise of 'consumer culture' or as a reflection of changing sexual politics. Our own evidence suggests that men's magazines have succeeded commercially through the commodification of men's gender anxieties. As men have been encouraged to 'open up' previously repressed aspects of their masculinities, they face a growing sense of anxiety and risk to which the magazines have responded by providing a form of 'constructed certitude', or what one of our focus group participants referred to as a sense of false security (London unemployed men). Like other consumer goods, magazines provide a kind of cultural comfort zone, giving men the discursive resources to handle their changing circumstances and experiences. Given the uncertainties surrounding contemporary masculinities, however, the magazines have tended to hedge their bets, offering advice but doing so in a humorous or ironic way that avoids being taken too seriously, turning potentially unpalatable advice into a source of 'harmless fun'. This is as true of the delicate balance involved in editing the magazines (chapter 3) as it is of the diverse ways in which different individuals and groups of men attempt to 'make sense' of the magazines (chapter 5).

Such a view maintains a considerable distance from such recent high-profile studies as that of Faludi (1999), which, like our own work, look at changing gender relations and men's cultural responses. Faludi argues that men in American society have lost their communal function. Postwar society has 'stiffed' American men by making them a whole series of promises concerning their role in the family, the workplace and the political community, which it has failed to deliver. A society built upon patriarchy, which sustained male values such as stoicism, the need to protect and provide and make sacrifices for others, has been replaced by more consumerist ethics. The more productive aspects of postwar manhood, such as the need to contribute to building and sustaining a society, have been lost through a series of betrayals, under-fathering and the allure of celebrity culture. According to Faludi, American men are condemned to gain a sense of social worth largely free from the norms of their fathers' worlds and by participating in a consumerist culture. Men have lost a useful role in our public culture and have been 'invited to fill the void with consumption and a gym-bred display of his ultra-masculinity' (1999: 40).

While there is much to agree with (and to question) in Faludi's study, we shall confine ourselves to two points. First, while Faludi identifies social change in terms of decline and loss for men, men's magazines in Britain have been successful, in that they speak of some of the opportunities and pleasures that are available to contemporary men. While this is often caught up in a language of misogyny, irony and laddism, they are at least aware of some of the potential gains in autonomy that may currently be available for men with the appropriate cultural capital (as discussed in chapters 4 and 5). Second, while Faludi argues that contemporary men are oppressed by an ornamental culture, we have argued that, in the British context, a far more diverse set of cultural and commodified responses are available than Faludi seems to have identified in the USA. While we agree that the cultural realm continues to be defined in masculinist terms, she seems unaware of some of the pleasures, ambivalences and critiques that are available to men in a variety of different social spaces.

Finally, our study reveals, across a range of concerns, that both celebratory and moralistic dispositions towards contemporary commercial cultures are misplaced (cf. Jackson, 1999). Rather than identifying with either of these extremes, our research has uncovered a range of readings of the magazines that are indicative of some of the ambivalences and instabilities of contemporary masculinities. The magazines have succeeded commercially, we argue, through their symbolic resolution of these ambiguities, offering a form of 'constructed certitude', the constructedness of which is demonstrated by the magazines' characteristic use of ironic humour to distance readers from any serious commitment to personal or social change. As such, we reiterate, the magazines demonstrate the potential for significant change in gender relations and identities, while simultaneously reinscribing traditional forms of masculinity.

Appendix: Researching Men's Magazines

In this Appendix we describe how we carried out the research for *Making Sense of Men's Magazines*. For reasons that will become obvious, we are suspicious of other, similar research, which appears too tidy and straightforward. We consider it important to recognize what is often the hidden, unacknowledged, behind-the-scenes work of a project such as this. However, we are not just recounting our recruiting problems, the interviews that 'got away', etc., simply to impress the reader with our hard work, but in order to reveal the ways in which the 'research *as process*' – our assumptions, methods, problems, revisions of questions and so on – shaped the final product.

As Morgan (1983) argues, 'assumptions make messes research-able', as researchers can use their initial, pragmatic assumptions to make sense of the complexities of the research. We would add that *messes* make *assumptions* researchable, in that the messy way in which research occurs – the seemingly blind alleys, the apparent 'failure' of particular methods, the puzzling ambiguity of one's material – can enable the researcher retrospectively to examine their own assumptions and expectations about how the project would take shape. The ways in which we went about recruiting focus groups, for example, helped us, in retrospect, to examine our original assumptions of what the range of 'ways of reading' would be and what type of group would represent each particular way of reading. The difficulties we had in getting hold of anyone who described themselves as a 'committed reader' also led us to consider, in our final analyses, issues surrounding researching 'popular culture' and how we should be aware of our respondents' own perceptions about our roles as interviewers and of the project itself.

We are explicit about our methodology here for two broad reasons. First, we believe such an account, as honest as it is, can help other researchers embarking on similar projects. Second, such a discussion can and should raise questions about the processes of such research, and the wider methodological traditions of which this research is a part. Ideally, there is enough material available in this Appendix for readers to make their own evaluations.[1]

The project used three basic types of method: one-to-one interviews with magazine editors and writers, content analyses of the magazines themselves, and focus group discussions with a wide range of men (and a smaller number of women).

Editorial interviews

Editors were initially contacted by phone (usually via their PA) and if an interview could not be arranged over the phone there and then, this initial contact was followed up by a letter explaining about the project in more detail. Where possible, editors were also emailed. As we discuss in chapter 3, some of the more prominent editors declined to be interviewed. In these cases, we used press interviews and articles in order to glean appropriate information. As we were analysing the interviews in terms of how the editors represented their role and the magazine to us, rather than as a straightforward source of information, the ways in which they presented themselves in, or were presented by, the press, was equally useful and relevant to our research. Fortunately, the project coincided with an intense amount of press attention on these new lifestyle magazines, as we discussed in chapter 2. Frustratingly, one editor had gone on honeymoon when we arrived for the interview at the agreed time and place; another agreed to an interview and subsequently cancelled; and another never replied to our repeated requests for an interview.

Most interviews took place in the editor's office. One magazine website editor was interviewed by phone, and another via email. As with the focus groups, we devised a loose schedule of questions so that each editor was interviewed on the same topics (although we did discuss briefly with Gill Hudson, her thoughts on being currently the only female editor of a men's magazine). Each interview was transcribed and analysed separately by each of the researchers. The schedule of topics for discussion included the editors' personal and professional biography, the process of launching a new magazine, their target market, the relationship between editorial and advertising content, the magazine's style and concept of 'lifestyle', changes in contemporary masculinities, the reasons behind the current boom in men's magazines, the selection of cover images, questions of irony and the future of magazine publishing.

In the course of the project some further interaction with the magazine editors took place, providing access to a number of those who had declined to be interviewed. During interviews on Radio Sheffield, for example, Nick Stevenson participated in a discussion on men's happiness with the editor of the health magazine *ZM* (who advocated greater intake of zinc as the most effective means of promoting men's health and happiness), while, in a separate interview, Peter Jackson engaged in conversation with Phil Hilton, editor of *Men's Health*, concerning the balance between entertainment and advice in the magazines. (The conversation was provoked by Peter's suggestion that men's magazines offered 'quick and dirty' solutions to men's complex problems – a charge that Phil Hilton was keen to repudiate.) In this and other ways, we came to participate in the public discourses about masculinity that were the object of our study, reinforcing the need for the kind of reflexive research practices that we have attempted to describe in this Appendix.

Our analysis of the editorial transcripts and press interviews aimed to increase our understanding of the connections between the consumption phase of the 'circuit of magazine culture' (discussed in chapter 5) and the ways in which the magazines are produced, edited and distributed (the production phase of the circuit, discussed in chapter 3). We also undertook content analyses of a number of the magazines themselves, in order to triangulate our transcript material with our own analyses.

Content analyses

We used the regular meetings of the research group to photocopy and pass round what we took to be the most interesting articles from the magazines, concentrating on those that addressed questions of sexual politics (cf. Stevenson et al., 2000a). We added to this file of articles on a regular basis. Focusing on what seemed to us the prominent articles in the magazines gave us a way in to talking about their content. The magazines were very difficult to study in this respect, as they are not organized in terms of a coherent narrative. Men's lifestyle magazines are generally organized into sections (editor's page, pictures of women, jokes, fashion, reviews, items on consumption, feature articles, etc.), the order and construction of which are largely dependent upon the magazine in question. Our initial problem that the magazines (like soap operas) displayed little by way of narrative unity was partially resolved by collecting articles over a period of time. The sense of internal coherence was also enhanced by the emergence of the new lad. The shift in the magazines' overall style helped us track some of the more definite shifts in meaning. That is, the ideological coherence of the various texts could be found in metaphors associated with laddish lifestyles. However, as we saw in chapter 4, the figure of the new lad was not embraced in the same way by all the magazines.

By focusing on magazine content we hoped to reveal the different meanings that have become attached to the new lad from the point of view of the magazines. Further, by analysing certain stories, we hoped to give a more informed account of the magazines' actual content without relying only on the views of readers (and non-readers) or editors. This was considered important in order that the horizons of the texts did not disappear into the interpretations of either the editors or the participants in our focus groups. We would argue, then, that an analysis of the internal structural dynamics of magazine culture is a valid dimension of analysis. Yet it remains limited if it is examined in isolation from the other circuits of media production and consumption.

Our goal in respect of the magazines was to tap into some of the different narratives that have become connected with the magazines. We did this by concentrating on the way the magazines sought to create different positions for identification, constructing different subject positions and mobilizing particular fantasies within the text. Such an analysis sought to look at the magazines in terms of their corresponding ideologies without presupposing the effects that they had on their audience(s). In this respect, works by McRobbie (1982), Radway (1987) and Walkerdine (1990) were particularly helpful in framing our own analysis.

Recruiting the focus groups

Our principal methodology involved the recruitment of a wide range of focus groups. Initially, we had planned to do a number of small group-based interviews in Sheffield and in London. These cities have very different traditions and reputations: while Sheffield is a post-industrial 'northern' working-class city (as documented by Taylor et al., 1996), most of the men's magazines are London-based, as are many of their readers. Whilst recent developments in Sheffield, such as its developing 'cultural industries quarter' and the (struggling) National Centre for Popular Music, mean it is following its more fashionable neighbours, Leeds and Manchester, in trying to reinvent itself as a 'city of culture', we considered it to be different enough from London to be able to make comparisons between individuals and groups of men in both places. We also wanted to interview 'non-readers' or those who were not the magazines' target audience of young, white, metropolitan, heterosexual males, involved in or aspiring to successful, consumerist lifestyles. We wanted to know what unemployed men made of these magazines and how they were read by men from ethnic minority backgrounds, by older men, gay men and women.

Whilst we were aiming for diversity, we were not attempting to construct a representative sample of 'readers in Sheffield', 'readers in London', 'gay readers' and so on. What we wanted was as interesting a range of responses as possible, with which to study how these new men's lifestyle magazines were being read, used and talked about across a number of dimensions of difference.

Our first step was to construct a speculative 'wish list' of the types of groups we would like to talk to. After our first 'brainstorming' session, we came up with the following general categories:

- working/middle class;
- city/suburban/rural;
- northern/southern;
- casual/committed readers;
- anti-/non-readers.

Within and crossing over these general categories, we wanted, ideally, to encompass a range of the following variations:

- female readers/non-readers;
- gay readers/non-readers;
- ethnic minorities (readers/non-readers);
- different districts in Sheffield and London (e.g. trendy/non-trendy);
- men in fashion and media industries;
- men in health professions (including for example, bodybuilders);
- readers/non-readers of different ages – young/old, fathers/non-fathers;
- single men/men in relationships;
- religious groups.

Needless to say we did not manage to interview all of these 'types'. Nevertheless, such a checklist was useful when we went about recruiting our groups, and afterwards when we began the analysis, as we will go on to discuss. We had two main methods of recruitment. One was to distribute cards asking for people to talk to us, in newsagents and other shops (a doomed endeavour, as we explain below). The other was what Hermes (1995) and others have termed, 'snowballing' or 'friendship pyramiding', using our personal contacts (which proved more effective).

We asked colleagues, friends, friends of friends, friends of colleagues' friends, our students, anyone who said they read the magazines or had glanced through one in a doctor's waiting room, or who had never read one – in other words, we explored all avenues. Because of existing contacts in other areas, and particularly when it seemed that our card recruitment method was proving fruitless, we decided to change the initial remit of Sheffield and London and go further afield, eventually including Bristol, Derby, Manchester and Taunton. All these places offered opportunities to explore a different range of readings: Manchester is similar to Sheffield in that it is a deindustrialized northern city, yet its shopping and clubbing scene now arguably rivals that of London (Champion, 1990); Derby is also in the process of reinventing itself: the Saddlergate shopping area is now home to a significant number of new, up-and-coming designer outlets; Bristol, like Manchester and Sheffield, has a large student population, although it is arguably a more affluent, less 'trendy' city, with its anti-consumerist, reggae/'hippy' subcultures (Johnson, 1996); and Taunton is a large market town in the South-West, usually described in tourist brochures as 'sleepy', and more famed for cream teas than Calvin Kleins.

Such an approach yielded some interesting 'surprise' groups: whilst we were waiting for our group of student journalists, for example, we got talking to an avid reader of *Loaded* and a male model in the college café, who formed an interesting, impromptu focus group of very differing opinions concerning the magazine; a chance meeting with an old friend on a London tube resulted in another London focus group; a visit to relatives resulted in a large group interview of Taunton bikers.

Some groups failed to materialize, of course. Via one contact we had hoped to talk to high wage-earners with prestigious jobs in banking, but because of time and organizational constraints, this never happened. We also contacted the UK Men's Movement, which was at the time newsworthy for its condemnation of feminism as 'the greatest evil of this century',[2] and a women's group which had

debated at Sheffield Student Union on the Union's stocking of both
Loaded and the *Sun*. Both groups were contacted, first over the
phone, then via a follow-up letter, and then were phoned again, but,
in the end, we had to admit defeat. We spent a lot of time in the
early stages of the project waiting for people to get back to us
(editors and focus group participants alike), and there is a fine line
between asking contacts to 'help us with some research we're doing'
and hectoring them to do what we asked. Personal contacts proved
most fruitful, for the obvious reasons that friends are possibly more
likely to be willing to help out. With such contacts, too, a degree of
trust has already been established, although coming to a focus group
with this type of commitment has important implications for our
findings, as we will discuss.

For our other recruitment method, we devised flyers with our
address on the back, asking for anyone who had anything to say
about men's magazines to post the flyer back to us, including their
name, address, age and occupation, telling us why they bought – or
didn't buy – men's magazines. We planned then to organize the
replies into focus groups according to age, as age was thought to be
most significant in terms of shared cultural references and thus group
rapport, and according to readership. Ideally, we wanted a combination of group types: whilst our 'snowballing' methods would give
us pre-existing groups, such as friendship groups, the second method
would enable us to include groups we had arranged ourselves which
could include homogenous groups or regular/non-readers and some
non-homogenous groups, to see what debates and discourses
occurred.

We distributed 200 flyers in Sheffield and London. These were left
in newsagents, music shops, men's fashion shops, café-bars and
hairdressers. Some newsagents promised us that they would give the
flyers out when anyone bought a magazine. Within the first week,
we already had seven responses, and eventually the grand total of
returned flyers was eleven, including two illegible/joke replies (unless
Englebert Humperdink really was enjoying a drunken afternoon in a
Sheffield café-bar). Out of these, two were interviewed in their
workplace (a fashionable menswear shop) and seven agreed to turn
up to a focus group at the university. But even the promise of a £5
gift voucher – which we gave all our participants as a contribution
to their expenses – did not tempt those mysterious six potential
participants who had gone so far as to fill in the form, buy a stamp
and post the reply. In the event, only one turned up – and we later
discovered that the tape-recorder microphone had failed to work
after the first ten minutes of the interview.

Most groups were men only, although three (the London counsellors, London journalists and Bristol lecturers) were mixed gender and one group was women only (the Derby women). Our aim was not to focus on gender differences per se, but to explore different ways of talking about the magazines – hence our reference (in chapter 5) to 'men's talk' about the magazines might be more strictly cast as 'popular discourses'. Our eventual list of focus groups therefore encompasses a wide range of ages, sexualities, (dis)abilities, classes and ethnic backgrounds (see p. 110).

We have included our original checklist here as well as this final list in order to make a point about our own expectations of the different types of readers and non-readers we would find. For example, we wanted to talk to people 'in the media' expecting them to take a distanced or 'expert' view of the magazines. However, the group of journalism students we spoke to were much less distanced and more emotional in their opinions than we had expected, talking at great length about what they saw as the unacceptable (pornographic) content of the magazines. We also expected a group of young male, media studies students to be more likely to engage in debates about 'masculinity in crisis' and thus to be more ambivalent about the magazines than, say, a group of working-class Sheffield teenagers. However, despite being interviewed by their female ex-lecturer, the students were firm believers that what they had done 'about semiotics and all that crap' did not dampen their obvious enthusiasm for the 'pretty women' in *Loaded*.

So, whilst we tried to have an open approach to recruiting our focus groups, intending to investigate as wide a range of 'readings' as possible (rather than a representative sample), we referred back to this original list when beginning to analyse the transcripts, as it enabled us to be reflexive about our own prior assumptions and expectations of who read or didn't read these magazines and why, what differences we were initially expecting and so on.

Carrying out the focus groups interviews

Apart from the one card response and our pilot group of postgraduates, all the focus group interviews took place either at the participants' home or in their place of work. As Janice Morse observes: 'those doing research always cause some degree of inconvenience [and] self-consciousness for those who are being observed or interviewed' and therefore 'reciprocity is as essential in fieldwork as good manners were to our mothers' (1998: 147). Gifts, such as drinks, food or money provide an important message: 'I understand I am causing you inconvenience with my presence . . . please let me put it right . . . without you, I have no data.' Whilst Morse observes that in her case, it took 'a lot of donuts to get good data,' we gave our participants tea, coffee and biscuits, or wine and crisps (depending on the participants and the time of day) or bought drinks and snacks if the focus group took place in a café or bar. After the meeting, participants were given a feedback form asking them for any additional thoughts on the discussion and a £5 gift voucher. A voucher, rather than money, was, we felt, more of a 'thank-you' gift than a payment for time, and thus helped keep the situation as informal as possible. Handing it out with the feedback form was perhaps a subtle way of saying, 'please now feel obliged to fill in this form and send it back to us in return'. We did, in fact, get almost all our feedback forms returned.

All focus groups were tape-recorded and transcribed. Each session began with us introducing ourselves and the purpose of the project. Where possible, we took some magazines with us to act as a prompt or ice-breaker, which tended to work well: people would flick through them as they talked, or something in them would trigger off a conversation. At the very least the magazines were, in traditional waiting-room style, useful time-fillers for participants whilst we were setting up the tape-recorder or waiting for other people to arrive. Obviously, non-readers found them useful starting points, such as the journalism students who had apparently not read any before and thus were able to give us their initial reactions to the magazines.

The feedback form, given out at the end, had a number of functions. We asked each participant to fill in their name, occupation, ethnic origin, age, and area of the city or town in which they lived. This gave us useful information for groups of 'friends of friends', for example, whom we had not met before the focus group session and about whom we would otherwise have known very little. The form was designed to give us information that could be used to investigate the possible differences in readings or uses of men's magazines according to age, class, gender and ethnic origin. We also gave them space to jot down anything they wanted to say that they either hadn't thought of during the session, or felt they couldn't or didn't want to say in public. This material, such as comments on the questions asked and the structure of the session, was taken into account during our continual assessment of the questions we were asking, and how those questions were worded. Additional thoughts from participants were added as a postscript to that particular interview's transcript.

Usually, however, participants used the forms to give their views on the session itself, the most frequent comments being that they had found the focus group 'informal' and 'relaxed'. Finally we asked them to sign their agreement to our using the interview for research, assuring them of anonymity and confidentiality (via the subsequent use of pseudonyms). Giving out the form, and the voucher, was also a useful means of signalling closure of the session, when it seemed appropriate.

We devised a schedule of topics, so that instead of a question-and-answer routine we had a series of grouped headings on a theme, such as buying the magazines, thoughts on the imagery in the magazines, and so on (see figure A.1). Grouping the questions like this meant that, ideally, themes would arise as naturally as possible from the general discussion and the moderator could then introduce related topics in what would hopefully seem like an 'ordinary' conversational manner, and not as an abrupt change of subject. Having a set of themes like this meant they were easier to remember, so the moderator didn't have to keep referring to a list of questions, and also that, as far as possible, we could be sure that each of us was discussing the same themes at different focus groups.[3] Generally, the groups that seemed most successful were those – as both Hermes (1995) and Barker and Brooks (1998) have observed – at which participants felt like they weren't being interviewed at all but were just 'having a chat'.

Holding focus groups with personal contacts and groups of friends has its advantages and disadvantages. Because we were usually reliant on our 'contact' doing the recruiting for us, we could not really stipulate who would be there. Also, long-established groups of friends can have their own 'patterns of vocabulary' and can use the focus group as a springboard to continue long-running debates (such as the journalism students' pornography debate) or in-jokes (such as the frequent teasing of one of the Pimlico group 'trying to be an intellectual' whenever he attempted to be reflexive about his reading pleasures). In our experience, however, friendship groups tend to be more relaxed, are perhaps less reticent in voicing their opinions (unless the group dynamic forbids 'intellectualizing', of course) and, as we found, were easier to set up.

Introduction to the project and to each other.

- What magazines do you buy (if any)? When do you usually buy them? How do you read them (when, where)? Do you subscribe? What makes you choose one magazine rather than another one? When did you first start reading them? What did you read before?

- Have you ever bought/looked at/read any of these new magazines for men?

- What made you buy/look at/read it? Would you buy it again? Who do you think they appeal to?

- Why don't you buy these magazines? What would make you read them? What would your ideal magazine be?

- What do you like/dislike about the magazines? What do you think of the pictures/articles? Anything you particularly like/dislike/remember from those you've read?

- What would you say are the similarities and differences between the magazines? Who do they target? You? What would you like to see included that isn't already there? Anything that should be excluded?

- What are your thoughts about the images of men in the magazines? Do you think they show an 'ideal' of a successful man? What kinds of lifestyles do you think the magazines are appealing to?

- Have you ever talked about these magazines to anyone (partner, friends, work-mates etc.)? What do they think of them? What kind of things do you/would you talk about? What do you do with the magazines when you've finished reading them?

- How different are these magazines from other types of magazine (women's magazines, special interest magazines, top-shelf magazines etc.)?

- In the last ten years, many new men's magazines have appeared. Why do you think that is? Do you think men are changing? (in what ways?)

Figure A.1   Focus group themes

Thinking about the focus groups

Using focus groups has become an increasingly popular research method, generating a considerable literature, including authors such as David Morgan and Richard Krueger (Morgan, 1988; Morgan and Krueger, 1997; Krueger and Casey, 2000). Focus groups in the social sciences are essentially group interviews, with the focus on group interaction. The researcher supplies the topic, moderates the discussion and keeps it focused on the topic whilst enabling participants to say what they want, in order that the researcher can then gain insight into their 'natural vocabulary'. That is, the ideal focus group involves:

> a high level of group interactive discussion on a researcher-given topic, focused yet casual, moderated by the researcher who guides but does not lead, controls but does not inhibit the conversation, and who (among other things) ensures everyone has equal opportunity to express their natural vocabulary: in short, the researcher is a perfect combination of 'understanding empathy' and 'natural detachment' whilst the respondents are orderly, natural, interactive and utterly self revealing. In other words, impossible. (Barker and Brooks 1998: 24)

Talking about magazines is one thing. To talk about them to university researchers is a different kind of commitment. Even before the interview itself, the means by which we contacted a potential focus group inevitably set up expectations as to who we were and what we wanted: were we, for example, friends and colleagues, even relatives, asking for help on yet another project, or were we 'humourless feminists' and/or 'new men' looking to 'prove' how the magazines corrupted the young. Or were we simply misguided, ivory tower researchers doing one of 'those' trendy media studies projects on the blindingly obvious. The fact that we had got a grant to study men's magazines was greeted with amusement not only in the magazines themselves but also by our colleagues, as Frank Mort (1988) also found when embarking on his original study of men's style magazines in the 1980s.[4]

In the end, our data could be criticized as being mostly of university-educated and/or middle-class participants. Inevitably, since we work in universities, our social networks are heavily biased in this direction. Second, perhaps, to be prepared to discuss opinions with university researchers is a social activity involving particular skills and is therefore a situation in which those who are not used to participating, as students or researchers, may not feel comfortable. In addition, since we relied heavily on personal contacts, some of the groups were perhaps there simply to 'help out' and thus didn't feel they had much to say on the magazines themselves. As Hermes (1995) found, attempting to talk to people about a leisure pursuit which is commonly assumed to be about escapism, relaxation, something you 'just do' when you don't really want to do anything else, can be a difficult and frustrating phase of one's research. Perhaps also, participants may have felt self-conscious about talking about their pleasures in the magazines, with a female friend or colleague.

The most common response to our request to join a focus group was the reply: 'well I don't really *read* the magazines . . .'. Initially, in the early stages of the project when we were trying to set up the focus groups, this seemed like a major stumbling block. However, the frequency of this response raised interesting questions for the project in general. Hermes writes of her surprise that after her first set of interviews with readers of women's magazines, she also found that readers did not have much to say. This leads her to question what she calls, the 'fallacy of meaningfulness' within such research traditions which may therefore exclude 'theorising the mundaneness of media use'. In other words, for Hermes, the relationship that readers had to women's magazines was marked by meaninglessness and mundaneness, where readers neither absorbed nor actively resisted any textual 'message': reading magazines was an endlessly repeated, but purposeless, routine activity. Janice Radway's (1987) study of women readers of romantic fiction also reports on how such books can be put down and then picked up again quite effortlessly. However, a key part of the story that Radway tells is the importance of reading in negotiating leisure time for women (a refuge from household duties) and the significance of the romantic narratives themselves. Thus readers strongly valued (even to the point of reading the end of the book first) a strong yet nurturant idea of masculinity which allowed the readers 'the experience of being cared for' (1987: 97). As these examples suggest, there are many ways of 'reading' the readers of magazines and popular fiction.

Our transcripts initially seemed to be saying the same thing as Hermes: that magazines were there to be flicked through. Noone seemed to take them seriously. Even the act of choosing and buying them was relatively 'meaningless': as one participant said: 'If I'm bored . . . because usually I'm doing something all the time and if . . . I'm just sat here, I'll pick up something to read . . . [but] it's the same old crap in a different cover.' However, unlike women's magazines, which have after all been around for over a century and are tradition-ally part of women's domestic culture (often handed down from mother to daughter), men's magazines were not only relatively new but also somewhat controversial. In fact, our findings reveal consider-able ambivalence in the way these magazines are consumed. On first looking at the transcripts, it seemed significant to us that, despite their newness and the controversy surrounding them, the overwhelm-ing majority of our participants appeared to treat men's magazines as mundane. That is, while the magazines are seen as meaningful, readers rarely (if ever) remembered specific articles or story lines (like Radway's women). This puzzle led us eventually to develop our analytical tools of discursive repertoires and discursive dispositions, and also to explore our own positionalities within the project, as we now go on to discuss.

Reading the transcripts

Initially, all three members of the research team listened to the tapes and read the transcripts repeatedly, independently noting key phrases, ways of talking, patterns of responses and so on, meeting regularly to discuss a number of transcripts at a time. We also made notes after each focus group, concerning our own reactions to the group, a brief summary of what had been discussed and what we had thought of each session. This served as extra information on the group, 'back-up' if some of the tape was unclear, and was also an attempt to address the sticky issue of interviewer/interviewee relationships.

Early on in the project, we had considered, and rejected, using the types of computer packages that identify frequency of phrases, links and associations. It was important for our mapping out of discourses and dispositions that we acknowledged, for example, the possibility that frequency does not always equal significance: a long-established group of gay men, for example, who met regularly as an informal discussion group, would not feel the need to repeatedly articulate how they read magazines 'as a gay reader', but would take that articulation as implicitly assumed by the group.

When we began to look at our transcripts more analytically we needed to decide what segments of interviews were meaningful: to be sensitive to individual responses, and the ways in which individuals voiced those responses, and also to how they positioned themselves and their responses in relation to wider discourses and social practices. In addition, we also wanted to try to understand why so many of our participants, even those who read them regularly, talked about their lack of commitment to the magazines, as it seemed that there was more to this than Hermes's (1995) assumption of her readers' relatively meaningless 'everyday routines', given the supposed newness of men's lifestyle magazines and the public controversy surrounding them, as reflected in the media discourses reported in chapter 2.

In her analysis, Hermes develops the notion of 'interpretive repertoires', as 'ways . . . of talking about women's magazines, recon-structed from interview fragments. . . . [T]he cultural resources that speakers fall back on and refer to. Which repertoires are used depends on the cultural capital of the individual reader' (1995: 3). However, when we began to look at the ways in which speakers positioned themselves in relation to *us*, as well as in relation to the magazines themselves, we found that whilst participants referred to culturally specific 'repertoires' of reading – celebratory, condemna-tory and so on – they did so in different ways. They would use phrases such as, 'you know what I mean' or 'it's one of those things . . .', acknowledging that ideas, responses, ways of talking do not exist within each individual as self-contained or internally con-sistent, but as part of a wider social context, in which we as researchers played a part. We were, in other words, either assumed to share their position ('you know what I mean') or to be naively unaware of it ('what men really want . . .') or defensive of it ('I know it's sad/sexist but . . .') and so on.

Whilst recent work on women's magazines and their readers advocates for the researcher a position of 'celebration' or 'respect' versus the 'modernity discourse' of concern (Hermes, 1995), our relationship to readers of men's magazines was often more ambiva-lent.[5] It was, after all, our desire to explore our own ambivalences about the ways in which these magazines could be read in terms of contemporary masculinities that had inspired the project in the first place. Thus, a post-focus group debriefing often helped us examine our own positions in relation to these magazines and their readers, and also served as an opportunity to off-load any particular frustra-tions from the experience, when for example one's neutral stance as an interviewer meant having to listen, but not respond, to sexist and occasionally offensive remarks about what 'you women' were like, the 'failures' of feminism and so on.[6]

It is important, then, to say something more about our own subject positions and feelings towards the magazines and their readers. For example, many feminists have pointed towards the idea of sharing experiences with their research participants. This is particularly evident in a series of studies where the researcher describes herself as a fan of a particular cultural form (e.g. Ang, 1982). Like Gray (1992) and Walkerdine (1990), they have offered a more reflexive account of their involvement with different cultural forms and the partici-pants in their studies. Ours is a potentially more complex problem in this regard, as our research involves the labour of three different researchers. We thought it important at this point to speak in our own voices, to talk of the different levels of investment we had in the magazines and the project as a whole. This is done not to overly personalize the account, but to make the reader aware of some of the tensions within our own positions.[7] Also, given that we are committed to demystifying the research process, we want to confront our own positionalities in order to allow the reader to make their own evaluations of our work. We also want to point out that our personal differences enabled us to discuss the magazines in an open and fruitful way, and that the degree of commonality was enough to make the research possible and highly enjoyable. In other words, we found that tensions between researchers can be productive as well as difficult and troubling.

Peter Jackson

My interest in men's magazines dates back to January 1990 when the British edition of GQ first went monthly. Researching a paper on the cultural politics of masculinity (Jackson, 1991), magazines like GQ provided an opportunity to explore alternative (non-hegemonic) constructions of masculinity. This period coincided with the emergence of the much-hyped 'new man' and some softening of the boundaries of dominant models of gender and sexuality. The sense of optimism which this generated at the time was subsequently eroded during the course of the current project. This was partly as a result of changes in the magazines themselves, as the commercial success of Loaded led to changes in the content and style of all the other titles. But it was also a response to the unrelenting sameness of the magazines whose content seemed remarkably unvaried from month to month.

As a project, we had subscribed to around a dozen monthly titles which meant that a new magazine was arriving every two or three days. Aside from the sarcastic comments of colleagues who questioned the seriousness of the research (while casting their eyes over whichever magazine happened to be on my desk at the time), it proved hard to remain enthusiastic about the magazines or to maintain our commitment to reading each issue of each magazine as it arrived. As our focus groups and interviews soon made clear, the magazines were not intended to be read in this way and it is perhaps no surprise that my initial sense of reading for pleasure rapidly diminished.

The level of media interest in the magazines gave a fillip to the research, as the launch of each new title generated its own trail of publicity. But the magazines themselves were a disappointment, conforming to what came to be known as 'laddish' versions of masculinity rather than sustaining their early promise of providing a space for exploring new and more progressive alternatives. My enthusiasm was rekindled by the response of our focus groups, where it became clear that the magazines were being read in a variety of ways, not all of which corresponded with the predominantly laddish way of making sense that was being emphasized in the press. Our emphasis on ambivalence and contradiction allowed us to differentiate more clearly among the magazines and between different readings, allowing me to remain optimistic about the discursive spaces that the magazines have opened up for thinking about masculinity in new ways, even though this is not the predominant way in which the magazines are read. A 'professional' interest in magazine culture came to replace a more 'innocent' sense of reading for pleasure. This is rather different from feminist accounts of women's magazines where much of the analysis has focused on the 'guilty pleasure' of reading for enjoyment or escapism. As the project came to an end, I found myself still stimulated by the focus group discussions but much less interested in the magazines themselves.

Nick Stevenson

My interest in the magazines began in 1995 when I started to buy *Maxim* and *FHM*. I had been aware of some of the debates about 'new men' and 'lifestyle' in connection with some of the more upmarket titles, but had never read these with much personal interest. I suppose I perceived them to be about a metropolitan lifestyle that seemed far removed from my own as a lecturer in Sheffield. *FHM* at this time was quite different from the magazine that appears on the shelves today and was possibly targeted at professional men like myself. *Maxim*, on the other hand, was more overtly laddish but seemed less downmarket than *Loaded*, which I was aware of but did not buy. I kept the magazines that I bought literally 'under the bed', as my partner at the time did not really approve of them and our conversations would often end in sharp disagreements. I enjoyed reading the magazines but was worried about the fact that they seemed to be overtly politically incorrect, and that the conversations with my partner were becoming increasingly heated.

On a more unconscious level, the magazines tapped into different levels of my psyche. I remember after a hard day dashing home with a magazine and opening it up with a sense of excitement. They seemed to be telling me that being a man could be great fun, enjoyable and not dogged by guilt or ethical complexity. However, when I put the magazines down I would start to feel depressed at the thought that my life at least did not seem to be quite so straightforward. I was also aware that many of my male friends were also buying the magazines and had a less concerned attitude than my own. I was often told I was taking them too seriously or that I was a typical academic in that I just didn't know how to enjoy myself. I became acutely aware that the magazines provided an interesting cross-over point between my academic and more personal interests. Again, I think unconsciously, I was motivated to discover how 'other' men might enjoy the magazines in a more guilt-free way and how this connected to different definitions of masculinity.

For the project, as we have already mentioned, we subscribed to all the current titles. This proved difficult, as in 1996 and 1997 a new magazine seemed to appear each week. Probably because I had to read so many of the magazines and because of their increasingly laddish nature, I quickly went off them. At this point I felt it necessary to distance myself from some of the material in the magazines in order to 'make sense of them' and because if you read too many of them they quickly become repetitious and boring. In particular, I went through a period of thinking that *Men's Health* was the acceptable face of men's magazines, only to become disturbed by its obsessive stress upon bodily perfection. This was during a period when I became ill (taking 9 months off work) and was becoming increasingly aware of the 'limits of the body' during my late thirties. During this period, I didn't take much pleasure in reading the magazines and became irritated by the slavish way they all seemed to follow the market leader. However, at this point, I was (like Peter Jackson) more interested in what our focus groups were saying about the magazines. This gave me some impetus to think about them again, but reading them seemed more like an arduous task than a form of pleasure. That is not to say I did not gain pleasure from analysing the magazines, but that they were more like work than relaxation.

Towards the final phases of the project, I began to enjoy reading the magazines again. While I had no particular favourite, I found myself buying at least one magazine a month, usually as a treat to be enjoyed on a train journey or as part of an evening in. Over the course of the project I built quite a collection of magazines, which I displayed on a coffee table in my hallway. My new(ish) partner also developed a curiosity with the magazines and we occasionally read them together, laughing with and against them. However, there have also been moments when we have shared our 'concern' about the ways in which both men and women are represented. Our conversations have moved quickly between laughter and deeper forms of reflection. I have also noticed how many of my male friends have initially made fun of the pile of magazines only to be found reading them later. Their responses, you will not be surprised to hear, often come close to those we discovered in the focus groups.

It's not that I don't think there are many critical questions you could ask of the magazines politically, it's more that I have learnt that they can be fun too. That is, the magazine's glossy and visual nature can be enjoyed, while I also realize that there are a number of more political questions that might be asked. Doing the project has enabled me to develop a more reciprocal relationship between my identity as an academic and as a fan of the magazines than might otherwise have been possible. My own relationship to the magazines would resist the idea that they can only be read by people of low intelligence or misogynists, while maintaining a concern with their evident sexism and depressing cultural conservatism. For me, the magazines are part of an ambivalent social experience.

Kate Brooks

Like Nick and Peter, I had a much more optimistic approach to the magazines when the project began. My initial impression of them was that they seemed to reflect contemporary culture in a much more entertaining and relevant way than did women's glossies, which relied on the standard formula of make-up tips and advice on 'getting your man to commit'.

Loaded, in particular, played around with the conventions of such formats. So I was interested in finding out about the magazines, both in terms of how they represented a new generic form, and also in terms of who they were read by, and what they represented, to readers and non-readers alike.

What seemed to change, I think, during the time this project was carried out, was the way in which such magazines stopped being satirical, and became more blatantly sexist. When the project began, for example, *Loaded*'s strapline was 'for men who should know better' – an almost self-deprecating acknowledgement, I had assumed, that feminism had changed things, and that these magazines were for self-indulgent 'guilty enjoyment' and not therefore an outright reactionary backlash to feminism itself. By August 1999 the strapline read: 'for men who should knob better' – an indication that such self-deprecation and defensiveness are no longer necessary.

Throughout 1997, we read thirteen magazines a month, and also gathered as many press articles on the magazines as possible, during the time when tabloids – and some broadsheets – were celebrating them as heralding the end of humourless political correctness. This celebratory mood could also be found in the focus groups. As I carried out the majority of the focus groups, I seemed to spend most of the time being told how 'feminism had failed' or was 'irrelevant', or indeed had 'prevented' men from saying and doing what they wanted when feminism had 'gone to the extremes' in the 1980s. Then I would go home and read press cuttings which also told me that 'at last' there was 'no need' to 'bang on about feminism'. On more than one occasion I found myself wondering where exactly I had been to miss this apparent Golden Age when feminism was taken so seriously by everyone that men had been severely oppressed by the experience.

Nevertheless, I found it difficult to voice my growing dislike of the magazines, mainly because it was difficult to argue against the common-sense notions of the magazines as 'harmless fun'. Like Nick and Peter, I was accused of taking them too seriously, of not getting the joke and so on, and also accused of being envious of the bodies of the women on display. This last point possibly has some truth in it, as having to look at page after page of young, toned, tanned, female bodies did begin to affect me: having never been a regular reader of women's glossies, I realized I had managed to avoid a lot of the anxieties perpetuated by these magazines about one's appearance and, especially, ageing. Now, faced with image after image of the 'Top 100 Babes', of pull-out posters of lingerie models, of pin-up calendars and the like, I began to look at myself much more critically than I had done before, and was also irritated with myself for doing so, when I should 'know better'.

Unlike feminist studies of women's pleasures in popular culture, which tend either to be concerned studies aiming to 'enlighten' their subjects, or celebratory in that such pleasures are championed as forms of 'resistance' to the dominant patriarchal norms, our position here is, I think, a difficult one to define. In retrospect, I think I would have liked to have spent more time during the project talking about how we each felt about the magazines and the readers, and I wonder to what extent the fact that I was a female assistant working for two men on a study concerning new forms of masculinities made us all feel self-conscious about doing so. Like the groups of friends we interviewed as focus groups, I think we also usually skirted the issue with ironic banter, which made the working experience enjoyable, if not as reflexive as we perhaps could have been.

There were times that year where I felt almost overwhelmed by the amount of sexist images, jokes, and stories I was having to read and look at. I do think there are parts of some of these magazines which are witty and amusing and enjoyable, and perhaps if I had read the odd one like a 'normal' reader I wouldn't have spent most of the time feeling permanently bemused and negative about what I was reading and hearing. I am glad I did read them and that I carried out most of the focus groups, because now I know not to take what I have assumed were the gains of feminism for granted, and that I still have to argue my position in the face of common-sense sexism about what men and women are 'really like'.

For me, this project raised important issues about the nature of the relationship between researcher and researched, which I am still fascinated by. I can't say, however, that I still read any magazines – although I did enjoy *Men's Health* which at least acknowledged that men have relationships with women they like and don't necessarily refer to as 'the missus'.

These quite different (if overlapping) accounts not only point towards our different relationship with the magazines, but also hint at some of the mistakes we might have made. On the whole, they emphasize that our different takes on the magazines are poorly represented by a wholly oppositional stance (the magazines as a false ideology) or as fans (the magazines as pleasurable texts we all enjoyed). The shifts in our own accounts over the course of the project and the differences between them are all evidence of how 'ambivalence' became such a key word during the research process. Unlike Hermes, then, we are unable to separate questions of concern and critique from those of respect, given that we all took the gendered nature of the magazines seriously. The line we were all seeking to hold was an investigation of the magazines that was attendant to certain ideological features, while being aware of the different forms of subjectivity they helped open out. Further, and surely a point worth making, is that the different genders and experiences of the research team were a definite bonus for the project. We were motivated to investigate our own responses to the magazines and use our different subjectivities to ask different questions of the research process. Our aim here was to produce knowledges of men's magazines that resisted bland descriptions of reading patterns, but also to break with essentialist accounts of gender identities. In this respect, we follow Hearn (1988: 808) in the hope that 'it might be possible for men to work towards forms of knowledge that are different from yet overlapping with women's'.

Given that Kate Brooks undertook most of the focus groups, we also share McKee and O'Brien's (1983) concern that a female interviewer of men is sometimes put in a difficult moral position. McKee and O'Brien's own experiences as female researchers interviewing fathers led them to feel that by adopting the traditional stance of a 'non-judgemental viewing mode' they had felt powerless and uneasy about their 'silences and failures' in not challenging men about their sexist remarks. However, we would argue that it is perhaps at the level of analysis, rather than interview, that is the appropriate and most effective place to challenge the sexism of our respondents, through investigating the ways in which such talk is articulated, justified or defended in interaction (as for example, 'common sense' in the face of the academic's assumed naiveté, or disapproval). To take up a challenging position at the focus group would contravene the implied contract of neutrality set up beforehand, where we have asked participants to come along and talk to us about their magazine reading and pleasures, not to come along and justify to us or be challenged by us. Plus, we would perhaps get little in the way of useful material.

We would also take issue with McKee and O'Brien's assumption that an easy division can be made between 'neutral' interviews and 'challenging' interviews. Since complete neutrality is impossible, we obviously *did* respond to sexism and other offensive remarks, either inadvertently through body language such as facial expression, or jokingly in the form of a laugh, grimace or ironic response. Furthermore, we need also to consider how far sexist remarks were said in order to 'wind us up' as 'right-on' academic researchers, or indeed, as 'hypocritical' or naive New Men, who needed to be reminded what women were 'really' like.

Similarly, we question McKee and O'Brien's assumption that this is necessarily a 'male–female' issue, not only to get away from the well-worn and unhelpful cliché, which can be summed up as 'women are sensitive and good; men are sexist and bad', but because we also think it necessary to explore the issues of men interviewing men about masculinities.

Further, we should also add that Nick Stevenson was present at about a third of the focus groups (running a number on his own). This raised a related if different set of questions in terms of the relationship between the researcher(s) and members of the focus groups. First, the question of sexism was evident again, and there was a concern that, as a male researcher, Nick might become complicit with such assumptions. However, we also noticed that participants were likely to correct themselves as there was an assumption that we would all be 'new men' given that we work in a university and are evidently studying gender. During one group moderated by Nick (the Turnpike Lane graduates) the discussion was interrupted by a phone call. The participants asked for the tape to be turned off and a telephone conversation began between a member of the household and his girlfriend. When the call was over one of the group remarked that 'she's always ringing up when she thinks we are having fun'. There was then a pause and a lot of laughter after one of the group remarked that that was a potentially 'incriminating statement'. Such an incident could be interpreted in a number of ways. First, it is evident that the men are 'enjoying themselves' and that the focus group was working well in a conversational and relaxed atmosphere. Second, that the moderator's role in respect of the rest of the group is unclear. There are evidently two competing assumptions about the role of a man running a focus group. The first is that their shared masculinity tied moderator and participants together in their evident enjoyment of the magazines and as a group of men who are of similar ages. The second, which emerges through the laughter, is that there is a suspicion that the moderator was trying to catch them out or stitch them up. In other words, the moderator was viewed less as a person facilitating discussion and more as a potential source of normalization. The men therefore would need to be careful not to reveal too much. This then articulates a slightly different set of concerns from the groups that were moderated by Kate. During the focus group sessions with a male researcher there was a concern on the moderator's part about being seen as complicit with overtly sexist language without wanting to act in a way that was censorious. This placed us in an inevitably contradictory situation. That is, it put the researcher in the potentially impossible situation of running a focus group without conveying a sense of mutual agreement or outright disagreement. Further, it was also important to listen to what the men had to say without turning them into 'others'. There is a tendency in some research into masculinity to convert the subjects into hapless victims of ideological strategies that are easily seen through by the researcher. More broadly, as male researchers, both Nick and Peter would argue that many of the men in our focus groups were dealing with sets of complex contradictions that we were also aware of in our own lives. That is, while we did not always agree with what we heard, we did not see it as our role to try and police the men into a less polluted form of masculinity.

Transcript analyses: discourses and dispositions

Having independently noted key phrases, and discussed with each other our interpretations of the significant aspects of each interview, we would then label these key phrases as 'markers', where speakers were, for example, positioning themselves according to their assumptions of us and our positions, or in reference to an assumed common-sense discourse about what the magazines represented. Such markers enabled us to start to identify particular repertoires (e.g. reading the magazines as 'harmless fun') and also take into account the possibility that articulating such a repertoire did not necessarily mean it was endorsed by the speaker ('we're supposed to think these magazines are just a laugh'). Thus, we argue, participants took what we term 'discursive dispositions' to the available, publicly acknowledged, 'repertoires'.[8]

We then began the process of mapping out the discourses and dispositions, and investigating the puzzle of non-committal readers, by asking questions of our transcripts. For example, when people say they aren't *readers*, does this mean we should talk more about 'using' rather than 'reading' magazines? After all, flicking through a magazine in the bathroom, or whilst waiting for the kettle to boil or watching TV or while waiting to see the doctor (because, as one participant said, 'you have to read something, you're too embarrassed to look someone in the eye'), or even looking at the pictures of women in a magazine in bed when – as one respondent put it – 'now't else was happening' with your partner at that moment, are all very different ways of 'using' a magazine, which can't necessarily be talked about accurately as just 'reading'.

To describe oneself as 'not *really* a reader' might also be interpreted as a defensive rejection of such categorizations, positioning oneself in this instance as not one of 'those' readers of 'those' magazines. During the course of this project (1997–9) men's magazines were often in the press – their phenomenal success, their seemingly controversial stance of 'anti-political correctness' and their association with hedonistic forms of 'new laddism' meant that such magazines might be assumed to be both controversial and 'trashy' by academics, especially feminist academics. As we have already suggested, any study of popular culture tends to be treated in the common-sense discourses of the tabloid press, either as an absurd search for meaning where it's obvious there isn't any, it's just for fun, or where it is automatically assumed that any study must be looking to prove the harm of such forms – particularly in research on popular films. Such cases are usually mocked both for their pretentious 'reading into' the text, and for their assumed search for damaging effects on the audience.[9] Similar problems beset this project, as we were regularly regarded as 'sad' academics who failed to share the magazines' and their readers' sense of humour because our assumed political correctness prevented us from seeing that the magazines were meant to be enjoyed as harmless fun with little if any political significance.

We did, however, find that for some groups, the opportunity to talk about masculinities as participants in our focus groups had been an interesting and novel experience. For example, one group of established friends told Nick Stevenson after the session that they had never before talked like that between themselves. Similar comments on our feedback forms, given out at the end of the session, described the experience as 'enlightening', 'stimulating', 'thought-provoking', 'informal and honest'. So, whilst our respondents tended to be keen to distance themselves from the magazines, participating in the focus groups had the potential to raise their awareness of gender issues in ways that might not otherwise have occurred. As one man wrote, for example, 'this is a topic I had not considered before – as it turned out I had some fairly strong opinions!'. We can conclude, then, that the focus groups did not simply mirror everyday conversations that might have taken place, irrespective of the research context, but that research can itself play a role in opening up new discursive spaces in which to reimagine and, hopefully, 'make sense' of the changing shape of contemporary masculinities.

Notes

1 Introduction

1 We recognize that the terms 'lad' and 'laddishness' are problematic. While they are analytically problematic, however, the terms were in widespread usage during the late-1990s. Commonly employed in media discussions of the magazines (as discussed in chapter 2), the terms also had a clearly understood and widely shared popular meaning (as is confirmed by our focus group evidence, discussed in chapter 5).

2 Feminist accounts of magazine reading as 'very specifically associated with femininity and *women's* culture' reached similar conclusions: 'Men do not have or need magazines for "A Man's World"; it *is* their world, out there, beyond the shelves: the culture of the workplace, of politics and public life, the world of business, property and technology' (Winship, 1987: 5–6).

3 'Lifestyle' is defined by Chaney (1996: 4) as 'patterns of action that differentiate people', 'embedded in a culture of consumerism' and 'invested with ethical and aesthetic significance' (ibid.: ix–x). Interviewed in the *Guardian* (8 November 1993), the late Michael VerMeulen, founder editor of *GQ*, defined 'lifestyle' more succinctly as a euphemism for fashion and 'neat shit to buy'.

4 A full account of the research design and methodology is provided in the Appendix.

5 Frank Mort (1996) provides a similar list of masculine 'types' from the 'gentleman' of the nineteenth century to the 'yuppie' and 'gay urban *flâneur*' of the 1980s, all of whom have been the target of advertising and other forms of commercial culture.

6 Where McRobbie's work does connect with readers is in her emphasis on the casual and inattentive way that women's magazines are read. Readers 'flick through' *Jackie*, skim-reading in a highly selective way

(1991b: 142–3) – similar to our own findings on men's casual engagement with magazines (see below, chapter 5).

7   Hermes makes a similar comment on the Janus-faced nature of women's magazines: agent of change and progress, but also the devil in disguise, agent of alienation, anomie and despair in the powerfully seductive guise of provider of entertainment and excitement (1995: 1–2). Rather than adopting a high moral tone, she suggests that readers of all kinds, including academics, should accept that we enjoy texts in some contexts that we are critical of in other contexts.

8   Despite the title of her book Hermes makes only a limited engagement with women's actual *reading practices* as opposed to what readers say about what and how they read (their *discursive practices*). Such an emphasis would require a more thoroughly ethnographic approach than an account (like Hermes's or our own) which is based primarily on interviews or focus groups. While we follow Hermes's approach in much of what follows, we place more emphasis on differences between the various magazines than Hermes, who insists on the virtual irrelevance of the magazines' content.

9   The neglect of 'laddish' masculinities in recent academic work contrasts with the popular media's virtual obsession with the 'new lad', starting with Julie Burchill's 1986 essay in *The Face* and proliferating rapidly in the 1990s (see chapter 2).

10 Chirato and Yell (1999) also draw on Butler's theorization of gender as performance in their analysis of the 'new' men's magazines in Australia (*Ralph, Max, Men's Health* and *FHM*). Like us, they see the magazines as a discursive site for the production and circulation of 'new' forms of masculine subjectivity. Of the magazines they analyse, *Ralph* is closest to the irreverent tone of British magazines like *Loaded*. With an emphasis on sport, cars, alcohol and women, the title comes from an ocker word for vomit. Chirato and Yell conclude that the magazines aren't meant to be taken seriously, representing a self-conscious performance of an outmoded model of masculinity that is acknowledged to be anachronistic. While this is tenable as an academic interpretation, the authors privilege their own reading of the text without presenting any evidence of how other readers 'make sense' of the magazines.

11 Hall's own work has also developed considerably since his early theorization of the 'encoding/decoding' of meaning, as suggested by his more recent work on cultural representations and signifying practices (Hall, 1997).

2   The Media and the Market

1   Many novels were, of course, serialized in newspaper and periodical form during the nineteenth century, the blurring of genres continuing to the present day with magazines (for men and women) including

complimentary paperback books or CDs as an inducement to
purchase.

2   The publisher of *The Gentleman's Magazine*, Edward Cave, is said to
have coined the term 'magazine' (Davis, 1988: 4). Long-established
political and literary reviews such as the *Edinburgh Review* (founded in
1802) and *The Quarterly Review* (founded in 1809) were also aimed
overwhelmingly at male readers.

3   The 'illicit pleasures' of women's magazines, described by Beetham
(1996: viii) and others, are paralleled in our discussion of the contradictions and ambivalences evoked by men's magazines (see chapter 5).

4   The decline continues. In January 1997 Britain's daily newspapers
together sold just over 14 million copies. In January 1999 that figure
had declined by more than 500,000. Sales of the Sunday titles have also
declined by almost a million in two years (*Guardian*, 15 February
1999).

5   Similar tensions are characteristic of the current generation of men's
magazines, as the discussion of editorial interviews in chapter 3
confirms.

6   The transformation of *FHM* from a trade journal for the fashion
industry (first published in 1984) into a fully fledged men's 'lifestyle'
magazine (following its acquisition by EMAP in 1994) is particularly
instructive, highlighting the close relationship between the magazine
industry and the business of fashion. As Beetham (1996: 8) observes,
from the very early days of magazine publishing, one commodity, the
magazine, gave entry into a world of other commodities.

7   As an indication of their market share (estimated at around 30%), IPC
publish more than 40 'specialist' titles in fields such as music and sport
(16 titles), leisure (12 titles) and science and special interest (13 titles).

8   Sean Nixon (1993) quotes this phrase in the title of his paper on the
publishing and advertising strategies of contemporary men's magazines
(and subsequently in his book: *Hard Looks*, 1996).

9   The distinction between 'upmarket' and 'downmarket' titles is a problematic one, but was frequently employed by our focus group participants to distinguish magazines such as *Arena* and *Esquire*, with artistic
and literary pretensions, and those such as *GQ* and *Men's Health* with
a 'serious' interest in fashion or health, from titles such as *Loaded* and
Maxim, which had a more populist appeal. While there are class and
age differences in the readership profile of the magazines, the distinctions are sometimes difficult to maintain, particularly from the mid-
1990s when the commercial success of *Loaded* led all of the magazines
to move 'downmarket' in their pursuit of readers.

10 Since 1997, *FHM* has out-sold *Cosmopolitan* (*Independent* 15 August
1997). Our focus groups also confirm that men's magazines are passed
from hand to hand and read in public places such as doctors' and
dentists' waiting rooms. Like women's magazines, therefore, their
readership is likely to be at least two or three times higher than the
recorded sales figures.

11   Women's magazines are often significantly longer – with more than 400 pages in *Marie Claire*, for example, over 50% of which is advertising. The November 1997 issue of *GQ* (the first to be edited by James Brown, following his much-publicized move from *Loaded*) provoked press comment, with 197 of its 300 pages devoted to advertising or 'advertorial' (*Guardian*, 20 October 1997).

12   The list of titles included in our research is, to some extent, arbitrary. We have excluded some titles, like *Sky*, *T3* (Tomorrow's Technology Today) and *Q*, which have a predominantly male readership but which are not marketed specifically as men's lifestyle magazines. The market is also extremely dynamic, with several new titles, including *Later*, *ZM*, *Front* and *Men's Quest*, having been launched since we concluded our research.

13   See chapter 4 for a further discussion of 'irony' in the magazines' editorial content, and chapter 5 and the Appendix for a discussion of irony as both a discourse and a disposition. The nature of irony is indeed a common thread throughout this book.

14   This is similar to Hermes's (1995) notion of 'repertoires'. However, we would argue that she fails to examine how the reputation of women's magazines can have a bearing on how her respondents talk to her about their pleasures in reading them.

15   Another popular image of the 'soft yet strong' male was the (in)famous Athena poster, *L'Enfant*, depicting a muscular man gently cradling a baby. If the *New Statesman* and the *Guardian* had their doubts about the 'new' man, girls' magazine *Minx* confirmed them: in April 1998 the magazine carried a feature entitled, 'I Scored with the Athena Poster Man' which related, alongside that famous image, how the model Adam Perry claimed to have slept with more than 3,000 women, was really 'sordid and horrible', had sold his story to the *Sun* and then 'pissed off to Miami' (*Minx*, April 1998).

16   See also Joanna Bourke's (1996) *Dismembering the Male* for an excellent account of the social and cultural impacts of the Great War on constructions of modern masculinities.

17   Thus, Janice Winship (1987: 162) concludes her study of women's magazines by arguing that 'We might learn much from the "style" and young women's magazines' in terms of making feminist politics 'accessible' to a wider audience.

18   Incidentally the 1960s cult 'trash' road film, *The Wild Angels*, features the line: 'We wanna get loaded and we wanna have a good time', as sampled in Primal Scream's 'Loaded'.

19   The failure of readers to live up to the magazines' aspirations was a frequent subject of media commentary, as in this extract from Simon Hoggart: 'The new men's magazines are about chaps in Hugo Boss suits, sleeping with gorgeous women, skiing in Vervier, and facing that tough choice between a Saab and an imported Mustang. Yet the lads I see reading them are almost all spotty oiks, some in shambling sweats and dirty trainers, others in estate agent uniform of gun metal grey suit

and polyester tie, chaps whose idea of a great motor is either a Ford Fiesta with spoiler, or a Routemaster bus. And you never see them with a woman on their arm' (*Guardian*, 22 February 1997).

20 See Hunt's (1998) entertaining discussion on the 1970s as the perceived 'Golden Age' of 'unfettered straight masculinity' for '90s 'lads' and *Loaded* readers. For these men, Hunt argues, 'the fall, clearly, was via the "castrated" New Man of the 1980s'.

21 Promising 'new attitude', the short-lived *Fresh!* (published by Hair and Beauty Ltd.), celebrated ''90s bad girls' who were not only 'feisty and in yer face' but also 'turning years of sexism on its head. Once . . . it was a man's prerogative to screw his way through the female sex and sick up a few vindaloos en route. . . . Women have had enough of wiping the metaphorical sick off the bedsheets. Anyway, why wipe up the vomit when you can chuck up some of your own?' And to help readers achieve this post-feminist utopia, *Fresh!* provides another handy list of attributes: who Bad Girls are (Paula Yates, Fergie, Barbara Windsor, Eve), what they do (take control of their lives, wear crotchless knickers, get off with strangers, swear) and what they do not (wear wide belts, smile sweetly, and 'sit around drinking mulled wine talking about the world's problems') (*Fresh!* March 1997).

22 In the same edition of the newspaper, poet Martin Newell's column described: '[T]hose Lost Boys / Shaven headed creatures / Twoccing cars and downing pills / Faces pressed to window grilles / Lacking in those reading skills / For those *Loaded* features.'

3   Editorial Work

1 We have already sought to problematize the distinction between 'upmarket' and 'downmarket' magazines in chapter 2 (note 9).

2 Our expectation that the editors might have a commitment to 'men's issues' was derived from published accounts of Nick Logan's battle to find a publisher for the pioneering men's magazine, *Arena*. Logan projects an image of himself (described below) as having a 'vision' of the future of men's lifestyle magazines which he struggled heroically to sell to a hard-nosed, and initially sceptical, publishing industry.

3 Previous attempts to establish a 'general interest' men's magazine had been described as like searching for the Holy Grail (Nixon (1996: 130), quoting the advertising weekly *Campaign* (29 August 1986)).

4 Southwell's 'insider story' of working for *Loaded* also has its darker side: 'Working at such a breakneck pace, indulging in all manner of stimulants and generally experiencing all this crazy success led to lots of problems' (1998: 182), including the sectioning of deputy editor Michael Holden to a mental hospital in Southampton in December 1995.

5 James Brown's departure as editor of *GQ* has also been linked to negative reactions from blue-chip advertisers such as Ralph Lauren ('Growing pains hit the lad mags where it hurts', *Guardian*, 21 February 1999).

6 'Attitude' could also be said to involve a sense of 'hip', of 'knowingness' and confidence which can equally apply to women – as evidenced by the new range of young women's magazines promising 'attitude' such as *Minx* and *Fresh!*. Notably, women with 'attitude' tend to be defined as 'ladettes' ('Girls just like to have fun with booze and sex', *Guardian*, November 1996).

7 A distinction should perhaps be drawn between 'aspirational' in terms of the consumption of designer goods and 'aspirational' in terms of being skilled in dangerous sports (though there are clearly some overlaps in terms of the sale of designer-label sportswear, for example). Both are part of a lifestyle that can be lived in the imagination as much as in practice.

8 By contrast, Tim Southwell disavowed the use of irony in *Loaded*'s editorial content and among the magazine's readers: 'Now what I've always thought about *Loaded* was there was no irony to it at all, everything was done from the heart. . . . Half a million people are buying it and that means that about a million and a half are going to be reading it. These people aren't reading it ironically and it's not being written ironically' (1998: 254).

9 We make further use of Beck's concept of 'constructed certitude' in our interpretation of magazine content (chapter 4) and readership (chapter 5).

10 James Brown's short-lived editorial reign at *GQ* was described in similar terms as 'walking a difficult tightrope'. According to Nicolas Coleridge, managing director at Condé Nast: 'If you don't have babes [on the cover] you get punished at the news-stand. On the other hand, you've also got to appeal to more cerebral readers who want more than the lowest common denominator' ('Growing pains hit the lad mags where it hurts', *Observer*, 21 February 1999).

11 An 'aspirational' lifestyle runs counter to the ideal of nonchalant success that magazines like *Loaded* constantly claim to represent. The magazine's heroes include the wealthy and successful but also 'platinum rogues', like George Best, who have experienced fame and wealth but have risked 'losing it all' through over-indulgence of various kinds. While some of the magazines (notably *Men's Health*) emphasize the virtues of sport and fitness, others (like *Loaded*) celebrate the value of 'getting away with it'. Other lifestyle titles, such as *Dazed and Confused*, celebrate a 'slacker' lifestyle (*Independent*, 28 July 1997), similar to the values that are portrayed in recent TV commercials such as the ad for Strongbow cider which extols the virtues of 'loafing'.

12 Cf. the late Michael VerMeulen's uncompromising attitude towards his gay readership while he was editor of *GQ*: 'Most men are heterosexual and I want to sell a lot of magazines. I make exactly the same

accommodation for gay readers as Sainsbury's makes for gay shoppers' (interviewed in the *Observer Review*, 2 April 1995).

4   Questions of Content

1   Tim Edwards's (1997: 79) content analysis of the six leading men's magazines in May 1995 showed a variation in advertising content from 19% in *Maxim* to 35% in *Arena* (with *GQ* a close second at 34% and *FHM* third with 33%). Coverage of 'sex/women' varied between 0% in *Esquire* to 15% in *Maxim*. 'Health/fitness' ranged from 0% in *Loaded* to 10% in *Esquire*. Edwards did not include men's fashion as a separate category but noted that a high proportion of advertising was devoted to fashion (ranging from 8% in *Maxim* to 25% in *GQ*).

2   The recent addition of *Men's Fitness* to an expanding men's magazine market does, however, point to the possibility of more laddish health magazines. The August/September 1999 issue features a picture of Keith Richards on the front cover under the ironic title: 'live fast and die young'.

3   The issue of lengthening working hours and time is becoming a major political issue. See Polly Toynbee, 'Time is not on our side' (*Guardian*, 27 August 1999).

4   This might also suggest that men's fitness and health regimes are class-specific: that it is culturally acceptable for professional men with stressful jobs and limited time to work out for the necessary health benefits but that for working-class or unemployed men, with too much time on their hands, a concern for bodily fitness may be considered obsessive or potentially pathological (as represented by Travis Bickell in Martin Scorsese's film, *Taxi Driver*).

5   Readings

1   For a general review of masculinity and the media, see Craig (1992). For research on the new visual codings of masculinity, see, in particular, Nixon (1997) where he argues that it was in men's fashion and lifestyle magazines that these new images of masculinity first emerged and where they were most extensively elaborated.

2   For some examples of research on reading practices, see Radway's (1987) account of women's complex encounters with romantic fiction; Pearce's (1997) reflections on the volatile relationship between readers and texts; and Chartier's (1994) cultural history of the relationship between readers, authors and libraries, which includes some insightful comments on the rebellious and vagabond nature of reading.

3   Hermes (1995) includes a number of descriptive repertoires such as 'easily put down' and 'relaxation' as well as interpretive repertoires of 'practical knowledge', 'emotional learning' and 'connected knowing'. More analytical repertoires include those of 'vanguard', 'moral duty' and 'liberal-individualist'.

4   The development of reader-response criticism signalled a welcome break from text-based studies which virtually ignored the role of readers in the determination of literary meaning. Our own emphasis is on the social process of reading and meaning creation, the construction of interpretive communities and the relationship between individual readings and the wider discourses of which they are a part.

5   Ambivalence can be defined as a situation in which contradictory impulses and emotions co-exist, with positive and negative aspects remaining in opposition without easy resolution. As in Parker's (1995) work on maternal ambivalence, from which this definition is derived, ambivalence need not only be thought of as disabling but can also be creative.

6   This also allows us to illustrate the diversity of 'readings' *between* focus groups as well as noting any significant differences *within* each group. An earlier analysis of the transcripts (Jackson et al., 1999) presented a slightly different list of discourses. We regard the revised interpretation presented here as the definitive one.

7   That these rather dismissive public forms of talk might disguise more complex reading practices was confirmed by the fact that another member of this group later admitted to keeping back issues of one of the magazines, stacked neatly at his bedside.

8   That changes in contemporary masculinities may be only 'skin deep' was stressed by several groups. The idea is also reflected in the magazines' frequent advertisements for cosmetics such as Clinique's range of 'skin supplies for men'. To distinguish them from 'feminine' products, men's cosmetics commonly use names like 'facial scrub', including one product called 'deeply superficial', an extra-strength exfoliating scrub (*GQ*, November 1997).

9   The suggestion that 'you could get all theoretical' about the magazines implies that this is an acknowledged (and erroneous) response that we, as analysts, are assumed to endorse. It is a good example of the distinction which we are attempting to draw between discourses and dispositions which also helps us to reflect on our own role as analysts in terms of how we were positioned by the focus group participants.

10 'Honesty' is also a key value in the way the magazines' editorial staff present themselves (as discussed in chapter 3). Explaining *Loaded*'s appeal to its readers, for instance, Martin Deeson claimed 'We were the only organisation that was being totally honest about ourselves' (Southwell, 1998: 101). Other editorial staff at *Loaded* shared this view, including Mick Bunnage, who argued that 'We were really honest about it.' (ibid.: 163).

11 The fact that some groups saw the 'new lad' as a more natural form of

masculinity compared to the media construction of the 'new man', while other groups (such as the media professionals in Stoke Newington) thought of the 'new lad' as a media fiction (compared adversely to the 'lost moment' of the 1980s new man), only serves to demonstrate that all masculinities are socially constructed. What strikes one group as a media creation appears quite 'natural' to another group. Significantly, however, some constructions (including, we would argue, the image of the 'new lad') are more widely accepted as natural – and hence incontestable – as our discussion of media representations in chapter 2 also confirms.

12 Cf. the distinction between homosocial and homosexual desire made by authors such as Mort (1996) and Sedgwick (1991).

13 We should, however, be wary of projecting our own values onto the focus group participants. Insisting that the magazines should be read 'for a laugh' might not always imply a defensive strategy, denying their political significance. Some readers might genuinely feel that the magazines have no political significance or that any such significance is irrelevant or unimportant.

14 Irony is a key feature of the magazines and of our interpretation of them. The concept has already been discussed in our analysis of magazine content (in chapter 4). Here, we draw attention to the way that irony appears *both as a discourse* on which men draw in making sense of the magazines, *and as a disposition*, adopted by different individuals and groups towards a range of discourses. Thus, it is possible to recognize a discourse of irony without oneself endorsing that discourse, but it is also possible to take an ironic stance towards a variety of other discourses (ironizing the notion of magazine reading as 'harmless fun', for example).

15 These are, of course, examples of different dispositions to the notion of 'harmless fun', ranging from outright hostility through compliant acceptance to outright celebration.

16 Irony was, in fact, surprisingly rare in our content analysis of the magazines, given the extent to which it is regarded as fundamental to the genre in most media accounts. Contrary to such accounts, laddishness was embraced in an uncritical and unreflexive manner in most magazines rather than via an ironic sense of distance. While irony was present in *Loaded* ('for men who should know better') and even occasionally in *Xtreme* ('we've dropped the e'), there was very little irony in magazines like *XL for Men* or *Escape*. The magazines are themselves easily ironized, however, as in the Biff cartoon character's claim that 'I only buy New Man Quarterly for the articles' (*Guardian*, 22 April 1995).

17 That the magazines' editors are themselves conscious of these contradictions is suggested by Mike Soutar (former editor of *FHM*) in his reflection on the magazine's typical readership: 'These are guys who don't just want to go out in a gang, get pissed, eat curry and try and shag everything in a skirt. But they aren't settled down yet either. Most

guys in their twenties have one foot in either camp. They want to have fun, but they're ambitious too. They want mates, but they also want a girlfriend' (*Guardian*, 17 February 1997).

18 The contradictory notion of 'women as Other' as applied to (ultra-) feminists is also encapsulated in a *GQ* article which argued that 'Good looking feminists give me a real rise . . . they're a challenge . . . [but] most of us couldn't cope with her in real life' (March 1992).

19 The idea of 'resistance' implies a degree of coherence and intentionality, as well as a self-conscious ability to specify what is being resisted (cf. Pile and Keith, 1997). Similarly, the identification of 'oppositional' readings would imply a singularity and coherence in the 'dominant' meanings attributed to the magazines, for which there is little evidence in our focus groups.

20 Pearce's own work concentrates on differences between groups of feminist readers who might initially be thought of as members of a single interpretive community. Looking at reading as a process where readers are 'implicated' (with the text and with other readers) she focuses on declared positions (where readers engage with or reject a text according to 'prepared grids') and on covert processes (involving notions of interpretive community, audience and text–reader interactions). Unlike our own work, however, Pearce focuses on readers' *written responses* rather than on transcripts of their conversations.

21 Comments such as 'I'm sorry but . . .' are important indicators of participants' assumptions about our own positionality as researchers. Here, for example, the speaker adopts a defensive, semi-apologetic disposition concerning the alleged harmlessness of the magazines, assuming that we, as researchers, do not share this hostility or may even be adopting a more celebratory position. Our awareness of the researcher–researched relationship enables us to take the analysis beyond the identification of interpretive repertoires in the previous work of Hermes (1995) and others. The distinction between discourse and disposition also allows us to go beyond crude oppositions between an undifferentiated 'laddishness' and an equally problematic celebration of 'consumer resistance' through an analysis of ambivalence and contradiction such as we have attempted here.

22 Compare the editor's claim that all the material in *FHM* should be sexy, funny or useful – and preferably all three (*Guardian*, 17 February 1997).

23 This was the same man who described feminism as having involved 'a kicking for men' (above).

24 Their 'refusal' to theorize the magazines could, of course, be understood in a variety of ways – as defensiveness, as denial or as indicating the perceived irrelevance of theory.

25 Where such stories do appear, they are written in a predictably ironic manner. See, for example, the discussion of parenting in *FHM* (September 1998) entitled 'Know your enemy' which includes a section on calculating 'the price of a baby'. Another exception to the general

silence on fatherhood was *Maxim*'s short piece on 'How to be a better dad' (June 1998).

26 In employing Bourdieu's notion of cultural capital, we are aware of the recent critiques of his tendency towards sociological reductionism, including his implication that all judgements are based on people's material interests; see, for example, Crang (1997) and Sayer (1999).

27 Compare Mort's (1996) analysis of the various forms of discursive knowledge and complex professional alliances that facilitated the emergence during the 1990s of specific commercial cultures associated with changing forms of masculinity.

28 There is a clear parallel here with feminist analyses of women's magazines, where 'the effective operation of the commodity system requires the breakdown of the body into parts – nails, skin, breath – each one of which can constantly be improved through the purchase of a commodity' (Mary Ann Doane, cited in Radner, 1995: 154).

29 A Mintel report on 'British Lifestyles' showed that men's anxieties focused on money and health with a third of 20–54 year olds worried about losing their jobs within the next five years and nearly half anxious about their health. The same report showed a significant increase in expenditure on treats and rewards, such as chocolates, jewellery and magazines (*Guardian*, 12 February 1997).

Appendix

1 In this, we are particularly influenced by Joke Hermes's (1995) account of her 'research as process' in which she is refreshingly frank about the time-consuming difficulties she encountered when interviewing readers of women's magazines. We are, however, aware of some problematic issues in her work, particularly concerning race: see Brooks and Smith (1998).

2 'Militant Men Declare War on the "Social Evil of Feminism"' (*Independent*, 4 February 1997).

3 Most of the groups were moderated by Kate Brooks, assisted in some cases by Nick Stevenson or Peter Jackson. Four of the London groups were undertaken by Nick Stevenson.

4 The project featured in a *GQ* magazine article satirizing academic research ('We're paying for that: ten great pieces of university research we're funding', December 1998).

5 For example, whilst Radner (1995) argues against the notion that women's magazines operate as forms of ideological oppression and can instead be read as offering readers a potential site for resistance to patriarchal norms, we have difficulty finding cause for similar celebration in these magazines or in the focus group transcripts.

6 Such debriefing sessions occasionally raised some interesting insights into the different ways in which the same discussion can be perceived.

In one session, for example, moderated by both Nick Stevenson and Kate Brooks, each felt afterwards that they had had to be extra pleasant to compensate for the other's 'obvious' dislike of the participants.

7   Indeed, we are aware of recent debates about the difficulties of making our positionalities more 'transparent' (Rose, 1997), suggesting that more complex models of reflexivity need to be developed.

8   We have elaborated further on this distinction in chapter 5.

9   For example, a previous project on which one of us was working on popular action films was described variously as 'a bizarre, irrelevant, cocktail of PC nonsense' and also as having taken place at the 'University of the West of England – in other words, a poly with pretensions' in the tabloids at the time (quoted in Barker and Brooks, 1998: 2).

References

Abercrombie, N. and Longhurst, B. 1998: *Audiences*. London: Sage.

Adam, B. 1995: *Timewatch*. Cambridge: Polity.

Adorno, T. and Horkheimer, M. 1973: *The Dialectic of the Enlightenment*. London: Allen Lane.

Ang, I. 1982: *Watching Dallas: Soap Opera and the Melodramatic Imagination*. London: Methuen.

Ballaster, R., Beetham, M., Frazer, E. and Hebron, S. 1991: *Women's Worlds: Ideology, Femininity and the Woman's Magazine*. London: Macmillan.

Barker, M. and Brooks, K. 1998: *Knowing Audiences*. Luton: University of Luton Press.

Baudrillard, J. 1991: *Symbolic Exchange and Death*. London: Sage.

Bauman, Z. 1992: *Mortality, Immortality and Other Life Strategies*. Cambridge: Polity.

Bauman, Z. 2000: *Liquid Modernity*. Cambridge: Polity.

Beck, U. 1992: *Risk Society: Towards a New Modernity*. London: Sage.

Beck, U. 1997: *The Reinvention of Politics: Rethinking Modernity in the Global Social Order*. Cambridge: Polity.

Beck, U. and Beck-Gernsheim, E. 1995: *The Normal Chaos of Love*. Cambridge: Polity.

Beck, U., Giddens, A. and Lash, S. 1994: *Reflexive Modernization: Politics, Tradition and Aesthetics in the Modern Social Order*. Cambridge: Polity.

Beetham, M. 1996: *A Magazine of Her Own? Domesticity and Desire in the Woman's Magazine, 1800–1914*. London: Routledge.

Bell, D., Caplan, P. and Karim, W. J. (eds) 1993: *Gendered Fields: Women, Men and Ethnography*. London: Routledge.

Benjamin, J. 1990: *The Bonds of Love: Psychoanalysis, Feminism and the Problem of Domination*. London: Virago.

Benjamin, J. 1995: *Love Subjects, Love Objects*. New Haven and London: Yale University Press.

Bewes, T. 1997: *Cynicism and Postmodernity*. London: Verso.

Blount, M. and Cunningham, G. P. (eds) 1996: *Representing Black Men*. London: Routledge.

Bourdieu, P. 1984: *Distinction*. London: Routledge.

Bourdieu, P. 1990: *In Other Words: Essays Towards a Reflexive Sociology*. Cambridge: Polity.

Bourdieu, P. 1993: *Sociology in Question*. London: Sage.

Bourdieu, P. and Passeron, J.-C. 1977: *Reproduction in Education, Society and Culture*. London: Sage.

Bourke, J. 1996: *Dismembering the Male: Men's Bodies, Britain and the Great War*. London: Reaktion Books

Breazeale, K. 1994. In spite of women: *Esquire* magazine and the construction of the male consumer. *Signs: Journal of Women in Culture and Society*, 20, 1–22.

Brittan, A. 1989: *Masculinity and Power*. Oxford: Basil Blackwell.

Brooks, K. and Smith, C. 1998: *Reading Hermes' Reading Women's Magazines* Unpublished paper, University of the West of England.

Buber, M. 1958: *I and Thou*. Edinburgh: T. and T. Clark.

Burchill, J. 1986: Lad overboard. *The Face*, 70, 28–31.

Butler, J. 1990: *Gender Trouble: Feminism and the Subversion of Identity*. London: Routledge.

Butler, J. 1993: *Bodies That Matter: On the Discursive Limits of 'Sex'*. London: Routledge.

Campbell, B. 1993: *Goliath: Britain's Dangerous Places*. London: Methuen.

Carey, J. 1989: *Communication as Culture: Essays on Media and Society*. London: Unwin Hyman.

Carrigan, T., Connell, B. and Lee, J. 1985: Toward a new sociology of masculinity. *Theory and Society*, 14, 551–603.

Castells, M. 1996: *The Rise of the Network Society: The Informational Age: Economy, Society and Culture, Vol. I*. Oxford: Basil Blackwell.

Castells, M. 1997: *The Power of Identity: The Information Age: Economy, Society and Culture, Vol. II*. Oxford: Basil Blackwell.

Castoriadis, C. 1997: *World in Fragments: Writing on Politics, Society, Psychoanalysis, and the Imagination*. Stanford: Stanford University Press.

Champion, S. 1990: *And God Created Manchester*. Manchester: Wordsmith.

Chaney, D. 1996: *Lifestyles*. London: Routledge.

Chapman, R. 1988: The great pretender: variations on the new man theme. In R. Chapman and Rutherford, J. (eds), *Male Order: Unwrapping Masculinity*, London: Lawrence and Wishart, 225–48.

Chapman, R. and Rutherford, J. (eds) 1988: *Male Order: Unwrapping Masculinity*. London: Lawrence and Wishart.

Chartier, R. 1994: *The Order of Books*. Cambridge: Polity.

Chirato, T. and Yell, S. 1999: The 'new' men's magazines and the performance of masculinity. *Media International Australia*, 92, 81–90.

Chodorow, N. 1978: *The Reproduction of Mothering: Psychoanalysis and the Sociology of Gender*. Berkeley: University of California Press.

Clarke, J. and Critcher, C. 1985: *The Devil Makes Work: Leisure in Capitalist Britain*. London: Macmillan.

Connell, R. W. 1987: *Gender and Power*. Cambridge: Polity.

Connell, R. W. 1995: *Masculinities*. Cambridge: Polity.

Cornwall, A. and Lindisfarne, N. (eds) 1994: *Dislocating Masculinities: Comparative Ethnographies*. London: Routledge.

Craib, I. 1994: *The Importance of Disappointment*. London: Routledge.

Craig, S. (ed.) 1992: *Men, Masculinity and the Media*. London: Sage.

Crang, P. 1997: Cultural turns and the (re)constitution of economic geography. In R. Lee and J. Wills (eds), *Geographies of Economies*, London: Arnold, 3–15.

Davis, A. 1988: *Magazine Journalism Today*. Oxford: Focal Press.

de Certeau, M. 1984: *The Practice of Everyday Life*. Berkeley: University of California Press.

du Gay, P. 1996: *Consumption and Identity at Work*. London: Sage.

Duncombe, S. 1997: *Notes from the Underground: Zines and the Politics of Alternative Culture*. London: Verso.

Dyer, R. 1992: *Only Entertainment*. London: Routledge.

Edley, N. and Wetherell, M. 1997: Jockeying for position: the construction of masculine identities. *Discourse and Society*, 8, 203–17.

Edwards, T. 1997: *Men in the Mirror: Men's Fashion, Masculinity and Consumer Society*. London: Cassell.

Ehrenreich, B. 1983: *The Hearts of Men: American Dreams and the Flight from Commitment*. Garden City, New York: Anchor Press/ Doubleday.

Ekinsmyth, C. 1999: Professional workers in a risk society. *Transactions, Institute of British Geographers*, 24, 353–66.

Elias, N. 1985: *The Loneliness of the Dying*. Oxford: Basil Blackwell.

Elliott, A. 1996: *Subject to Ourselves: Social Theory, Psychoanalysis and Postmodernity*. Cambridge: Polity.

Falk, P. 1996: Expelling future threats: some observations on the magical world of vitamins. In S. Edgell, K. Hetherington and A. Warde (eds), *Consumption Matters*, Oxford: Basil Blackwell, 183–203.

Faludi, S. 1992: *Backlash*. New York: Vintage.

Faludi, S. 1999: *Stiffed: the Betrayal of the Modern Man*. London: Chatto and Windus.

Featherstone, M. 1991: The body in consumer culture. In M. Featherstone, M. Hepworth and B. S. Turner (eds), *The Body: Social Process and Cultural Theory*, London: Sage, 170–96.

Fiske, J. 1987: *Television Culture*. London: Methuen.

Fiske, J. 1989: *Understanding Popular Culture*. London: Routledge.

Forrester, J. 1992: What do men want? In D. Porter (ed.), *Between Men and Feminism*, London: Routledge, 105–20.

Foucault, M. 1977: *Discipline and Punish*. London: Penguin.

Franks, S. 1999: *Having None of It: Women, Men and the Future of Work*. Cambridge: Granta.

Frazer, E. 1992: Teenage girls reading *Jackie*. In P. Scannell, P. Schlesinger and C. Sparks (eds), *Culture and Power*, London: Sage, 182–200 (originally published in *Media, Culture and Society*, 9 (1987), 407–25).

Giddens, A. 1984: *The Constitution of Society: Outline of a Theory of Structuration*. Cambridge: Polity.

Giddens, A. 1991: *Modernity and Self-Identity: Self and Society in the Late Modern Age*. Cambridge: Polity.

Giddens, A. 1992: *The Transformation of Intimacy: Sexuality, Love and Eroticism in Modern Societies*. Cambridge: Polity.

Giddens, A. 1994: *Beyond Left and Right: The Future of Radical Politics*. Cambridge: Polity.

Gray, A. 1992: *Video Playtime: The Gendering of a Leisure Technology*. London: Routledge.

Gripsrud, J. 1989: 'High culture' revisited. *Cultural Studies*, 3, 194–207.

Habermas, J. 1971: Technology and science as 'ideology'. In *Toward a Rational Society: Student Protest, Science and Politics*, London: Heinemann Educational, 81–122.

Hall, C. 1992: *White, Male and Middle Class: Essays in Feminism and History*. Cambridge: Polity.

Hall, S. 1980: Encoding/decoding. In S. Hall, D. Hobson, A. Lowe and P. Willis (eds), *Culture, Media, Language*, London: Hutchinson, 128–38.

Hall, S. (ed.) 1997: *Representation: Cultural Representations and Signifying Practices*. London: Sage (in association with The Open University).

Hall, S. and Jefferson, T. (eds) 1976: *Resistance Through Rituals: Youth Sub-Cultures in Post-War Britain*. London: Hutchinson.

Harvey, D. 1998: The body as an accumulation strategy. *Environment and Planning D: Society and Space*, 16, 401–21.

Hearn, J. 1987: *The Gender of Oppression: Men, Masculinity and the Critique of Marxism*. Brighton: Harvester Wheatsheaf.

Hearn, J. 1988: Theorizing men and men's theorizing: varieties of discursive practices in men's theorizing of men. *Theory and Society*, 27, 781–816.

Hermes J, 1995: *Reading Women's Magazines*. Cambridge: Polity.

Hornby, N. 1992: *Fever Pitch*. London: Victor Gollancz.

Hornby, N. 1995: *High Fidelity*. London: Victor Gollancz.

Horrocks, R. 1994: *Masculinity in Crisis: Myths, Fantasies and Realities*. London: Macmillan.

Hunt, L. 1998: *British Low Culture: From Safari Suits to Sexploitation*. London: Routledge.

Hutcheon, L. 1994: *Irony's Edge: The Theory and Politics of Irony*. London: Routledge.

Jackson, P. 1991: The cultural politics of masculinity: towards a social geography. *Transactions, Institute of British Geographers*, 16, 199–213.

Jackson, P. 1995: Gender trouble – or just shopping? *Gender, Place and Culture*, 2, 107–8.

Jackson, P. 1999: Commodity cultures: the traffic in things. *Transactions, Institute of British Geographers*, 24, 95–108.

Jackson, P. Making sense of qualitative data. In M. Limb and C. Dwyer (eds), *Qualitative Methodologies for Geographers*. London: Arnold, in press.

Jackson, P., Lowe, M., Miller, D. and Mort, F. (eds) 2000: *Commercial Cultures: Economies, Practices, Spaces*. Oxford: Berg.

Jackson, P., Stevenson, N. and Brooks, K. 1999: Making sense of men's lifestyle magazines. *Environment and Planning D: Society and Space*, 17, 353–68.

Johnson, P. 1996: *Straight Outa Bristol*. London: Hodder and Stoughton.

Johnson, R. 1986: The story so far: and other transformations. In D. Punter (ed.), *Introduction to Contemporary Cultural Studies*, London: Longman, 277–313.

Kenny, M. and Stevenson, N. 1998: Cultural studies or cultural political economy? Cues from the long revolution. *Cultural Policy*, 4, 249–69.

Key Note Market Report 1996: *Men's magazines*.

Kimmel, M. 1987: The contemporary 'crisis' of masculinity in historical perspective. In H. Brod (ed.) *The Making of Masculinities: The New Men's Studies*, London: Allen and Unwin, 121–53.

Krueger, R. A. and Casey, M. A. 2000: *Focus Groups: A Practical Guide for Applied Research*. London: Sage (3rd edn).

Laclau, E. 1977: *Politics and Ideology in Marxist Theory*. London: Verso.

Lash, S. 1994: Reflexivity and its doubles: structure, aesthetics, community. In U. Beck, A. Giddens and S. Lash (eds), *Reflexive Modernization: Politics, Tradition and Aesthetics in the Modern Social Order*, Cambridge: Polity, 110–73.

Lash, S. and Friedman, J. (eds) 1992: *Modernity and Identity*. Oxford: Basil Blackwell.

Lash, S. and Urry, J. 1994: *Economies of Signs and Space*. London: Sage.

Longhurst, B. and Savage, M. 1996: Social class, consumption and the influence of Bourdieu. In S. Edgell et al. (eds), *Consumption Matters*, Oxford: Blackwell, 274–301.

Lyndon, N. 1992: *No More Sex War: the Failures of Feminism*. London: Sinclair-Stevenson.

Mac an Ghaill, M. (ed.) 1996: *Understanding Masculinities: Social Relations and Cultural Arenas*. London: Sage.

Mackay, H. (ed.) 1997: *Consumption and Everyday Life*. London: Sage.

Malbon, B. 1999: *Clubbing: Dancing, Ecstasy and Vitality*. London: Routledge.

Mangan, J. and Walvin, J. (eds) 1987: *Manliness and Morality: Middle-Class Masculinity in Britain and America 1800–1940*. Manchester: Manchester University Press.

McClintock, A. 1995: *Imperial Leather: Race, Gender and Sexuality in the Imperial Contest*. London: Routledge.

McDowell, L. 1991: Life without father and Ford: the new gender order of post-Fordism. *Transactions, Institute of British Geographers*, 16, 400–19.

McKee, L. and O'Brien, M. 1983: Interviewing men: 'taking gender seriously'. In E. Gamarinkow, D. H. J. Morgan, J. Purvis, and D. Taylorson (eds), *The Public and the Private*, London: Heinemann, 147–61.

McRobbie, A. 1982: The politics of feminist research: between talk, text and action. *Feminist Review*, 12, 46–57.

McRobbie, A. 1991a: *Jackie* magazine: romantic individualism and the teenage girl. In *Feminism and Youth Culture*, London: Macmillan, 81–134 (orginally published as *Jackie*: an ideology of adolescent femininity. In Centre for Contemporary Cultural Studies Women's Group, *Women Take Issue*, Hutchinson: London, 96–108).

McRobbie, A. 1991b: *Jackie* and *Just Seventeen*: girls' comics and magazines in the 1980s. In *Feminism and Youth Culture*, London: Macmillan, 135–88.

McRobbie, A. 1999: *In the Culture Society*. London: Routledge.

Melucci, A. 1996: *Challenging Codes: Collective Action in the Information Age*. Cambridge: Cambridge University Press.

Merck, M. (ed.) 1998. *After Diana*. London: Verso.

Middleton, P. 1992. *The Inward Gaze: Masculinity and Subjectivity in Modern Culture*. London: Routledge.

Miller, D. (ed.) 1995: *Acknowledging Consumption*. London: Routledge.

Mintel Market Intelligence 1997: *Men's lifestyle magazines* (http://www.mintel.com).

Moore, S. 1989: Getting a bit of the other – the pimps of postmodernism. In R. Chapman and J. Rutherford (eds), *Male Order: Unwrapping Masculinity*, London: Lawrence and Wishart, 165–92.

Morgan, D. 1988: *Focus Groups as Qualitative Research*. London: Sage.

Morgan, D. and Krueger, R. 1997: *Focus Group Kit*, vols 1–6. London: Sage.

Morgan, G. 1983: *Beyond Method: Strategies for Social Research*. London: Sage.

Morley, D. 1988: *Family Television: Cultural Power and Domestic Leisure*. London: Routledge.

Morley, D. 1992: *Television, Audiences and Cultural Studies*. London: Routledge.

Morse, J. 1998: It takes a lot of donuts to get good data. *Qualitative Health Research*, 8, 147–8.

Mort, F. 1988: Boy's own? Masculinity, style and popular culture. In R. Chapman and J. Rutherford (eds) *Male Order: Unwrapping Masculinity*, London: Lawrence and Wishart, 193–224.

Mort, F. 1996: *Cultures of Consumption: Masculinities and Social Space in Late Twentieth Century Britain*. London: Routledge.

Mouffe, C. 1993: *The Return of the Political*. London: Verso.

Mulvey, L. 1989: *Visual and Other Pleasures*. Basingstoke: Macmillan.

Nava, M. 1992: Consumerism and its contradictions. In *Changing Cultures: Feminism, Youth and Consumerism*, London: Sage, 162–8 (orginally published in *Cultural Studies*, 1(2) (1987)).

Nixon, S. 1992: Have you got the look? masculinities and shopping spectacle. In R. Shields (eds), *Lifestyle Shopping*, London: Routledge, 149–69.

Nixon, S. 1993: Looking for the holy grail: publishing and advertising strategies for contemporary men's magazines. *Cultural Studies*, 7, 467–92.

Nixon, S. 1996: *Hard Looks: Masculinities, Spectatorship and Contemporary Consumption*. London: UCL Press.

Nixon, S. 1997: Exhibiting masculinity. In S. Hall (ed.), *Representation: Cultural Representations and Signifying Practices*. London: Sage, 291–336.

O'Hagan, S. 1996: Here comes the New Lad! In D. Jones (ed.), *Ten Years of Arena: Sex, Power and Travel*, London: Virgin Publishing, 154–8.

Parker, R. 1995: *Torn in Two: The Experience of Maternal Ambivalence*. London: Verso.

Pearce, L. 1997: *Feminism and the Politics of Reading*. London: Arnold.

Pfeil, F. 1995: *White Guys: Studies in Postmodern Domination and Difference*. London: Verso.

Pile, S. and Keith, M. (eds) 1997: *Geographies of Resistance*. London: Routledge.

Radner, H. 1995: *Shopping Around: Feminine Culture and the Pursuit of Pleasure*. London: Routledge.

Radway, J. 1987: *Reading the Romance: Women, Patriarchy and Popular Literature*. London: Verso.

Rorty, R. 1989: *Contingency, Irony, and Solidarity*. Cambridge: Cambridge University Press.

Rose, G. 1997: Situating knowledges: positionality, reflexivities and other tactics. *Progress in Human Geography*, 21, 305–20.

Rose, N. 1989: *Governing the Soul: The Shaping of the Private Self*. London: Routledge.

Rutherford, J. 1992: *Men's Silences: Predicaments in Masculinity*. London: Routledge.

Sanderson, T. 1994: *Mediawatch: the Treatment of Male and Female Sexuality in the British Media*. London: Cassell.

Sayer, A. 1999: Bourdieu, Smith and disinterested judgement. *The Sociological Review*, 47, 403–31.

Sayers, J. 1995: *The Man Who Never Was: Freudian Tales*. London: Chatto and Windus.

Schilling, C. 1993: *The Body and Social Theory*. London: Sage.

Sconce, J. 1995: Trashing the Academy: taste, excess and an emerging politics of cinematic style. *Screen*, 36, 371–93.

Sedgwick, E. K. 1991: *Epistemology of the Closet*. Brighton: Harvester Wheatsheaf.

Segal, L. 1990: *Slow Motion: Changing Masculinities, Changing Men*. London: Virago.

Seidler, V. J. (ed.) 1991: *The Achilles Heel Reader: Men, Sexual Politics and Socialism*. London: Routledge.

Seidler, V. J. 1997: *Man Enough: Embodying Masculinities*. London: Sage.

Sennett, R. 1998: *The Corrosion of Character: The Personal Consequences of Work in the New Capitalism*. New York and London: W. W. Norton.

Sibley, D. 1995: *Geographies of Exclusion: Society and Difference in the West*. London: Routledge.

Simpson, L. C. 1995: *Technology, Time and the Conversations of Modernity*. London: Routledge.

Slater, D. 1997: Integrating consumption and leisure: 'hobbies' and the structures of everyday life. Paper presented at the European Sociological Association subgroup on the Sociology of Consumption, Essex, 27–31 August.

Sloterdijk, P. 1988: *Critique of Cynical Reason*. London: Verso.

Smith, C. 1998: *Creative Britain*. London, Faber.

Sontag, S. 1966: Notes on 'camp'. In *Against Interpretation and Other Essays*. New York: Farrar, Strauss and Giroux, 275–92.

Southwell, T. 1998: *Getting Away With It: The Inside Story of Loaded*. London: Ebury Press.

Stevenson, N. 1995: *Understanding Media Cultures: Social Theory and Mass Communication*. London: Sage.

Stevenson, N. 1999a: *The Transformation of the Media: Globalisation, Morality and Ethics*. London: Longman.

Stevenson, N. 1999b: Globalization and cultural political economy. In R. Germain (ed.), *Globalization and its Critics*, London: Macmillan, 91–113.

Stevenson, N., Jackson, P. and Brooks, K. 2000a: The sexual politics of men's lifestyle magazines. *European Journal of Cultural Studies*, 3, 366–85.

Stevenson, N., Jackson, P. and Brooks, K. 2000b: Ambiguity in men's lifestyle magazines. In P. Jackson, et al. (eds), *Commercial Cultures: Economies, Practices, Spaces*, Oxford: Berg, 189–212.

Stewart, D. W. and Shamdasani, P. N. 1990: *Focus Groups: Theory and Practice*. London: Sage.

Strauss, A. L. 1983: *Qualitative Analysis for Social Scientists*. Cambridge: Cambridge University Press.

Stringfellow Jr, F. 1994: *The Meaning of Irony: A Psychoanalytic Investigation*. Albany, NY: New York State University Press.

Taylor, I., Evans, K. and Fraser, P. 1996: *A Tale of Two Cities: Global Change, Local Feeling and Everyday Life in the North of England – A Study in Manchester and Sheffield*. London: Routledge.

Tompkins, J. P. (ed.) 1980: *Reader-Response Criticism: From Formalism to Post-Structuralism*. Baltimore and London: The Johns Hopkins University Press.

Tracey, D. J. 1997: *Remaking Men: Jung, Spirituality and Social Change*. London: Routledge.

Turner, B. S. 1991: Recent developments in the theory of the body. In M. Featherstone, M. Hepworth and B. S. Turner (eds), *The Body: Social Process and Cultural Theory*, London: Sage, 1–35.

Urry, J. 2000: *Sociology Beyond Societies: Mobilities for the Twenty-first Century*. London: Routledge.

Walby, S. 1990: *Theorizing Patriarchy*. Oxford: Basil Blackwell.

Walby, S. 1997: *Gender Transformations*. London: Routledge.

Walkerdine, V. 1990: *Schoolgirl Fictions*. London: Verso.

White, C. L. 1970: *Women's Magazines 1693–1968*. London: Michael Joseph.

Willis, P. 1990: *Common Culture*. Milton Keynes: Open University Press.

Winship, J. 1978: A woman's world: *Woman* – an ideology of femininity. In CCCS Women's Group (eds), *Women Take Issue*, London: Hutchinson, 133–45.

Winship, J. 1987: *Inside Women's Magazines*. London: Pandora Press.

Wolf, N. 1990: *The Beauty Myth*. London: Chatto and Windus.

Zizek, S. 1989: *The Sublime Object of Ideology*. London: Verso.

Index